Relocating Middle Pc

This book examines how two middle powers, Australia and Canada, engaged in the difficult process of *relocating* themselves in the profoundly altered international political system of the late 1980s and early 1990s. Arguing that the concept of middle power has continuing relevance in contemporary international relations theory, the authors present a number of case studies to illustrate the changing nature of middle power behaviour. In particular, they examine the trend towards the amalgamation of the foreign and trade ministries in both Canada and Australia. They also look at the unique case of the Cairns Group and examine the growing importance of regional trading blocs, particularly Asia-Pacific Economic Cooperation and the North American Free Trade Agreement. Australian and Canadian roles in the Gulf War are also scrutinized.

Relocating Middle Powers is the first book to explore the similarities and differences in the foreign policies of two middle powers in a new era of international relations, and it shows how and why middle powers will continue to be important international actors in the 1990s and beyond.

Andrew F. Cooper is an associate professor in the Department of Political Science and director of the International Studies Program, University of Waterloo, Ontario.

Richard A. Higgott is a professor in the Department of International Relations, Research School of Pacific Studies, Australian National University, Canberra.

Kim Richard Nossal is a professor and chair of the Department of Political Science, McMaster University, Hamilton, Ontario.

Andrew F. Cooper, Richard A. Higgott, and Kim Richard Nossal

Relocating Middle Powers: Australia and Canada in a Changing World Order

UBCPress / Vancouver

ISBN 0-7748-0447-5 (hardcover)
ISBN 0-7748-0450-5 (paperback)

ISSN 0847-0510 (Canada and International Relations)

Published simultaneously in Australia by Melbourne University Press

Canadian Cataloguing in Publication Data

Cooper, Andrew Fenton, 1950-
  Relocating middle powers

  (Canada and international relations, ISSN 0847-0510; v. 6)
  Includes bibliographical references.
  ISBN 0-7748-0447-5 (bound) – ISBN 0-7748-0450-5 (pbk.)

1. Canada – Foreign relations. 2. Australia – Foreign relations. 3. Canada – Foreign
economic relations. 4. Australia – Foreign economic relations. 5. International
relations. 6. Middle powers. I. Higgott, Richard A. II. Nossal, Kim Richard. III. Title.
IV. Series.   FC630.C66 1993   327.71   C93-091279-9   F1034.2.C66 1993

This book has been published with the help of a grant from the Social Science
Federation of Canada, using funds provided by the Social Sciences and Humanities
Research Council of Canada. An additional grant was provided by the Australian
National University, Canberra.

UBC Press gratefully acknowledges the ongoing support to its publishing program
from the Canada Council, the Province of British Columbia Cultural Services
Branch, and the Department of Communications of the Government of Canada.

UBC Press
University of British Columbia
6344 Memorial Rd
Vancouver, BC V6T 1Z2
(604) 822-3259
Fax: (604) 822-6083

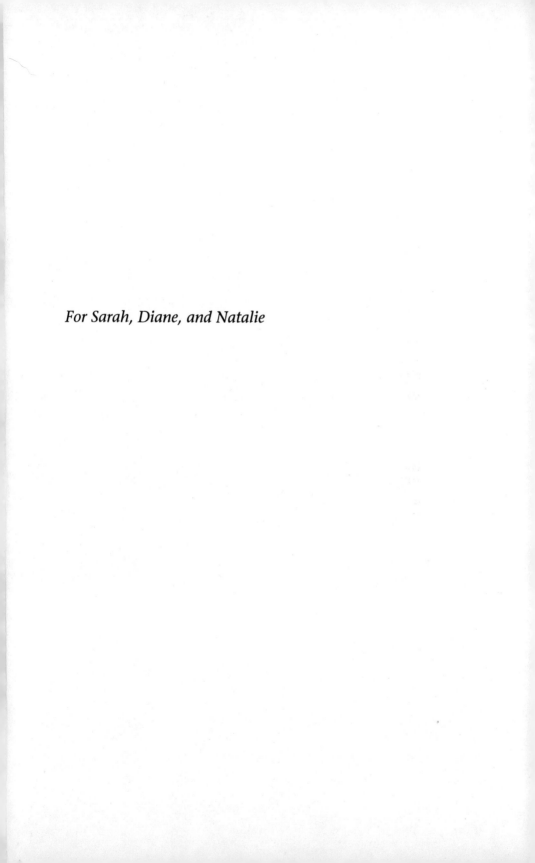

For Sarah, Diane, and Natalie

Contents

Preface and Acknowledgments

This book on Australian and Canadian middle power diplomacy evolved out of the authors' shared interest in how their two countries were seeking to respond to the profound challenges they confronted in the changing international political economy in the late 1980s and early 1990s. In writing it, we incurred a large number of debts.

We would particularly like to thank External Affairs and International Trade Canada in Ottawa and the Canadian High Commission, Canberra, which awarded Murdoch University, with Richard Higgott as the principal researcher, the Canada-Australia Bicentennial Institutional Research Award for 1990. The purpose of this award – a gift from the Government of Canada to Australia on the occasion of the Australian bicentennial in 1988 – is to encourage research cooperation between the two countries. Indeed, the generous terms of the grant afforded all three authors an opportunity to overcome the 'tyranny of distance' imposed by the Pacific Ocean. We would like to offer a special personal thanks to Ron Hughes of the Canadian High Commission, Canberra, who was so helpful in the administration of the award at all stages. Needless to say, what has resulted from this trans-Pacific collaboration does not in any way represent the views of the Government of Canada.

Cooper and Nossal gratefully acknowledge the support of the Social Sciences and Humanities Research Council of Canada through research grants they both held at various stages of this project.

We would also like to express our gratitude to the Australian National University and to the Aid to Scholarly Publications Programme of the Social Science Federation of Canada for financial assistance in the publication of this book.

At the time the Canada-Australia Bicentennial Award was granted, Higgott was a member of the faculty of Murdoch University, and we thank the university for administering the grant. We owe particular thanks to Murdoch's vice-chancellor, Professor Peter Boyce – himself a political scientist with an interest in the comparative study of Australia and Canada – and also to Hugh Collins, professor of government and politics, for hosting the valuable one-day seminar at which we presented the major themes of the book, which were in turn subjected to critical scrutiny by a most lively audience.

In addition to the contributions from professors Boyce and Collins, we benefited greatly from the comments of Robert Bruce, Curtin University of Technology, and Scott Spencer and Paul O'Callaghan, from the Australian Department of Foreign Affairs and Trade. O'Callaghan acted as discussant-at-large on the day's proceedings and did much to convince us of the utility of academic speculation and distance for a better understanding of the policy process.

This book has also been much improved because of the generous input of other scholars and practitioners in both the Australian and Canadian foreign policy communities, who read different sections of the manuscript or offered their comments and suggestions. We would particularly like to thank Stuart Harris, Richard Leaver, John Ravenhill, and J.L. Richardson, all of the Department of International Relations, Research School of Pacific Studies at the Australian National University; Lorraine Eden of the Norman Paterson School of International Affairs, Carleton University; Lorraine Elliott, Department of Political Science at the ANU; Peter Field and Peter Gallagher of the Australian Department of Foreign Affairs and Trade; Tony Payne, University of Sheffield; John English, Department of History, University of Waterloo; Richard Stubbs, Department of Political Science, McMaster University; Nancy Viviani, Griffith University; T.K. Warley, University of Guelph; Geoff Wiseman, the Ford Foundation; and the foreign service trainee graduate students in Australian foreign policy at the ANU for their astute comments.

A special thanks to Michael Berry, Canadian high commissioner to Australia, for taking the time out of his busy schedule to read and comment on the entire manuscript. We are also particularly grateful to the two anonymous reviewers engaged by the University of British Columbia Press and the Social Science Federation of Canada for their full and helpful suggestions on an initial draft of the book.

Parts of chapters 3 and 4 have been published previously as 'Middle Power Leadership and Coalition Building: Australia, the Cairns Group and the Uruguay Round of Trade Negotiations' (*International Organization* 44 [Autumn 1990]:589-632) and 'Asia Pacific Economic Cooperation: An Evolving Case Study in Cooperation and Leadership' (*International Journal* 40 [Autumn 1990]:823-66). Although the chapters in which these case studies appear have been extensively rewritten, updated, and, indeed, augmented by new material, we nonetheless thank the MIT Press and the Canadian Institute of International Affairs for permission to republish here.

Finally, our thanks for technical assistance to Lynne Payne of the Department of International Relations, Australian National University; Joanne Voisin of the Department of Political Science, University of Waterloo; Dr. Toni Makkai of the Department of Sociology, Research School of Social Sciences, Australian National University; and Gerald Bierling of the Department of Political Science, McMaster University.

Andrew F. Cooper
Richard A. Higgott
Kim Richard Nossal

Abbreviations

AD	Australian Democrats
ALP	Australian Labor Party
ANZUS	Australia-New Zealand-United States security treaty
ANZCERTA	Australia New Zealand Closer Economic Relations and Trade Agreement (usually CER)
APEC	Asia-Pacific Economic Cooperation
ASEAN	Association of Southeast Asian Nations
AUSPECC	Australian Pacific Economic Cooperation Committee
BQ	Bloc Québécois
CANZ	Canada-Australia-New Zealand
CAP	Common Agricultural Policy
CER	Closer Economic Relations (see ANZCERTA)
CEDAW	Convention on the Elimination of All Forms of Discrimination Against Women
CF	Canadian Forces
CFCs	chlorofluorocarbons
CFMSA	Committee of Foreign Ministers on Southern Africa
CHOGM	Commonwealth Heads of Government Meeting
CIDA	Canadian International Development Agency
COMECON	Council for Mutual Economic Assistance
CRAMRA	Convention on the Regulation of Antarctic Mineral Resource Activities
CSBMs	confidence and security-building measures
CSCA	Conference on Security and Cooperation in Asia
CSCE	Conference on Security and Cooperation in Europe
CWC	Chemical Weapons Convention
DEA	Department of External Affairs (Canada); after 1989: EAITC

DFAT	Department of Foreign Affairs and Trade (Australia)
DITAC	Department of Industry, Technology and Commerce (Australia)
DND	Department of National Defence (Canada)
DRIE	Department of Regional Industrial Expansion (Canada)
EAITC	External Affairs and International Trade Canada (before 1989, Department of External Affairs)
EC	European Community
EEP	Export Enhancement Program
E&I	Department of Employment and Immigration (Canada)
ESCAP	Economic and Social Commission of Asia and the Pacific
FAO	Food and Agriculture Organization
G-7	Group of Seven industrialized countries
G-77	Group of Seventy-Seven Less Developed Countries
GATT	General Agreement on Tariffs and Trade
IAEA	International Atomic Energy Agency
ICER	Interdepartmental Committee on External Relations (Canada)
IMC	Informal Meeting on Cambodia (same as JIM)
IT&C	Department of Industry, Trade and Commerce (Canada)
JACADS	Johnston Atoll Chemical Agent Disposal System
JIM	Jakarta Informal Meeting (on Cambodia; same as IMC)
LDC	less developed country
MITI	Ministry of International Trade and Industry (Japan)
MTN	multilateral trade negotiations
MSERD	Ministry of State for Economic and Regional Development (Canada)
NATO	North Atlantic Treaty Organization
NDP	New Democratic Party (Canada)
NIEO	New International Economic Order
NIE	Newly Industrializing Economy
NGO	nongovernmental organization
NORAD	North American Aerospace Defence Command
NPCSD	North Pacific Cooperative Security Dialogue
NPT	Non-Proliferation Treaty
ODA	official development assistance
OECD	Organization for Economic Cooperation and Development
OPEC	Organization of Petroleum Exporting Countries
OPTAD	Organization for Pacific Trade and Development

P-5	five permanent members of the UN Security Council
PAFTA	Pacific Free Trade Area
PAFTAD	Pacific Trade and Development Conference
PBEC	Pacific Basic Economic Committee
PC	Progressive Conservative party
PCO	Privy Council Office (Canada)
PECC	Pacific Economic Cooperation Conference
PICC	Paris International Conference on Cambodia
PSE	producer subsidy equivalent
SAARC	South Asia Association for Regional Cooperation
SCOR	Secretaries' Committee on Overseas Representation (Australia)
SNC	Supreme National Council (of Cambodia)
SPARTECA	South Pacific Regional Trade and Economic Cooperation Agreement
SQ	Sûreté du Québec
T&C	Department of Trade and Commerce (Canada)
UNCED	UN Conference on Environment and Development
UNCLOS	UN Conference on the Law of the Sea
UNCSW	UN Commission on the Status of Women
UNCTAD	UN Conference on Trade and Development
UNEP	UN Environment Program
UNESCO	UN Economic, Social and Cultural Organization
UNICEF	UN International Children's Emergency Fund
UNIFEM	UN Development Fund for Women
WMO	World Meteorological Organization

Relocating Middle Powers

Introduction

Students and practitioners of public policy in Australia and Canada have always paid considerable attention to politics and public policy in the other country. However, this comparative focus has tended to be fixed primarily on domestic issues: comparative federalism, comparative approaches to natural resources or Aboriginal peoples, questions of social welfare, and so on. Much less attention has been paid to the similarities and differences in the way the two states have pursued their foreign policies in the 1980s.[1]

This is an unfortunate omission. Australia and Canada have much in common and faced many of the same problems in the international political and economic systems in the last quarter of the twentieth century. Both states were part of the post-1945 Western alliance system: Canada through the North Atlantic Treaty Organization (NATO) and the North American Aerospace Defence Command (NORAD), and Australia through its membership in the Australia-New Zealand-United States (ANZUS) alliance. Both are members of the economic club of developed nations, the Organization for Economic Cooperation and Development (OECD), yet both suffer, much more than most of their OECD partners, from being principally, but not exclusively, commodity-dependent economies. In the pursuit of their foreign policies, both were typically 'first followers' of their major ally, the United States, in the decades following the Second World War. Their external policies inexorably reflected a sensitivity to the actions of the strong and a commitment to the economic and security systems established under American hegemony after 1945.

The changes that occurred in the international system over the 1980s, however, required both states to engage in a considerable rethinking of their international roles. From the coming to power of Mikhail S.

Gorbachev in the Soviet Union in 1985 and the subsequent transformations in international politics – the fall of the Berlin Wall in 1989, the wrapping up of the Council for Mutual Economic Assistance (COMECON) and the Warsaw Pact, the reunification of Germany the following year, and, finally, the disintegration of the USSR itself in 1991 – all brought declining tensions between the two superpowers and then the end of the Cold War itself. These developments meant that, for Australia and Canada, some of the more traditional foreign policy concerns of a military-strategic nature were increasingly replaced by a mounting concern over the future of the international economic system.

In the context of the international political economy, neither state flourished in the latter part of the 1980s and early 1990s. Both experienced severe problems in an international economy that saw the emergence of new economic powers. On the one hand, the European Community (EC) remained committed to greater integration and also greater economic cooperation with its Eastern European neighbours after the end of the Cold War. On the other hand, we have seen the emergence of a new centre of economic activity in the Asia-Pacific region. These developments, accompanied by the declining economic power of the United States and growing American economic nationalism, generated growing tensions in international economic confidence that had not been seen since the Great Depression of the interwar years. Both Canada and Australia became increasingly susceptible to the vicissitudes of a more interdependent, but more unpredictable, global economic order in the 1980s and 1990s than that which prevailed in the early decades of the post-Second World War era.

Consequently, both states had to address and, in many senses, to redefine their roles vis-à-vis the traditional structures of the international environment. The principal component of this redefinition was the raised salience of the economic dimension of their foreign policies – especially trade policy. Thus, both countries moved – within five years of each other – to restructure their bureaucracies in an effort to give greater emphasis to the economic dimensions of their foreign policies.

Likewise, both states came to recognize that the vulnerability of the system's middle-sized states dramatically increases when there is an absence of leadership from a hegemonic power on the one hand or a general agreement to share leadership responsibilities between the major economic powers (the United States, the European Community, and Japan) on the other. Attempts to resolve economic conflict between the major economic powers bilaterally, whether it was the United States and Japan looking for a mythical 'level playing field' or the United States and the EC engaging in a subsidy war over agricultural products, often led to the smaller states being 'third party' or 'sideswipe' victims to such bilateral dealings.

It is, therefore, not surprising that both Australia and Canada invested considerable time, money, intellectual capital, and political energy in attempts to mitigate the growth of economic conflict between the major powers in the 1980s. In particular, both countries tried to achieve what they felt was their best 'first option' for the 1990s: both generally preferred an open multilateral trading system bound by an agreed set of principles and rules. It is true that the major powers also professed to seek this goal. However, the evidence from the 1980s would suggest that this was true primarily at the rhetorical level; their actual behaviour would suggest a less than wholehearted commitment to the preservation of the liberal trading system in circumstances that do not suit their immediate interests. It is for this reason, for example, that Australia and Canada cooperated, along with other non-great powers, in the formation of the Cairns Group to secure agricultural reform in the Uruguay Round of trade negotiations. In so doing, they were playing the important role of building coalitions of states to secure reform in the international system.

The coalition-building activity of Australia and Canada – in this and other areas – is important as an indicator of how powers of middle size and rank might assist in the fostering of cooperation in the international system in the 1990s. This is not to suggest that the military dimensions of international relations disappeared in the early 1990s. On the contrary: there are those who argue that the disappearance of the discipline imposed by the Cold War opened the way to such conflicts as the war in Yugoslavia in 1991 and 1992 or the breakdown in order that led to the multinational intervention in Somalia in 1992 and 1993. Rather, it is to suggest that, as the nature of leadership in international politics evolves, it is probable, as P.J. Boyce has argued, that we will see less reliance on traditional sources of power, such as military capability and economic strength, and more reliance on diplomatic capability and policy initiatives.[2]

Indeed, in an analysis of United States foreign policy in the 1990s, Stanley Hoffmann suggested that 'games of skill will replace tests of will' in American statecraft.[3] Hoffmann, we would suggest, overstates the case. While it is unlikely that games of skill will replace tests of will completely, they will become much more important tools of statecraft in a post-Cold War world than at any time since the Second World War. Further, Hoffmann was, of course, referring to the international system's great powers. Yet we believe that his characterization applies with equal, if not more, force to some secondary actors in the international system.

Aims of This Book

The title of this book, *Relocating Middle Powers*, is intentionally ambiguous in order to reflect its dual aims. On the one hand, we try to demonstrate the efforts of two states in the international system, Australia and Canada, to engage in the difficult process of 'relocating' themselves in the rapidly changing international system of the 1980s and 1990s. With the dramatic shifts in both the economic and political systems – with the alignments, the institutions, and the understandings that came with the aftermath of the Second World War withering away, or collapsing, or being dismantled – these middle powers faced profound dislocations. The chapters that follow chronicle and analyze the attempts of these states to engage in the 'games of skill' that relocation required. Our analysis provides an alternative perspective on the international policymaking process – one that stresses the importance of secondary players in the international system. The role of smaller states in the resolution of contemporary international problems is all too often overlooked, or given short shrift, by both the policymakers and scholars of the major powers. Our contention is that both leadership and followership are crucial elements for an understanding of the dynamics of contemporary management of international problems. In this book, we explore some alternative approaches to these questions in both a theoretical and empirical manner.

We begin by taking issue with the degree to which hegemonic stability theory has served to distort our understanding of the processes of policymaking for the international community and the management of international problems. The dominance of hegemonic stability theory in the Anglo-American literature on international relations has been subjected to substantial theoretical and methodological critiques,[4] but there has, to date, been little recognition of the manner in which the theory tends to deny autonomy of action to followers in a leader-follower relationship underwritten by hegemony. Without engaging the wider theoretical debate over the nature of hegemony, the introductory chapter explores the dynamics of leadership and followership in order to demonstrate the inadequacy of a leader-centred approach to contemporary international politics. Indeed, we conclude that there is a need for a more nuanced approach.

In our view, a more nuanced approach would begin by recognizing the importance of middle powers in international politics. The idea of middle power, as a distinctive category of actor in contemporary international relations, is, we recognize, problematic. However, the argument advanced in this book is that if the concept of middle powers were to be reformulated, it would clearly illustrate the leader-follower dynamic in international politics. Our reformulated perspective on middle power behaviour eschews traditional definitions anchored in criteria of size, power, and geographic location.[5] Rather, we develop an approach based on the technical and entrepreneurial capacities of states like Canada and Australia to provide complementary or alternative initiative-oriented sources of leadership and enhanced coalition-building in issue-specific contexts. We use this approach to examine what Australia and Canada actually do in contemporary international politics rather than to examine the empirical question of what characteristics they exhibit or the normative question of what they should be doing.

This dimension of our approach, we argue, is a departure from more traditional analyses of middle power behaviour in international relations, much of which was often couched in inspirational or celebratory terms. Even in the 1990s, the exhortatory approach to middle power analysis is still to be found. The perspective of Bernard Wood, a perceptive student of Canadian foreign policy, is illustrative of a view that is widely held with respect to the role of countries like Australia and Canada in world politics. In a discussion of the contemporary world order, Wood suggested that 'the world looks to Canada for special contributions to building this new order because of its capabilities, its historical record of innovation and participation.'[6] Such a view may provide a comforting self-perception for Canadians, but it does not throw much light on middle power diplomacy. By contrast, this book, as the title suggests, seeks to 'relocate' the notion of middle power in essentially theoretical terms.

We set out our theoretical approach in Chapter 1. We then explore a number of case studies from Australian and Canadian foreign policy in selected but specific issue areas in the 1980s and early 1990s. In Chapter 2, we examine the impact of changes in the international system on government structure and, specifically, how both governments sought to reorganize their bureaucracies for the conduct of a more economically oriented foreign policy. The chapter explores the amalgamations of the foreign and trade ministries, first in Ottawa in 1982, and then, five years later, in Canberra. In particular, we show how both governments sought to provide themselves with state agencies more closely geared to the kind of entrepreneurial and technical leadership initiatives we examine in later chapters.

In Chapter 3, we examine one of the key responses of both states to the growing frictions in trade between the United States and its major trading partners – the formation of the Cairns Group of Fair Trading Nations and its attempt to foster reform in agricultural trade in the context of the Uruguay Round of multilateral trade negotiations. We show that the Cairns Group was a novel, single-issue, transregional coalition in contemporary international economic relations. Led by Australia, the Group's actions exhibit precisely the kinds of middle power skills and approaches that we set out in Chapter 1. This chapter illustrates the attempts by the Group to influence the global trading system, whose decisionmaking processes are increasingly more frag-mented and complex, and whose major actors are becoming more intransigent in their attitudes towards cooperation. In the early phase of the Uruguay Round, the activities of the Cairns Group are shown to represent important advances in coalition-building in the contempo-rary international system.

In Chapter 4, we move from the global multilateral economic agenda to the regional one. The growing trends towards regionalism in inter-national economic relations in Europe and North America were matched by the growth of economic regionalism in the Pacific. Chapter 4 focuses on attempts to establish a wider economic dialogue in the Asia-Pacific region, following the November 1989 meeting on Asia Pacific Economic Cooperation (APEC), and contrasts developments in the Asia-Pacific region with the evolution of economic regional cooper-ation in a North American context, particularly the North American Free Trade Agreement (NAFTA) of 1992.

The chapter is thus a reflection of the renewed interest on the part of both scholars and practitioners of international relations in the question of institutionalism in world politics – defined fairly loosely to include the development of international regimes and the establishment of working conventions as well as that of formal organizations. This renewed interest was the result of a variety of developments, both negative and positive, in the international order in this period. The chapter provides an empirical and theoretical analysis of the evolution of APEC and NAFTA from the perspective of the new institutionalism.

This regionalism is seen to be a product of both increased interdependence in the international order and growing conflicts between the major actor. Regionalism, in short, was part of a wider crisis of multilateralism in international economic relations in the latter part of the 1980s. The process of cooperation in the Asia-Pacific region is shown to be substantially different from other forms of regional economic cooperation that emerged in the post-Second World War era. Unlike the European Community, APEC is constrained by the diversity of national political interests and levels of development. However, APEC nonetheless reflects a region-wide recognition of a mutuality of interest. It thus represents an evolutionary model with an institutional structure that allows for the continued expansion of communication on matters of regional concern. In so doing, the evolution of APEC, and especially the role of secondary players in facilitating its development, offers some interesting theoretical insights into the question of leadership in international economic cooperation in an era of 'waning hegemony.'

Finally, if the aim of our discussion of the Cairns Group in Chapter 3 was to focus on the coalition-building capabilities of middle powers in the latter part of the 1990s, then the aim of our discussion in Chapter 4 is to explore middle power approaches to leadership and followership. Again, as with the Cairns Group, we are as interested in process as we are in outcome. For it is our assumption that, while the structural determinants of power in the international system should never be underestimated, the structure of anarchy in international relations is by no means predetermined: states can, in short, make a difference.[7] While Australia's role in APEC offers us an illustrative case of middle power leadership in institution-building, Canada's role in the evolution of NAFTA demonstrates the continued relevance of followership.

Chapters 3 and 4 focus on what we call the second, or economic, agenda in international relations and fix on the exercise of leadership and coalition-building by middle powers in this issue area. While the case studies in these chapters highlight the opportunities for middle power activism in the contemporary international system, we are cognizant of the dangers of portraying the statecraft of these middle powers in exclusively celebratory terms. For, as we demonstrate in Chapter 5, the opportunities for middle power activism and coalition-building are highly dependent on the issue. A case study from the first, or security, agenda of international relations – the role of Australia and Canada in the coalition put together by the United States during the Gulf conflict of 1990-1 – reveals a rather different portrait of middle power behaviour, which we call the other side of coalition-building. In this case, we demonstrate the considerable constraints on middle powers and the more restrictive role options available to them. In contrast to the cases of the Cairns Group and APEC, where the middle powers were active coalition-builders and leaders, the Gulf conflict shows the passive side of coalition-building, in which secondary states like Australia and Canada are willing to allow themselves to be cast in the role of followers and let others build coalitions on them. Thus, the case of the Gulf conflict not only suggests the need for a more nuanced approach to the leadership-followership dynamic in international politics, it also reveals that when the more structural dimensions of power in international relations are at the fore, games of skill are of diminished importance.

Having drawn out the dualistic characteristic of the capabilities and constraints on Australia and Canada as actors in the economic and security agendas, we move, in Chapter 6, to a discussion of the response of both states to emerging agenda items in international relations. This is not to suggest, of course, that this widening agenda is distinct from the more traditional concerns of international relations. Indeed, a characteristic of this agenda is the interlocking nature of environmental and social issues with economic and strategic issues. The purpose of Chapter 6 is not to provide an exhaustive discussion of emerging items on the widening international agenda; rather, its aim is to present a series of specific cases representative of the concerns of states such as Australia and Canada and the manner in which such states addressed these cases.

We focus briefly on four specific sets of issues: (1) global security initiatives such as arms control and non-proliferation – which we see as old security issues approached in new ways; (2) regional politico-security initiatives, such as the attempt to secure a peaceful resolution of the conflict in Cambodia and efforts by both Australia and Canada to advance proposals for a Pacific security dialogue; (3) global functional issues, such as human rights, including Canada's approach to both the issue of Commonwealth-South African relations and newer functional issues such as women's and children's rights; and (4) symbolic internationalism, notably the protection of Antarctica and the issue of global climate change. We chose these case studies because they highlighted so well the scope, range, and multidimensional nature of Australian and Canadian diplomatic behaviour as they respond to an evolving international context.

On the basis of these cases, we demonstrate the appropriateness of the typology of middle power behaviour developed in Chapter 1. We show not only a commonality in Australian and Canadian diplomatic approaches to matters of substance but a disjuncture in matters of style. In exploring the question of style we develop two categories. The first, discrete instrumental internationalism, approximates much Australian foreign policy behaviour in the late 1980s and early 1990s. The second, diffuse internationalism, approximates much Canadian foreign policy behaviour during the same period. Finally, by way of conclusion, we try to draw out some wider analytical conclusions from our discussion of Australia and Canada.

In this brief outline of the book's aims, we should indicate what we are *not* seeking to do. This book is not intended to be a comprehensive comparative exploration of the totality of Australian and Canadian foreign policy in the late 1980s and early 1990s, even though it does touch on numerous aspects of contemporary policy. Nor do we purport to be offering a general model, let alone a blueprint, for successful middle power diplomacy in the pursuit of their national interests. Rather, we hope that by exploring particular facets of the foreign policy of these two states, we might demonstrate the continuing relevance of middle power behaviour in contemporary international politics.

1

Leadership, Followership, and Middle Powers in International Politics: A Reappraisal

Introduction

As the international system underwent a major transformation in the late 1980s, an important debate over the nature of leadership in the international order emerged in the international relations literature. This debate was provoked by a variety of theoretical and policy-related questions, largely centred on the argument about whether the United States was, or was not, in decline. While the intellectual controversy between the 'declinists' and their 'renewalist' critics tended to absorb much scholarly attention,[1] it can be argued that, in the long run, such parochial quarrels over the decline of American leadership may be less important than is the more general question of what, exactly, leadership in the international system entails and what the sources of that leadership might be. This question is clearly much wider than the issue of whether the United States lost the will or the capacity to lead in the 1980s.[2] Rather than focusing exclusively on the narrow question of American leadership in the contemporary international order, the subject of considerable speculation in the post-Cold War era[3], this chapter looks at alternative potential sources of initiative and innovation in international politics.

The essence of our argument is that under conditions of waning hegemony (or, to use Ruggie's term, hegemonic defection)[4] there is a need to pay much more attention to other sources of leadership. In particular, we examine what Oran Young has termed technical and entrepreneurial definitions of leadership,[5] a leadership style that contrasts with more traditional – and structurally determined – definitions of leadership that tended to prevail in the post-1945 period. It is clear that questions of leadership were of less interest to students of international relations during the period when the politico-economic hegemony of the United States was unchallenged, and the intellectual hegemony of the structuralist theoretical persuasion in the discipline of international relations was no less dominant. Globalization and inter-dependence have diminished the importance of structure in explana-tions of international relations. By contrast, the role of 'agents' in the international system has once again assumed greater importance in explanations of world politics,[6] especially for scholars and practitioners of international relations who are concerned with the question of international cooperation in an era of uncertainty and the role that secondary actors may play in the process of cooperation-building.

We start with the assumption that the sources of leadership in global politics are both systemic and domestic. However, while systemic strain may prompt policy responses or initiatives, domestic actors are the primary source of such initiatives or responses. As a consequence, our first concern is to extend the analysis to increase the number of actors which might have the potential to exercise non-structural forms of leadership. Second, we are attempting to widen the range of issue areas in which this non-structural leadership may be forthcoming. Our anal-ysis is driven by a recognition that changes in the international political and economic orders are less conducive to the unrestrained influence of a hegemon now than they were during the Cold War era, and that, as Stanley Hoffmann would have it, 'games of skill' are replacing 'tests of will' in the 1990s.[7]

As we noted in the Introduction, however, we are not suggesting that structural leadership by great powers is no longer the most important source of initiative in the international order in the 1990s. Rather, we contend that other categories of leadership can be significant in cata-lyzing the processes of reform and change – especially those requiring considerable cooperation and collaboration – in a variety of issue areas on the international agenda for the 1990s. Such a role may be performed by appropriately qualified secondary powers in a way that may not have been the case in the past. While we recognize that the term 'middle powers' is problematic, our purpose in this book is to reconsider the historical category of middle power and offer a definition of middle powers that takes account of the changing structure of the global order – especially the increased salience of economic, environmental, and human rights issues on the agenda of international politics in the second half of the 1980s and early 1990s.

Nor, it should be noted, are we arguing that the change in the relational power of the United States vis-à-vis the rest of the world over the two decades since 1970 was accompanied by a commensurate decline in what Susan Strange and others correctly identified as its residual and structural power.[8] Instead, the 1980s and the 1990s may be seen as something of an interregnum in which an old order is undergoing a process of change into an as yet to be defined new one. As Nye points out, the common assumption of an emerging multipolar world is fraught with ambiguity.[9] Not surprisingly, the analysis assumes a continuing central, although not hegemonic, role for the United States. But a strengthening of the tendency towards mitigating political and economic intellectual influences emanating from other centres of power is anticipated. Such influences will obviously come from the other principal centres of structural power in the international order, especially from the European Community and Japan.

This book attempts to look beyond even these influences, however; it suggests that such influences will not be the only sources of innovation in the search for international cooperation in the 1990s. We suggest that the analysis of international politics will have to feature less structurally determined approaches than did the theoretical approaches that held sway for much of the post-1945 era – traditional realism, dependency theory, or, more recently, neo-realist theorizing.[10] Theory-building will need to place much more emphasis on the complex and nuanced interplay of the agent-structure relationship and on the leadership capabilities and policymaking functions of foreign policymaking personnel and institutions in a large number of states. In short, we suggest that numerous factors modify and constrain the structures of anarchy, which are too often simply assumed as a given in neo-realist theory.[11]

Leadership and Followership

In particular, we argue that more emphasis must be placed on theorizing about leadership and followership in the international system. To this point, much of the discussion about leadership in world politics tends to fix on the leader alone. Perhaps not surprisingly (given its American pedigree), the international relations literature pays virtually no attention to the followers that are so necessary for leadership, relegating them to the status of residual and inconsequential categories.[12]

It is true that some of the theorizing about leadership in the global system bypasses the issue of leaders and followers altogether. It does so by eschewing the use of leadership in favour of hegemony. While hegemony and leadership were synonymous in meaning when first used in the English language in the nineteenth century, hegemony has acquired both a positive and a negative connotation in the international politics literature at the end of the twentieth century. In its more negative usage, hegemony tends to be used to describe systems of domination; leadership, with its more positive connotations, rarely makes an appearance in such discourse. In this view, because there is no leader providing leadership, there is little need for a careful examination of followers or followership. Indeed, it does not even make much sense to talk of followers of the hegemon; they are not follower states as much as they are simply subordinate or secondary states, subject to the hegemon's power to ensure that its interests prevail.

To be sure, there are more nuanced forms of structural analysis, be it Gramscian or neo-realist in origin. For example, Ikenberry and Kupchan seek to go beyond purely coercive explanations by exploring the degree to which hegemonic power is sustained by socialization patterns of political elites in secondary states, and the degree to which these elites come to share the larger 'vision' of the hegemon.[13] Likewise, Robert W. Cox stresses the interactive nature of the process: hegemony, he argues,

> means dominance of a particular kind where the dominant state creates an order based ideologically on a broad measure of consent, functioning according to general principles that in fact ensure the continuing supremacy of the leader state or states and leading social classes but at the same time offer some measure or prospect of satisfaction to the less powerful.[14]

However, in much of the literature, hegemony is used in a more positive way[15] – one that has no difficulty embracing the terminology of leadership. And, typically, the analysis tends to focus on the leader and the attributes or traits necessary for a leading state, on the leader's behaviour, and on the generally positive leadership role the hegemon plays, providing what are called 'international public goods,' like order, stability, and security.[16] With only a few exceptions,[17] most students seem interested in secondary states only in order to demonstrate the free rider principle in operation or to ascertain that these states do not possess the attributes of the hegemon – and therefore can be safely ruled out as 'contenders' or 'challengers' to the leading state.[18]

It can be argued that such an approach seriously distorts how we understand the nature of leadership in the international system. Focusing on the traits of leaders and would-be challengers may tell us a great deal about which states are bound to be the most powerful members of the international community (relatively speaking); but because such an approach tells us little about followership, it remains a surer guide to power than to leadership.

And most students of the phenomenon of leadership argue that there is an important distinction to be drawn between leadership on the one hand and headship or dominance on the other.[19] To be sure, such a distinction is not absent in the international literature,[20] but more often than not the leadership component of the leadership-dominance dichotomy tends to be inchoately defined.[21] More important, only rarely does the analysis touch on the dynamics of followership – what drives followers to follow.

By contrast, we believe that it is important to know why followers follow.[22] Like Richard Stubbs, who explores leadership and followership in the context of international relations in Southeast Asia,[23] we argue that the dynamics of leadership in international politics are more clearly revealed by an examination of followership. In the case studies that follow, therefore, we seek to explore the dynamics of leadership as well as followership in the international system and, particularly, the dynamics of how and why middle power followers such as Australia and Canada can embrace leadership roles in international politics.

Towards a Typology of Middle Power Behaviour

The changing nature of leadership and followership in the contemporary international system is one of the key reasons for wishing to reconsider middle power behaviour in international politics in general, and middle power leadership initiatives in particular, in a way that 'relocates' the idea of middle powers in the contemporary international system. Accompanying the hiatus in structural leadership in the international order, there would appear to be a growing awareness on the part of some of the smaller players of the need to substitute for this omission.[24] Such an awareness emanates from a recognition of both constraints and opportunity in the international order in the 1990s. While the increasing exposure of the United States economy to the vagaries of globalization demonstrates the degree to which the growth of interdependence in the international system has had an impact on even the largest of states,[25] there was another category of states which felt, even more acutely, the impact of increased interdependence – the secondary but still highly developed countries in the international system. Often thought of as quintessential middle powers, two of these – Canada and Australia – provide some empirical support upon which we attempt to reformulate middle powers as a useful conceptual category in international politics.

This section briefly reviews the evolution of the middle power concept in the postwar international politics literature, following which some of the applications of the concept are examined. Moving from a critique of the earlier literature, we then propose a reformulated model of the concept. This reformulation focuses on state activity and behaviour in given issue areas and suggests the relevance of an egoistic definition of interest rather than a structural definition. It thus differs from traditional analysis of middle power foreign policy, which has tended to focus on aspects of aggregate state power, 'location' in the hierarchy of states, or idealist normative influences. Above all, this approach – drawing on several examples of 'middle power' behaviour in the latter part of the 1980s – offers both an analysis of, and prognosis for, potentially significant innovation and initiative on the part of secondary, but not insignificant, players in the management of various aspects of the international agenda in the 1990s.

Although the term middle power has long been used in discourse about Australian and Canadian foreign policy in the post-1945 era, there is little agreement on what constitutes a middle power in international politics. We can identify at least four general approaches to the definitional problem.

It is most common to define a middle power by its *position* in the international hierarchy. In this view, middle powers are said to be those states occupying the 'middle' point in a range of bigness to smallness – usually measured by reference to such quantifiable attributes as area, population, size, complexity and strength of economy, military capability, and other comparable factors. Such an approach has its problems, particularly its dependence on quantifiable measures of power, but it does satisfy the intuitive desire to differentiate between those states which clearly are not great powers but are not minor powers either.[26]

Others, by contrast, have suggested that middle power derives from a state's *geography*. A middle power, it is asserted, is a state physically located 'in the middle' between the system's great powers.[27] The geographic approach has at least two variants. One suggests that states which are powerful within their geographic regions might usefully be thought of as middle powers. Another, common in the bipolar Cold War period, suggests that middle powers occupy a 'middle' position, ideologically, between polarized great powers.[28]

A third approach is the *normative* view of middle powers. In this view, middle powers are seen as potentially wiser or more virtuous than states positioned either 'above' them (the great powers) or 'below' them (the minor powers). Middle powers have been thought to be potentially more trustworthy because they can exert diplomatic influence without the likelihood of recourse to force. In addition, because of their past roles – for example, the participation of Australia and Canada in the First and Second World Wars and the Korean War – they are thought to have earned certain rights, at least from their hegemonic ally, the United States. Because of this, countries located 'in the middle' are portrayed as taking their responsibilities to the creation and maintenance of global order seriously; indeed, they have as a result often appeared less selfish than other states.[29]

Although buttressed by a long historical and philosophical pedigree, especially in Canada,[30] the limitations inherent in this emotionally centred view are numerous and significant. Viewed using normative lenses, middle power behaviour takes on a certain smugness, occupying the moral high ground of the politics of the 'warm inner glow.' Such a position, however, is often difficult to substantiate when the actual details of middle power foreign policy are examined more closely. Contrast, for example, Australian and Canadian rhetoric on Kuwait's sovereignty in the Gulf conflict of 1990-1 with their silence on Indonesia's invasion and annexation of East Timor in 1975. Likewise, Canada's reputation as an aid-giver in international emergencies can be contrasted with the hands-off approach adopted by Ottawa during the Nigerian civil war in the mid-1960s. These cases demonstrate the dangers of advocating a normative approach to middle power behaviour: middle powers can be asked to back their fine rhetoric with concrete actions or be susceptible to the charge of the 'arrogance of no power.'[31]

A more difficult problem with the normative approach is that it tends to exclude a wide variety of states which might reasonably claim membership in the ranks of the middle power tier according to other criteria. This problem is most clearly seen in the attempts of Cranford Pratt and his colleagues to examine 'humane internationalism' as it has been practised by middle powers.[32] Their 'middle powers,' in fact, comprise only a small selection of international actors, mainly states that are 'like-minded' developed northern states of middle size – Canada, the Netherlands, Norway, and Sweden – rather than a broader range of states that might include such countries as Argentina, Australia, Brazil, Hungary, India, Indonesia, Malaysia, Nigeria, or Poland.

Yet another problem with this normative approach relates to the demanding standards set for middle-power statecraft – standards which are difficult to meet even by the like-minded countries which have traditionally been opinion-leaders on North-South and development issues. The result, it may be suggested, is undue pessimism concerning the current direction of middle power diplomacy in the international arena. Instead of capturing the dynamism of middle power leadership in a variety of specific issue areas in the 1980s and 1990s, the present role (and future potential) of the middle powers appears to be in retreat, largely because of the uneven response of those countries to extremely broad and multi-layered topics with little hope of establishing workable agendas such as the New International Economic Order (NIEO).[33]

The central premise of this book is that the essence of middle power diplomatic activity is best captured by emphasizing not what this group of countries should be doing but what type of diplomatic behaviour they do, or could, display in common. This fourth approach, the *behavioural*, pays less attention to whether states remain on consistently high moral ground and more attention to a particular style of behaviour in international politics – a style that John W. Holmes termed, with considerable irony, 'middlepowermanship.'[34] According to this approach, middle powers are defined primarily by their behaviour: their tendency to pursue multilateral solutions to international problems, their tendency to embrace compromise positions in international disputes, and their tendency to embrace notions of 'good international citizenship' to guide their diplomacy.[35] Certainly, the foreign ministers of both Australia and Canada tended to embrace such notions in their public statements,[36] even when they did not use the words 'middle power.'[37]

Such middle power behaviour, it should be noted, is guided by healthy doses of enlightened self-interest: as Gareth Evans, the Australian minister for foreign affairs and trade, once stated, good international citizenship is not 'the foreign policy equivalent of boy scout good deeds.'[38] It is also guided by a belief in the technical and entrepreneurial ability to fulfil such a role – what Holmes saw as the functional resources for effective performance.[39]

Moreover, middle power behaviour has been far from static in nature. As the international system has changed, we have seen dramatic modification in the behaviour of these states. Middle power statecraft in the immediate post-1945 era was very much in support of that order established and underwritten by American hegemony. In particular, these states were especially active participants in, and supporters of, international organizations spawned by that order. Yet, constrained by the parameters imposed by tight bipolarity and the Cold War conflict, middle power diplomacy tended to manifest a reactive quality. With the international agenda dominated by geopolitical-security issues, middle powers had little room for manoeuvrability. For the most part, their diplomatic efforts were directed towards easing global tensions and, through peacekeeping and arms control, trying to avert the possibility of the outbreak of another world war. As Bernard Wood put it, 'For much of the post war period most of the middle powers may have felt themselves to be by-standers (or as basically acted upon rather than acting in these matters), with the implicit recognition that their role consisted in anticipating these external pressures and adjusting to them as swiftly as possible.'[40]

In certain circumstances, the role adopted by middle powers encompassed mediatory activity between two antagonistic Cold War blocs. This idea of middle powers acting as 'linchpins' or 'bridges' between East and West gained some prominence in the 1950s and 1960s. In particular, countries such as India (particularly under Jawaharlal Nehru) and Sweden frequently engaged in this type of inter-bloc diplomatic activity, but it was not limited to non-aligned or neutral states, as Canada's initiatives towards the Soviet Union in October 1955 indicate. More commonly, however, the statecraft of aligned middle powers tended to focus on intra-bloc relations: attempting to defuse tensions between bloc powers (during the Suez crisis of 1956, for example), or urging restraint on the alliance leader (during the Korean and Vietnam wars, for instance), or resisting renewed tendencies towards isolationism on the part of the bloc leader. Finally, a considerable amount of attention was paid by the middle powers to mediation and conflict-resolution with respect to regional 'brushfires,' which had the potential of escalating into more widespread conflicts.

To say that the middle powers were highly reactive in their diplomatic activity in the 1950s and 1960s[41] is not to suggest that this group of countries did not have an impact on the international system generally or on the hegemonic leader specifically. To use Keohane's analogy, many of these non-great powers were, indeed, 'able to lead the elephant' on occasion.[42] Cases of this type, however, remained, for the most part, atypical and were restricted to instances in which the United States was basically willing to be reined in. The overall impression one gets of middle power behaviour in that period, then, is not that of leadership but of what we term 'first followership' – a form of activity in which those actors loyally support the norms and rules of the international system and perform certain tasks to maintain and strengthen that system.

By contrast, adapting to new circumstances in the late 1980s and early 1990s, middle powers became increasingly quick and flexible in responding not only to some new conditions and circumstances but in taking different forms of initiatives in policy terms. While growing interdependence threw up more challenges and exposed these states to greater vulnerabilities, particularly in the international economic system, it also provided new windows of opportunities (or, perhaps more accurately, new windows of necessity) for middle powers. It seems clear that middle powers had greater freedom of action thrust upon them in terms of their diplomacy. Because of the gap in the power base, resulting from the relative decline of American resources (and, hence, the umbrella of structural leadership and willingness to lead), these actors were provided with an opportunity to take on greater – albeit selective – forms of responsibility. As part of a more general shift towards burden sharing, followers from the post-1945 era were well positioned to take advantage of the added available space in which to operate: as Puchala and Coate put it, 'numerous middle powers are now looking for ways to assert themselves in the context of the ... leadership void.'[43] Indeed, research in the field of organizational behaviour suggests that committed and able members 'in the ranks' tend to adopt new forms of creative action when confronted with altered circumstances or demands: over time, there is the possibility that followers may adopt leadership roles.[44]

Two other factors worked to reinforce the ability and willingness of middle powers to adopt a more activist, initiative-oriented approach in the international arena. The first is the change in the global agenda. Whereas 'high' policy issues – the first agenda of international relations – were dominant in the 1950s and 1960s, 'low' policy issues were ascendant in the 1970s, the 1980s, and the early 1990s. Concerns about economic security comprise the second agenda of contemporary international politics; this has been joined by a third agenda of social concerns such as environmental policy and human rights. This shift has, in turn, altered perceptions and definitions of national interest. The 'security agenda,' for example, took on a wider meaning in international relations generally.[45] For middle powers in particular, the search for national economic well-being and the maximization of economic sovereignty became as important as traditional conceptions of security, which fixed on physical or territorial conceptions of integrity.

A second significant factor impelling middle power activism is the accentuated intermeshing of domestic politics with foreign policy. With low issues increasingly in command, internal societal forces have been more involved in 'domestic' issues having international ramifications and in those 'international' issues which spill over into the national arena – ineluctably, as Putnam would have it, a two-level game.[46] In many cases, of course, this heightened form of internal pressure introduces a strong element of constraint on policy formulation and implementation. Despite high international expectations with respect to its role on an issue, for example, a given middle power may pull back from 'doing something,' because that action might cause pain to interest groups at home by making them more vulnerable to the exigencies of the changing international economic order. As Cutler and Zacher argue, the result is that, although middle powers such as Canada tend to be portrayed as having a firm attachment to multilateralism and international institution-building, their actual policy behaviour reveals that they have, at best, an uneven commitment to multilateralism.[47]

A classic case of this dynamic was the protectionism on textiles practised by a number of industrialized middle powers, Australia and Canada among them. While the government of Pierre Trudeau put a high priority on global economic development, it was also sensitive to the local needs and interests of Canadian industries – largely concentrated in Ontario and Quebec. With the political sensitivity of the issue heightened by the election of the Parti Québécois government in November 1976, and the run-up to the referendum on sovereignty-association in 1980, bilateral quotas were imposed on imports of clothing and footwear from low-cost sources.[48] Resistance to trade liberalization in this set of domestic industries was even stronger (and more effective) in the Australian case. Despite the cost imposed by such actions in terms of its economic and diplomatic relations with its neighbours in the Association of Southeast Asian Nations (ASEAN), the Liberal government of Malcolm Fraser responded to pressure by both manufacturers and trade unions to save jobs by imposing tougher new restrictions on imports of textiles, clothing, and footwear in the late 1970s.

If they can be a constraint on some issues, however, internal societal forces may push for stronger action or the exploration of more innovative options on other issues. Numerous examples of this pattern can be found in such areas as the environment, human rights, and development assistance – where non-state actors in general, and nongovernmental organizations in particular, can move out in front and provide pay-offs for governments that act expeditiously. For example, the Greens in Australia went well out in front of the government on a wide range of international environmental issues and were able to nudge policy along in the way they wanted. Thus, the Australian environmental movement was able to use the United Nations Economic, Social and Cultural Organization (UNESCO) World Heritage convention to transform the issue of wilderness conservation in South-West Tasmania and the rainforest areas of northern Queensland.[49] In Canada, the issue that stands out as a case in which societal forces led and government followed was the Ethiopian famine crisis, which took place between 1984 and 1985. Galvanized by television images of the catastrophe, the public responded en masse in Canada. While established nongovernmental organizations (NGOs), such as Inter Pares, Oxfam Canada, Care Canada, and the Canadian University Services Overseas, played an important role, one of the distinctive features of this campaign was the high degree of mobilization of ad hoc groupings such as Ethiopian Airlift and the Ethiopian Famine Relief Fund. Another was the scope of this type of activity, which ranged from high-profile campaigns of popular singers to create a 'Northern Lights' trust fund to widespread grass roots endeavours.[50] These public campaigns, in turn, prompted the government in Ottawa to accelerate its own efforts. Less than a year after the government had rejected a proposal for a massive relief operation as unnecessary, a special fund for Africa was initiated, and an emergency coordinator of African relief was appointed. As Joe Clark, Canada's secretary of state for external affairs, admitted, 'Governments, particularly democratic governments, are affected by public priorities.'[51]

What emerged in the 1980s and 1990s was not only a more segmented but a more multifaceted type of behaviour. Middle powers did not move to share structural leadership with the United States; nor, generally speaking, did they have the ability or the aspiration to move into a position of joint leadership on this basis. The leadership behaviour of middle powers was not of the classical type identified by James MacGregor Burns and other students of the phenomenon – that is, leadership based on coercion by brute strength.[52] Nor is it based on economic capability of the sort possessed by the country viewed by many as the 'incipient leader of tomorrow' – Japan.[53] Rather, middle power leadership and initiative-taking have been based on non-structural forms of power and influence associated with the imaginative and energetic use of their diplomatic capabilities. The skills they have utilized are not those of a giant but of a good dancer – what, in a plea for more deft American leadership, David Abshire referred to as 'persuasion, coalition-building, and the art of the "indirect approach."'[54] These are skills that the United States tended to underestimate in the late 1980s; by the early 1990s, Japan was still learning them. Although Japan, as the world's largest creditor and aid giver, had tremendous economic power, there was little sign that Tokyo was prepared to exercise agenda-based leadership. Japan's priority was primarily that of avoiding risks and danger. In contrast to the activism displayed by more skilful middle powers, its diplomatic approach remained exceedingly cautious and reactive in nature.[55] Far from taking the lead on specific issues, it tended to hang back and let other actors do the running.

In attempting to schematize the emergent pattern of middle power behaviour, we suggest that the dimensions highlighted by Oran Young serve as a useful starting point for mapping out categories of action.[56] A middle power approach to diplomacy (for this is what we are trying to demonstrate) emphasizes entrepreneurial flair and technical competence in the pursuit of diplomatic activities. Not only is this diplomacy devoted to building consensus and cooperation on issue-specific agendas, it is invariably differentiated and has an important temporal element as well. Consequently, an itemized pattern of middle power behaviour – changing over time – can be set out:

Catalyst: Entrepreneurial middle powers may act as a catalyst with respect to a diplomatic effort, providing the intellectual and political energy to trigger an initiative and, in that sense, take the lead in gathering followers around it.

Facilitator: In the early and middle stages the focus would be on agenda-setting. The actor (or actors) would be a facilitator for some form of associational, collaborative, and coalitional activity. As we will show in our discussion of both Canada and Australia, coalition-building on issue-specific questions is a central technique of leadership for middle powers, which do not have the structural sources of power available to the great powers. Instead, as Sylvia Ostry has rightly observed, 'Coalitions are a means of leveraging power.'[57] This type of work invariably entails the planning, convening, and hosting of formative meetings, setting priorities for future activity and drawing up rhetorical declarations and manifestos.

Manager: A third stage would be that of a manager, with a heavy emphasis on institution-building. Institution-building is used here in its broadest sense to include not only the creation of formal organizations and regimes but also the development of conventions and norms.[58] Central to institution-building is a work program that establishes a division of labour, the development of monitoring activity, and, possibly (but not necessarily), the establishment of a secretariat or bureaucracy. This managerial stage also requires the development of confidence-building measures and facilities for dispute resolution, in which trust and credibility are built up. Confidence-building also seeks to alleviate misunderstandings and misperceptions through liaison efforts, shuttle diplomacy, the use of alternative formal and informal fora, the creation of transparency, and other means to push a given process forward. In addition, this activity can be complemented by a push to demonstrate the relevance or importance of the initiative by operationalizing some of the more practical (and de-politicized) proposals and programs.

These roles depend on a small, core group of public officials and on the collection of data, which often requires the technical skills of specialists in the national bureaucracy or outside experts. It is also often the case that specialists have been involved in the process for a considerable time and have had continuing input into the genesis of a given proposal. This represents a substantial departure from past behaviour, which was premised on the belief that this activity was the exclusive 'turf' of diplomats.

Such activities are, of course, not the sole preserve of middle powers. Often the great powers have larger bureaucracies, more technical specialists, and greater resources in general at their disposal. However, they also invariably have larger agendas and a wider range of pressures and preoccupations than do middle powers, for whom one international issue may loom so large on their respective political agendas that they devote a larger proportion of their time, energy, and resources to it. In this regard, it is possible that there may be a considerable disjuncture between the overall structural capabilities of a given middle power on the one hand and its technical and entrepreneurial abilities and desires in a given policy area on the other.

This is what Gareth Evans, Australia's minister for foreign affairs and trade in the late 1980s and early 1990s, has called 'niche diplomacy.' It involves 'concentrating resources in specific areas best able to generate returns worth having, rather than trying to cover the field.'[59] How and why middle powers choose to allocate their technical resources to particular international policy issues is one of the more interesting and important questions for students of international relations to pursue in the 1990s. Several general comments may be made here. Concentration on the second and third agendas of international relations arises, in part, because, beyond the general question of potential global nuclear war, many of the developed middle powers do not feel themselves threatened by the issues on the first agenda of international politics – for example, the territorial integrity of the Scandinavian states, Australia, or Canada is not threatened from outside. On the other hand, technical and complex questions on the second and third agendas are threatening traditional high standards of living – for example, the Australian economy being hurt by a subsidy war between the United States and the European Community or the quality of the environment in Canada being under jeopardy from American pollution.

Significantly, these are not discrete foreign policy questions. Nor are they simply political questions manageable from within foreign ministries, using the traditional instruments of diplomacy. Invariably, they are technical questions, although no less political for that. They require not only international negotiators but also specialists from within and outside government to lay the knowledge basis for cooperative problem-solving activity on these matters at the international level. This required both countries to reassess their bureaucratic structures for the conduct of foreign policy. In the next chapter, we explore how, in the 1980s, both Canada and Australia radically reorganized their foreign ministries, giving them a new economic mission, in the hope that a new bureaucratic structure would give them the skills to operate more effectively in the international environment of the 1990s.

There is, thus, a potentially important role for capable middle powers, with appropriate skill levels, to build transgovernmental and transnational coalitions to facilitate policy coordination in important issue areas on the international agenda 'after hegemony.' Needless to say, we are not trying to overestimate the magnitude of this form of initiative in international relations. The influence of middle powers in agenda setting and policy coordination will be constrained by structural pressures; their influence will vary issue by issue, by institutional arena, and by the openness and receptivity to initiatives from other sources. In addition, early initiatives from middle powers in a given issue area are always likely to be easier than they will be in the later stages of any particular piece of policy implementation. Enforcing compliance to agreements will invariably require structural power and institutional support as well as technical and entrepreneurial innovation.

But the general approach to understanding middle power leadership activity as identified above has a number of advantages. First of all, by focusing less on positional attributes and more on the tasks performed on specific issues, a more systematic (and less arbitrary) assessment of the range of middle power leadership activities can be achieved. Rather than concentrating on the behaviour of a narrow group of 'like-minded' countries, for example, this mode of analysis opens up the possibility of studies on a wider range of middle-sized countries. While it is more inclusive, this approach does not devalue the currency of middle power leadership. To be included in the category of middle powers, countries have to act as middle powers. Further, this typology opens the way for a more nuanced portrayal of the diplomatic behaviour of individual middle powers – through a greater scrutiny of stylistic differences within this common middle power approach to diplomacy.

Issue-specific Behaviour: Australia and Canada Compared

To operationalize the model of middle power behaviour laid out above, we use Australia and Canada as useful test cases.[60] Historically, both of these countries may be characterized as committed 'first followers' of the post-1945 international order. Australia and Canada accepted (and, indeed, 'internalized') the norms and values of that system; they self-consciously accepted what Paul Painchaud called a middle power 'ideology,'[61] or what MacKay termed the 'doctrine of the middle powers.'[62] They also participated to a high degree in many of the diplomatic activities designed to support that order (especially at the founding of the United Nations in San Francisco in 1945), taking on a variety of functional responsibilities in areas in which they had some expertise or capacity.[63]

Australia and Canada have long had the potential to take initiatives on specific issues. Notwithstanding the traditional reactive nature of much of their diplomacy in such areas as peacekeeping and crisis management, both Australia and Canada were in the forefront of building international institutions (such as the Food and Agriculture Organization (FAO), for example), the strengthening of regimes such as the General Agreement on Tariffs and Trade (GATT), and economic development in the South (with schemes like the Colombo Plan of the early 1950s). Nor were Australia and Canada reluctant to criticize the

United States or other major powers in the Cold War era, when they believed that the behaviour of the great powers ignored or subordinated the rights of middle powers. It might be noted that, in such efforts, these middle powers frequently spoke for other countries as well.

Figure 1

Characterizing middle power behaviour

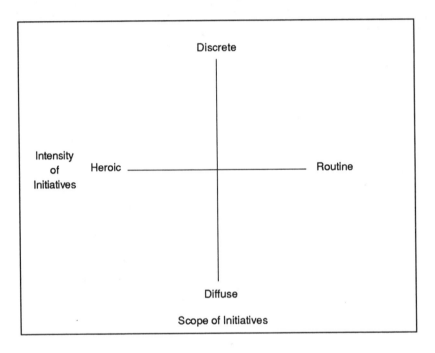

At the same time, however, Australia and Canada are useful to study because they appear to epitomize different styles of contemporary middle power behaviour.[64] To illustrate these differences, we characterize foreign policy behaviour on two intersecting axes, illustrated above. One axis indicates the intensity of the initiatives undertaken: at one pole, we locate what the public policy literature calls the 'heroic' approach to policymaking;[65] at the other pole are located 'routine' approaches. The other axis represents the scope of international initiatives. At one pole we identify initiatives that are diffuse in focus; at the other end are discrete initiatives – those that are more narrowly defined and more separate.

On the intensity axis, Australia generally took a more heroic approach to leadership in international affairs. Australian initiatives tended to be ambitious exercises involving a great deal of effort and risk-taking. They were also highly politicized, in the sense that activity in this form tended to require a high degree of assertiveness and political will. Thus, Australian initiatives were exemplified both by a tendency towards personal diplomacy and an effort to mobilize domestic societal forces behind the initiatives.[66]

Canada, by contrast, has long been viewed as a practitioner of a more 'routine' form of middle-power leadership, with a great deal of emphasis on external mediation and internal consensus-seeking. Heroic initiatives, such as Trudeau's North-South initiative of 1980-1 and his peace initiative of 1983-4 were the exception and not the rule of Canadian diplomacy.[67] Certainly, both of these high-profile initiatives received considerable criticism at home: such forays into personal diplomacy were viewed by many commentators as contributing to counterproductive swings in Canadian diplomacy.[68] If successful in focusing domestic societal (and media) attention on important international issues for a brief period of time, these efforts lacked the political impetus and bureaucratic backup to be effective in the long run. Facilitated by the debate generated after the report of the Commission on International Development Issues (the Brandt Report), Trudeau did get North-South issues onto the agenda at the July 1981 Group of Seven (G-7) Summit he hosted at Montebello, Quebec. But after the Cancún North-South conference – at which he served as co-chair – failed to achieve any agreement on future strategy, Trudeau appeared to lose interest in the issue.

A similar, even more exaggerated, illustration of this pattern may be discerned in Trudeau's peace initiative of 1983-4. This initiative was launched in response to the deepening East-West tensions that followed the shooting down of Korean Air Lines flight 007 in September 1983 and the widespread fear that war was imminent.[69] Trudeau chose to launch the initiative with a major speech at Guelph, Ontario, in October 1983. Key officials from the Department of External Affairs, the Prime Minister's Office, and the Privy Council Office devoted considerable time and resources to developing concrete proposals for negotiation. A heavy emphasis was placed on shuttle diplomacy by the prime minister: Trudeau carried his peace initiative to the Commonwealth Heads of Government Meetings in New Delhi and also to Washington, Moscow, various Western European capitals, Eastern Europe (including East Berlin), and Beijing. This initiative did appear to have some calming effect on the tenseness of the East-West relationship. But its impact was lessened considerably, because, as J.L. Granatstein and Robert Bothwell noted, 'his unilateral initiative had been hurriedly cobbled together ... and no effort had been made to build support for the initiative through patient low-level diplomatic discussions.'[70]

If we turn to the other axis – the scope of international initiatives – it is clear that Australian leadership tended to be discrete rather than diffuse. If Australian diplomacy tended to be deep, it was not broad. Insecure, and becoming more and more marginalized within the international political economy,[71] Australia tended to focus its activity on a small number of issues, where stakes were particularly high. Initiatives tended to be linked to attempts to reform the rules of the game in the international order. For all of the declaratory statements concerning Australia's relationship with the Third World as a whole, few initiatives were directed outside the Asia-Pacific region. Indeed, a concern with over-stretching Australian capabilities limited and curtailed these non-regional initiatives, even in situations in which Australia wanted to act as the archetypal 'good international citizen.' Nothing better illustrates the point than the failure of Australian aid initiatives in Africa.[72]

Conversely, initiatives in Canadian diplomacy were more diffuse. Being alone with the United States in North America tended to make Canadian governments fearful of excessive regionalism.[73] Instead, governments in Ottawa tended to concentrate on initiatives of a global or functional orientation. While overshadowed by the prime minister's personal diplomacy, Canadian diplomatic initiatives were characterized by their variety and diversification during the Trudeau period. Canada found itself having both the will and the means to take the lead on second and third agenda items, galvanized by both a desire to protect parochial national interests as well as a sense of international stewardship. Canada moved well out in front of both the United States and the major Western European countries on a number of environmental and resource issues in the 1970s. For example, the voyages of the American supertanker *Manhattan* in the Canadian Arctic in 1969 and 1970 and the *Arrow* oil spill off Nova Scotia in February 1970 catalyzed the Canadian government into enacting legislation in 1970 that was to provide an important stimulus for global action against ocean pollution.[74] Likewise, Canada was instrumental in helping to launch a new environmental regime through the United Nations Conference on the Human Environment held in Stockholm in 1972. Distancing itself from both the United States and Britain in these endeavours, Canadian diplomacy concentrated on building support for action along these lines among both other middle powers and the developing countries. A particular emphasis was placed on institution-building. At the administrative level, Canada pushed successfully for the creation of a new international agency within the UN. At the normative level, the Canadian priority was for the development of uniform anti-pollution standards or a universally accepted code of ethics.

These efforts, in turn, formed a component of Canada's wider approach to the Law of the Sea negotiations. Canadian behaviour on this complex and multifaceted issue area epitomized the global and functional orientation of Canadian diplomacy. Avoiding a high-profile campaign on the claims of sovereignty, Canadian diplomacy focused on low-key, detailed, sustained activity over a broad range of issues, extending from pollution control, fishing protection, international straits, and mining in the deep seabed. Using its coalition-building skills (through the Group of Twelve, and the Land-Based Producers' Group), and its reputation as a long-standing supporter of the development of international law in multilateral settings, the Canadian government was able to exert considerable influence over the outcome of these negotiations.[75]

It should be added in this context that Canadian officials played a prominent and diverse role in these types of initiatives. For example, Maurice Strong served as secretary-general of the Stockholm conference and was a strong and persistent advocate of the establishment of the United Nation Environment Program (UNEP). Likewise, the Department of External Affairs (DEA) showed a certain adaptability in its willingness to acquire and disseminate technical knowledge in the environment issue area. Not only did the DEA establish a Scientific Relations and Environmental Problems Division and an Environmental Law Section in 1970 (to complement the work of the newly formed Department of the Environment), the department also relied heavily on the Legal Division (headed first by Allan Gotlieb and then by Alan Beesley) within the DEA for specialized advice. Externally, this combination of 'diplomacy, law and science' facilitated on-going forms of technical collaboration between Canada and personnel from other countries.[76]

Conclusions

The purpose of this chapter has been to establish a framework for reassessing and, indeed, relocating the nature and role of middle powers.

We have been at pains to make clear that we are not entirely comfortable with this concept as it has evolved over the postwar period. Historically, the concept has tended to be a somewhat blunt instrument for 'locating' states such as Australia and Canada in an increasingly complex and interdependent world. Indeed, as it tended to be used in the postwar period, the concept of middle power came to lack definitional clarity. While some might be inclined to discard the concept altogether, we argue that the notion of middle power retains both validity and usefulness. The key, we suggest, is to try to move beyond the level of generality usually associated with discussions about middle powers. We argue that the notion of middle power becomes useful to the scholar and practitioner of international politics when we begin to consider the international agenda in an issue-specific manner and when we look at the behaviour of states rather than their positional or normative location in the international system.

As the remainder of this book will demonstrate, our attempts to operationalize the approach set out in this chapter has allowed us to identify a duality of behaviour patterns. At the first level, especially as exhibited in the security domain of international politics (as it has been traditionally understood and as we suggest in Chapter 5), there is a clearly identifiable legacy of followership and passivity. By contrast, on issues which appear on the second (economic) and third (social) agendas, we show that states like Australia and Canada have an opportunity to exercise technical and entrepreneurial leadership.

2

Changing with the International Agenda: State Reorganization and Middle Power Diplomacy

Introduction

We suggested in the Introduction that both Australia and Canada adopted a particular kind of diplomacy in the 1980s to deal with the changes in the international system. However, we also suggested that taking such middle power diplomatic initiatives required technical expertise, particularly concentrated in the bureaucracy. It perhaps should not be surprising, therefore, that in the 1980s, both countries had to confront the question of how best to organize their bureaucracies for the most effective and efficient conduct of entrepreneurial and technical diplomacy in both traditional 'high' policy issues and the newer 'low' policy issues dominating foreign policy. While this was an issue that was also exercising policymakers in numerous other Western states, both large and small,[1] it was particularly problematic for middle powers, such as Australia and Canada, as they sought to grapple with the profound changes occurring in the international political economy.

The question that confronted both Australians and Canadians was deceptively simple: should the state embrace a bureaucratic centralist model and give responsibility for the conduct for all the elements of the state's external intercourse to one central agency, which would be responsible for the panoply of the state's relations beyond its borders? Or should a kind of administrative pluralism be encouraged, where numerous specialized, and relatively autonomous, bureaucratic units would deal with the variety of different aspects of life in the international system? Should the foreign ministry deal only with the issues of 'high politics' – the great issues of war and peace that periodically face political communities? Or should it also try to deal with the numerous issues of 'low politics' that challenge a state's well-being on a more regular basis: economic development, trade, commodities, fisheries, energy, environmental protection, migration, and the like? Or would such issues be better dealt with by specialized line departments with the technical expertise that a foreign ministry could not hope to accumulate?

Some have noted that these are intractable problems, defying any obvious administrative 'solution.'[2] Others have noted the dialectical nature of the debate: in countries with a pluralist model, there are strong desires for an integrated foreign ministry, while in countries with an integrated foreign ministry, there are pressures to give foreign economic policy its own ministry.[3] Despite these obvious problems, political leaders have been persistently attracted to the idea that their foreign ministry could better serve the interests of the state if it were reorganized.[4]

Canada and Australia were no less affected by this broader tendency. Both countries were moved by changes in the international political economy in the late 1970s and 1980s to confront the effectiveness of their bureaucratic structures for the conduct of diplomacy in a changing world economy and in the face of a shifting international agenda. Both states ended up embracing what has long been the standard model for European states of middle size, which, like Australia and Canada, have open economies with a mix of industrialized and primary sectors heavily dependent on export markets and, thus, which needed a foreign ministry that could conduct both economic and 'political' diplomacy in defence of national interests.

Organizing for Economic Diplomacy: The European Model

The foreign ministries of European middle powers – Belgium, Denmark, Finland, the Netherlands, Norway, and Sweden – provide, or provided in the past, bureaucratic models for the conduct of foreign policy that is mainly economic in content and purpose. Each of these countries has long embraced amalgamated, or centralist, foreign ministries, in which the 'trade' and 'foreign policy' sides reside within the same bureaucratic unit.

In Belgium, amalgamation was a feature of the foreign ministry since the nation's founding in 1830, although separate ministers for trade and aid evolved in the postwar period.[5] In Denmark, while an amalgamated foreign ministry dates back to 1848, this tendency became more pronounced when the economic expansion of the latter part of the century 'naturally led to demands for the foreign service to be employed for economic ends.'[6] In Finland, Foreign Affairs is responsible for trade, but because of persistent demands for a separate ministry of trade, a minister for foreign trade was appointed to work as a 'second minister' at Foreign Affairs.[7] In the Netherlands, reorganizations in 1834 and 1841 split trade promotion from the foreign affairs side, with only foreign economic policy remaining with Foreign Affairs. A reorganization in 1876 increased the dominance of the trade side of the ministry: most permanent heads from 1840 to 1940 came from the Trade Affairs Department. In the post-1945 period, however, a series of reorganizations placed the coordination of Dutch foreign economic policy in the hands of an interministerial agency, the Directorate-General for Foreign Economic Relations, which was basically controlled by the Ministry of Economic Affairs.[8] Finally, Norway also created an amalgamated foreign ministry after its separation from Sweden in 1905, again because of the dominance of economic concerns in its foreign relations. A series of reorganizations and one royal commission increased the areas of the foreign ministry's responsibility.[9]

Sweden itself presents an illustrative example of the dialectical nature of the centralist/pluralist debate at work. In 1858, the foreign ministry underwent a major reorganization amid widespread criticisms that the ministry was 'too old-fashioned.' It was divided into three departments – political, legal, and trade – and retained that structure until the ministry was 'modernized' after the disintegration of the union with Norway in 1905. Because that reorganization judged that trade expansion was the key – and only – purpose of the Swedish foreign ministry, the political division was simply closed down. The First World War led to a rethinking of the importance of the political department, with the result that, after a complete reorganization in 1919, trade questions were handled by a resurrected political department; after 1928, trade was given its own department again, but the minister of commerce, not the minister of foreign affairs, was given responsibility for international trade. In the postwar period, there was continual criticism of this structure, including complaints about the trade department and a widespread belief that the amalgamated structure of Foreign Affairs was 'out of date.' As a consequence, in 1973, trade departments transferred to the Ministry of Commerce.[10]

Australia and Canada, of course, differ markedly from these European middle powers in a number of important respects. Neither are in the most obvious sense as 'small' as the European states, and both have rather different economic structures. Moreover, both are federal states in which the constituent governments – the Australian states and the

Canadian provinces – pursue their own aggressive foreign economic policies, frequently in a manner that conflicts with the interests and approaches of the central governments. Likewise, unlike the European states, Australia and Canada did not come to sovereign independence all at once; rather, as members of the British Empire, they enjoyed varying periods in a 'tadpole sort of existence,' as a Canadian politician once put it.[11] As a result, the development of the bureaucratic machinery necessary for operating as a sovereign state was slow and erratic. And, when it did develop, the model adopted was that of the Imperial government in London, with its bureaucratic division between 'Trade' and 'External Affairs.' As we will see, however, by the 1970s, both Australia and Canada did have one important attribute in common with the smaller European states: the general importance of foreign economic policy, particularly external trade, to national well-being and security. And, like the European states, both countries embraced a bureaucratic structure more suited to economic statecraft.

The 1982 Amalgamation in Canada

On 12 January 1982, the Canadian prime minister, Pierre Elliott Trudeau, used his authority to create a 'new' Department of External Affairs.[12] The 'new' department would result from the amalgamation of the 'old' Department of External Affairs, the Trade Commissioner Service, and the trade promotion units of the Department of Industry, Trade and Commerce (IT&C). Also included in the transfer was the Export Development Corporation, the agency responsible for providing credits and export guarantees, and the Canadian Commercial Corporation, a Crown corporation used by the government for state-to-state trading. Eventually, this department came to be known by its present name, 'External Affairs and International Trade Canada.'[13]

It should be noted that the amalgamation was part of a larger reorganization of the machinery of government, which, in turn, was part of the Trudeau government's strategy for dealing with the problems of economic development for Canada in the 1980s. The specific purpose of the reorganization was to encourage growth, both in the overall economy but also in the various regions of the country. As a result, the January 1982 decision affected all departments dealing with the economy. They were restructured, in the prime minister's words, 'to provide a Government-wide focus on regional economic development and to help exporters to successfully confront tough trade competition abroad.'[14] The Department of Regional Economic Expansion, the

Department of Industry, Trade and Commerce, and the 'old' Department of External Affairs were to be replaced by new agencies which, it was argued, could deliver a better and more effective mix of economic development programs: a Ministry of State for Economic and Regional Development (MSERD), a Department of Regional Industrial Expansion (DRIE), and a 'new' Department of External Affairs.

In short, much of Canada's economic recovery was going to be bureaucracy-led. The existing agencies for economic policymaking were going to be shaken up, and greater authority was going to be transferred to Cabinet ministers. Both were considered necessary to shake out the entrenched bureaucratic interests that had developed over time. Megaprojects, as a primary engine of economic development, were going to be encouraged by streamlining bureaucratic approval processes. Regional development policy was going to be made at Cabinet level rather than being left to bureaucrats.

This bureaucratic restructuring for economic development had an important external manifestation: a new Department of External Affairs, which was going to position Canada more solidly in the international economic system by focusing its 'foreign policy' energies on the promotion of the export trade. Henceforth, the Department of External Affairs would put 'a greater priority on trade objectives in the conduct of our international relations, give greater emphasis to the international marketing of resources and services, and strengthen Canada's ability to adapt to changing world economic conditions.' Likewise, the government expressed the hope that 'The reorganization of the DEA will allow it to act abroad with a better appreciation of strategic opportunities over the full range of Canadian interests. At the same time it will integrate the department more effectively into the broader economic policy process in Ottawa.'[15]

While the reasons offered for amalgamation focused on providing an institutional response to help confront the 'tough trade competition' facing Canada during this period,[16] the amalgamation must also be seen as the culmination of a long process of tension and debate about the proper organization of the federal government's foreign policymaking machinery. Some of this tension arose from the fact that the creation of two separate bureaucracies for the management of Canada's external relations was so time-lagged. When Canada became self-governing in 1867, there was no institutional machinery for the conduct of 'foreign' relations. Twenty-five years later, a ministry to encourage external trade was created.[17] And seventeen years after that a Department of External

Affairs was created – and Canada's external affairs department was not even a foreign ministry in the classical sense, since at this juncture Canada still lacked a separate personality in international politics.[18] The relationship between these two bureaucracies was rarely warm, and, until 1968, only twice was serious thought given to amalgamating them.[19]

The immediate background for the 1982 amalgamation can be traced back to 1968, which was when Pierre Elliott Trudeau became prime minister. Trudeau 'sneered publicly' at the Department of External Affairs,[20] not hesitating to denigrate it as largely irrelevant.[21] More important, his views were shared by those who were responsible for the machinery of government, such as Michael Pitfield, who was the deputy secretary (plans) in the Privy Council Office (PCO) and then clerk of the Privy Council and secretary to the Cabinet – Canada's highest civil servant. While Trudeau engaged in overt denigration of External Affairs, Pitfield was beginning a less public process of reorganizing the foreign policy machinery that was to extend over more than a decade.

It began in 1970 with what was known as 'integration' – a package of measures introduced under the direction of Pitfield at PCO. These included the establishment of a formal interdepartmental committee charged with the coordination of all of Canada's external relations, the introduction of 'country programming,' and the transfer to External Affairs of all the support staff of other departments. Some of these measures worked well: the integration of support staff, for example, was achieved without difficulty.[22] The Interdepartmental Committee on External Relations (ICER) fared less well. ICER comprised the permanent heads of External Affairs as chair; Privy Council Office; Industry, Trade and Commerce; Treasury Board Secretariat; Public Works; Manpower (later Employment) and Immigration; and the Canadian International Development Agency (CIDA). But there were no clear lines of authority, and 'infighting ensued (reportedly over trivial concerns), and then, as the protagonists grew weary of the fray, there was a wary truce.'[23]

These initiatives were followed in 1980 by 'consolidation,' again under the direction of Pitfield, by this time the clerk of the Privy Council. Under this scheme, all of the senior executive foreign service officers from the four departments with foreign operations (External Affairs; Industry, Trade and Commerce (as Trade and Commerce [T&C] had become); Employment and Immigration [E&I]; and CIDA) were fully integrated into the Department of External Affairs. From this common pool of senior executives would be drawn the heads of post for Canada's missions around the world.[24] Likewise, a common foreign service was to be created from among the non-executive ranks of CIDA and E&I. Only the Trade Commissioner Service was to be exempt. Amalgamation in 1982 can thus be seen as a logical end to a process that had begun two decades earlier.

But the 1982 amalgamation can also be seen as an attempt to give External Affairs policy 'relevance.' An examination of the views of officials in Ottawa reveals that there was wide attachment to the idea that the demands of a more interdependent and complex global economy required bureaucratic adaptation to a changing international economy and the demands of the so-called 'new diplomacy.'[25]

One of the primary exponents of the view that Canada had not responded appropriately to the changes in the international system was the prime minister himself. Trudeau's early scepticism about External Affairs would not change: when he wrote to Pamela McDougall in August 1980, outlining the tasks of the Royal Commission on Conditions of Foreign Service, he claimed that

> traditional concepts of foreign service have diminished relevance in an era of instantaneous, world-wide communications, in which there is increasing reliance on personal contacts between senior members of governments, and in which international relations are concerned with progressively more complex and technical questions. However, I am not convinced that our approach to foreign service adequately reflects this new era.[26]

This perspective was widely shared in Ottawa, or so it would appear. For example, Allan Gotlieb was the under-secretary of state for external affairs in the late 1970s. Like the prime minister, Gotlieb was convinced that the contemporary international system had undergone a major transformation and, thus, needed a different kind of administrative response. For example, it was no longer possible, he argued, to make distinctions between foreign policy and domestic policy, for this 'traditional distinction ... implies a hard and fast line which no longer exists.' On the contrary, domestic interests have international ramifications and international events have domestic consequences. This required a new kind of foreign ministry for Canada – a foreign ministry which would provide 'creative leadership' in the full range of Canada's response to the demands of the new diplomacy. Gotlieb was not at all convinced that the Department of External Affairs he had been appointed to head in 1977 had kept abreast of these changes. He claimed that External Affairs 'seemed to lack a clear and distinct idea of its role,' and that it 'had not yet decided on its role in the wake of substantial changes in the international and domestic environments which had occurred in the 1970s.'[27]

Many other officials in Ottawa were prepared to be more blunt than this. Pamela McDougall, who headed the 1981 Royal Commission on Conditions of Foreign Service, sought out the views of other public servants in Ottawa about External Affairs and reproduced a 'representative sampling' of these views in her final report.[28] The sample demonstrates the degree to which External Affairs was seen as increasingly irrelevant, given the 'new diplomacy.' For example, one official, unwittingly echoing Keenleyside's views from the mid-1940s quoted in note 19 above, observed that

> External has become irrelevant to the Ottawa game because it has lost sight of the fact that economic considerations led Canada to set up a foreign service in the first place ... Canada's external policies and its foreign activities must relate directly to our national interest, and that interest is 90 per cent oriented toward trade and commerce. Questions of peace and war are vital and should be understood and taken into account, but concern for economic issues must predominate.

Likewise, another official argued that External's 'irrelevance at home' stemmed from the department's 'inability to be an effective conduit of the national interest':

> The foreign service should be the essential prism through which domestic actions and policies are focused and reflected in our international concerns and through which, in return, external considerations illuminate domestic issues. Instead of functioning as a prism, the Service has ... become a transparent and passive interface.

Yet another official argued that the foreign service had lost its sense of purpose in 'the transition from its post-war "internationalist" preoccupation to the current requirement to focus on "the national interest."'

Of all officials, the most important was Michael Pitfield, who was clerk of the Privy Council and secretary to the Cabinet during much of the Trudeau period. Pitfield's views of External Affairs were crucial, for, as head of the civil service and, indeed, a confidant of Trudeau, his recommendations regarding the machinery of government would have a powerful impact on outcomes. Granatstein and Bothwell note that as a deputy secretary in the Privy Council Office 'Pitfield had initially despised External Affairs' elitist pretensions, and he had participated cheerfully in efforts to cut the department down early in the Trudeau years.'[29] As clerk in the late 1970s and early 1980s,[30] Pitfield was less concerned about cutting DEA down to size than about maintaining its policy relevance.

At a seminar in April 1982, Pitfield located the amalgamation firmly within the changing nature of the international system. Noting that Canada was 'living in a global village,' he suggested that 'the world has been further characterized by a growing instability that has rendered the intersection of political and economic factors more intense and problematic.' The difficulty, he argued, was that 'the existing foreign policy machinery in Ottawa contained some fundamental problems.' Among the deficiencies he noted were that a 'conceptual synthesis of policies and programmes' was impossible, for the existing structure did not facilitate policy integration or resource allocation in an era of restraint. Moreover, the existing system bred confrontation because it confused line and staff functions. The status quo did not provide a clear foreign policy line at home: in Pitfield's words, 'the foreign-domestic interface is complex, intellectual, and systemic. There is a tremendous need to ensure it works with clout.' In short, 'there was an intellectual and environmental failure of the system that had to be resolved.' To resolve this failure, two deputy ministers as 'centres of excellence' would 'provide the domestic-international integration that would be the trademark of success.'[31]

Not surprisingly, the official who was appointed to head External Affairs just prior to amalgamation shared these views. On Pitfield's recommendation, Trudeau appointed Gordon Osbaldeston to be the under-secretary of state for external affairs in 1981, after Allan Gotlieb was named ambassador to the United States. Osbaldeston was brought in from outside the department: he had been the deputy minister at the Department of Industry, Trade and Commerce. But he had no difficulty in overseeing the implementation of a scheme that would eliminate his old department. He fully supported the intent of reorganization: 'to pursue aggressively international export markets and to give greater priority to economic matters in the development of foreign policy.' But he noted that, prior to amalgamation, the institutional structure was not designed to do this. For example, he noted that in the case of the department he had headed, IT&C, it was designed to focus on one sector of the economy – secondary manufacturing – and, thus, did not adequately reflect the reality that much of Canada's trade was in areas other than secondary manufactures. Moreover, the structure did not reflect the reality that much trade with developing countries and centrally planned economies required government-to-government negotiations: Canada was ill-equipped bureaucratically for state-trading negotiations. In short, the government needed a restructured organization to 'bring policy-making in the trade and economic area into a closer relationship with foreign policy formulation.'[32]

The 1987 Amalgamation in Australia

In Canberra, Prime Minister Bob Hawke also exercised his prerogative to announce sweeping changes in the departmental structures of the Australian federal, or Commonwealth, government on 14 July 1987.[33] As part of the reorganization, a number of units from other departments with external policy responsibilities were transferred to the foreign ministry.[34] Among the most important were the units of the Department of Trade responsible for multilateral trade negotiations. As a result, Foreign Affairs became the Department of Foreign Affairs and Trade (DFAT). However, the unit responsible for trade promotion, Austrade, remained with the Department of Industry, Technology and Commerce (DITAC) until it was finally transferred to DFAT in November 1991.[35]

This amalgamation, like the one in Canada five years earlier, was part of a larger restructuring of the machinery of government. The prime minister's announcement of 14 July 1987 represented the most extensive reorganization of the public sector in Australian history. It included a reshaping of Cabinet: the usual Australian practice of a single-tiered ministry was replaced by a two-tiered ministry of thirty, comprising sixteen superministries presided over by cabinet ministers, supported by junior ministers not in Cabinet. This required significant changes in departmental structures, requiring amalgamations of a variety of key portfolios, particularly those which dealt with matters that affected social and economic conditions in Australia – education, health, infrastructure (such as transport, aviation, communications), and trade. Indeed, the reorganization saw eleven departments of government – and approximately 3,000 public service positions – abolished.[36]

Thus, the prime minister's own justification for the broader reorganization focused on the general administrative efficiencies and savings that would be accomplished by reducing the number of government departments, on the improvements in policy coordination that would come when interdepartmental debates over policy issues were perforce turned into intradepartmental debates, on the improved budgetary process, and on the enhanced ministerial control of departments that would flow from the restructuring. In turn, the changes in the machinery of government were part of a larger attempt by the Hawke government to try to manage the economic dislocations that were afflicting Australia, which, in the early 1980s, was in the trough of the worst recession since the Great Depression of the 1930s. Of immediate concern were the economic structural effects of the size of the national debt, the relative collapse of commodity markets after the resource boom that Australia had enjoyed during the 1960s and 1970s, and increasing pressure on agricultural commodities – the backbone of Australian trade – by a growing subsidy war between the United States, Japan, and the European Community. In short, as Australia's location in the evolving international division of labour changed, its share of international trade dropped from 2.5 per cent of world trade between 1939 to 1975 to 1.25 per cent in the 1980s; what many were calling Australia's increasing marginalization in the world economy was creating major and severe domestic dislocations.[37]

Throughout the 1980s, the Hawke government pursued a number of policy instruments for economic reform. These included what some have termed an Australian example of corporatism:[38] some old-fashioned Keynesian pump-priming macroeconomic policies interspersed with sharp contractions in government spending; deregulation and economic and market liberalization; and, most important, the floating of the Australian dollar. But the Hawke government also embraced the idea that domestic economic reform would be crucially aided by giving a new emphasis to Australia's foreign policy and the foreign policy machinery. As Gareth Evans, the minister for foreign affairs and trade, bluntly put it after he assumed the portfolio in 1988, 'A constant theme of this Government's economic policy has been to get Australia's external act together.'[39]

'Getting the external act together' meant a shift in emphasis to the economic dimension of foreign policy. The July 1987 restructuring saw the transfer of responsibility for bilateral and multilateral trade policy and negotiations to a new Department of Foreign Affairs and Trade, 'thus emphasizing the central importance of trade to our foreign relations.' It meant appointing a separate minister for trade negotiations, who would be advised by both DFAT and the Department of Primary

Resources and Energy. Likewise, although the trade promotion apparatus was not then to be moved to DFAT, the government did consolidate export promotion for both primary commodities and manufactures in DITAC. At the same time, responsibility for the administration of commodity agreements was left with Primary Resources and Energy because of the technical nature of these agreements.[40]

The impetus for giving a more central place to trade and economic factors in Australian diplomacy came from the changing context of the international economy in the 1970s and 1980s; the impetus to co-locate the two foreign relations bureaucracies within the same government department came from the domestic context of bureaucratic politics.

As in Canada, the Australian Department of External Affairs was created after a Department of Trade. While Australian trade commissioners were sent abroad beginning in 1918,[41] a Department of External Affairs was not created until 1935 – in its modern form, at least.[42] And, indeed, as in many jurisdictions where trade functions are performed by a different agency than are 'foreign policy' functions, the two departments were, as Evans himself asserted, 'separate and often warring.'[43]

Part of the reason for the historical tensions between Trade and Foreign Affairs in the postwar period can be found in the nature of domestic Australian politics. For much of the twenty-three years that the Liberal/Country party coalition dominated Australian politics in the postwar period, John McEwen was not only the leader of the party with a strong rural base, the Country party, but also the minister for trade. McEwen's portfolio was hardly coincidental: in the postwar period, the departments of both Trade and Primary Industry had been the fiefdoms of rural groups; moreover, Trade grew well beyond having merely an 'overseas' export role and took on a powerful domestic role as it developed sectoral policy expertise and control in agriculture, primary industries, and manufacturing. Thus, control of trade policy had been seen as essential for both rural interests (represented in the Country party) and manufacturing interests (represented in the Liberal party). McEwen was thus powerfully positioned within Cabinet to pursue an essentially bilateral trade strategy that tended towards protectionist policies for the benefit of rural and manufacturing interests. During this period, from 1958 to 1971, foreign economic policy and foreign policy in Australia tended to operate in two relatively autonomous spheres.[44]

Interbureaucratic tensions did not abate when the Australian Labor Party (ALP) government of Gough Whitlam was elected in 1972. There were considerable tensions between Foreign Affairs (as it had become in 1970) and other departments in Canberra, particularly between the former and the Department of Minerals and Energy.[45] With Overseas Trade (as it had become), the major problems were with policy coordination, overlap, and duplication, particularly in overseas missions,[46] and with the resistance of the department to attempts by Foreign Affairs to press its authority to coordinate all aspects of Australian foreign policy.

Problems of coordination were to be the focus of attention of the premier study of the machinery of government during this period, the Royal Commission on Australian Government Administration, chaired by H.C. Coombs. The 1975 Coombs Report, which advocated the 'integration' not only of the administrative and diplomatic streams with the Department of Foreign Affairs but also of Foreign Affairs within the broader bureaucracy in Canberra, did little to alter the basic structural problems surrounding policy overlap.[47] Nor, it might be argued, did any of the other seven reviews or studies of Foreign Affairs operations that were conducted between 1975 and 1981.[48] In short, it was not until the Hawke government's election in 1983 that there emerged a sustained examination of the respective roles of the two departments.

Hawke's election brought about two interrelated developments that would affect the historical separation of Trade and Foreign Affairs. The first was the ascendency in Canberra policymaking circles of those who embraced an 'economic rationalist' line in economic policy, both domestically and internationally.[49] The external manifestation of this economic rationalist impulse was a pronounced shift from bilateralism to multilateralism in foreign economic policy. In the economic rationalist view, Australia's traditional fixation with bilateral trade policy, particularly with Japan[50] and China, no longer served Australian interests. Rather, the economic rationalist perspective fixed firmly on the importance for Australia of the liberalization of the multilateral trading system.[51] This required the abandonment of the protectionism that had characterized Australia's traditional approach to foreign economic policy.[52]

The second was the desire of the ALP to capitalize on – and cement – the decline in the electoral fortunes of the National party (as the Country party eventually became). Implicitly, if not explicitly, this meant targeting the Department of Trade – the department so closely associated with the Country party and its rural and conservative interests. Thus the idea of dismantling the Department of Trade, and distributing its many functions around the Canberra bureaucracy, can be seen as also motivated by purely partisan electoral considerations.

As in Canada, personnel played an important role in the change in bureaucratic structure. Hawke's decision to appoint a secretary of Foreign Affairs from outside the department did not 'cause' the amalgamation, but it proved a powerful catalyst. While this abandoned a long tradition of filling the secretaryship from within the department,[53] it was in keeping with a broader tendency of the Hawke government to call on outside experts to fill senior bureaucratic posts.[54] On 3 September 1984, Hawke appointed Stuart Harris, professor of resource economics and director of the Centre for Resource and Environmental Studies at the Australian National University, to be the secretary of the Department of Foreign Affairs. Harris had served in the public service in the past: from 1967 to 1972, he had been the director of the Australian Bureau of Agricultural Economics, and, during the Whitlam Labor government from 1972 to 1975, he had been a deputy secretary in the Department of Overseas Trade.

Just as Pitfield catalyzed the amalgamation process in Ottawa, Harris was to press a view that he had put with considerable vigour in a 1982 article entitled 'The Separation of Economics and Politics: A Luxury We Can No Longer Afford.'[55] As the title suggests, Harris argued that, throughout the postwar period, Australians had compartmentalized their foreign relations into separate 'economic' and 'political' pigeon-holes, pursuing trade policies divorced from politico-security policies. In the meantime, the international system had changed dramatically, Harris argued, forcing an interlinkage between the economic sphere and conceptions of security.[56]

A first cut at breaking down this separation came in 1985 when John Dawkins, the minister for trade, announced that the Hawke government had decided to integrate a number of Australia's export marketing efforts 'with the aim of making them more efficient and vigorous' and 'to overcome Australia's difficult trading situation.' The new statutory authority, the Australian Trade Commission, or Austrade, would embrace the Trade Commissioner Service, the Export Development Grants Board, the Export Finance and Insurance Corporation, and the Australian Overseas Projects Corporation and was intended to be, in the words of the minister to whom it reported, a 'one stop trade shop.'[57] Austrade began operations in January 1986.

The integration of trade promotion functions into Austrade did not, however, settle the twin problems of coordination and overlap. Thus, a second cut at the problem would come in 1986, when Harris added one more report on Australia's foreign policy organization to the many which had accumulated over the previous decade. He authored the *Review of Australia's Overseas Representation*, released in 1986, which suggested that the separation of foreign economic policy and foreign policy could best be resolved by the establishment of a coordinating committee at the bureaucratic level. His suggestion was the creation of a Secretaries' Committee on Overseas Representation (SCOR), which would be chaired by the secretary of the Department of Foreign Affairs. Represented on the committee would be the permanent heads of the departments of Defence, Prime Minister and Cabinet, Immigration and Ethnic Affairs, Trade, Finance, and Local Government and Administrative Services. In addition, the managing director of Austrade and a member of the Public Service Board would sit on this committee.[58]

The 1986 review thus stopped short of embracing the logical bureaucratic solution to Harris's concern about the separation of bureaus into economic and political spheres: their amalgamation into one department. That, however, was to come in the following year, when the broader restructuring of government departments also embraced the departments of Trade and Foreign Affairs. It was not a development which Harris regretted.

In Harris's view – put in a number of addresses over the course of 1988[59] – the amalgamation would achieve a number of purposes. It would improve the advice to ministers on the full range of foreign policy issues and, in particular, those issues of greatest importance to Australian security – economic issues. It would 'enable us to focus more directly on the trade and related challenges that face us.' This rationale was repeated frequently by the two ministers for foreign affairs during this period, Bill Hayden and Gareth Evans.[60]

Conclusions

The amalgamations of the Australian and Canadian foreign ministries were of considerable importance to the evolution of the particular brand of middle power diplomacy pursued by both states in the 1980s. These amalgamations suggest that Canadians and Australians learned in the 1980s what European middle powers had learned last century: that foreign economic policy and, particularly, external trade are of vital importance to the well-being and security of states of middle size and rank, and an integrated foreign ministry is needed to reflect that importance. Australians and Canadians were learning that a bureaucratic structure that is not designed to reflect that reality will eventually lose its relevance.

And in both the Australian and Canadian cases, the changing location of these middle powers in the international political economy prompted a reconsideration. Economic developments – such as recession, collapsing prices of primary products, balance of payments problems, and growing protectionism by major trading partners – produced considerable domestic dislocation, prompting both federal governments to embrace strategies of adjustment to new economic realities. Because the economies of both states are highly dependent on trade, an integral part of their strategies for economic adjustment focused on export promotion and trade policy. In each case, therefore, the government was led to rethink the appropriateness of foreign policy machinery that had originally been created at a time when the two communities were not fully sovereign states, thus laying the groundwork for the separation of foreign economic policy and politico-security policy. In both cases, this rethinking occurred against a background of concern about the proper role of the foreign ministry in an era when the international agenda was burgeoning and changing. In both cases, the governments were led to the same view: the increasing connectedness between the domestic economy and the international economic developments meant that no longer could one maintain a foreign economic policy separate from foreign policy.[61]

Thus, in both cases, they were led first to attempts at bureaucratic coordination at the senior level (ICER and SCOR) and then to amalgamation (which, in both cases, was presided over by a permanent head, who had been brought into the foreign ministry via the trade ministry). As Harris said, amalgamation 'was a logical and indeed ultimately inevitable step' given the circumstances.[62] While he was referring to the Australian situation, he could just as well have been describing the Canadian situation.

'Inevitability,' of course, suggests that the amalgamations were predetermined, and that certainly was not the case. For example, it would have been unlikely for a Liberal/National coalition government in Australia to have undertaken the restructuring of the Department of Trade.[63] On the other hand, there is little doubt that by the 1980s, both Australians and Canadians alike were concerned to ensure that they were equipped with the bureaucratic expertise capable of supporting the kind of diplomatic initiatives we outlined in Chapter 1. This expertise was to be provided in the first instance by grafting the foreign trade and economic departments onto the foreign ministry, which dealt with traditional diplomatic/security affairs. It was then cemented in both countries by the establishment of formal training institutes for producing new recruits for the foreign ministry. In 1990, the Australian government inaugurated its Graduate Programme in Foreign Affairs and Trade at the Australian National University; the Canadian Foreign Service Institute began operations in 1992. Both programs sought to provide recruits for the new amalgamated departments with a more focused and systematic introduction to international political economy than had previously been the case.

Such expertise was crucial for the kind of middle power diplomacy we explore in this book. As we will see in the case studies of the Cairns Group (Chapter 3), regional economic cooperation (Chapter 4), and other global and functional issues (Chapter 6), the expanded focus of Canada's and Australia's foreign ministries was to be of considerable importance for the management of the changing foreign policy agenda in the 1980s and 1990s.

3
The Multilateral Economic Agenda: The Cairns Group and the Uruguay Round

Introduction

Relatively few studies are sensitive to the use of coalitions as vehicles for cooperation and regime-building in the global political economy. The major works that do discuss coalitions have, quite properly, focused principally on coalitions that involve a narrowly defined membership – usually circumscribed by a similarity of attributes and location in the international order – and are engaged in activities designed to secure a fundamental and wide-ranging change in the existing global structures of power. There is a need for studies which are more specifically and narrowly focused but which may, nevertheless, provide us with insight into broader theoretical questions about how to build cooperation in the global economic order on the one hand and the potential role of what we call 'non-hegemonic' actors in that process on the other. It is the purpose of this chapter to make a contribution to our understanding of these processes. Its focus is on what we see as an atypical coalition, a single-issue, cross-cutting group of like-minded states attempting to bring about change in one major area of the international trade regime.

The Cairns Group of Fair Trading Nations established itself as an international actor with considerable influence in the early part of the eighth round of multilateral trade negotiations that began at the Uruguayan resort of Punta del Este in 1986.[1] The Group was formed in Cairns, Australia, in August 1986; its main aim was to secure major reform in international agricultural trade. It was an economically and geographically diverse group from the four quadrants of the globe. Indeed, its very diversity makes it difficult to classify in terms of the traditional geopolitical criteria of North, South, East, and West. Our contention is that the emergence of the Cairns Group and its role in the early part of the Uruguay Round added a new dimension to the process of bargaining in multilateral trade negotiations (MTNs) under the auspices of the General Agreement on Tariffs and Trade. In particular, the activities of the Cairns Group offers substantial insight into the role that secondary states, acting in concert with thoughtful and focused programs of action, may play in contemporary international politics.

The Uruguay Round negotiating structure was headed by the Trade Negotiations Committee, which had overall responsibility for fourteen separate groups negotiating on goods and an additional group negotiating on services. In the final phase of the Uruguay Round, there were 108 countries participating in the negotiations – more than in any previous round. In addition, many states participating in the round were members of a variety of informal groups, such as the De la Paix Group, with its interests in GATT dispute settlement, safeguards, antidumping, tariff and non-tariff measures, and the functioning of the GATT system; the Canadian Informal Resource Exporters Group; the Morges Group on agriculture; the Pacific Group on safeguards; the 'Victims' Group on antidumping; the 'Friends' Group on trade-related aspects of intellectual property and trade-related investment measures; and the Rolle Group on negotiations about services.[2] Although we do not examine these groups in this chapter, they are, nevertheless, symptomatic of the inherent complexity of the negotiating process.

We argue that the institutional complexity and the changing configuration of power in the global political economy more generally diminished the ability of the major actors – in particular the United States and the European Community – to set the agenda and direct the negotiations in the Uruguay Round by themselves.[3] As Gilbert R. Winham, an astute observer of GATT negotiations, has noted, a 'pyramidal structure' of decisionmaking prevailed in previous rounds, allowing the major actors to establish the negotiating agenda: 'Once a tentative trade-off was established, the negotiation process was progressively expanded to include other countries. In this way, cooperation between the United States and the EC served to direct the negotiation.'[4] The essence of the pre-negotiation process (and, by extension, the negotiation process) was for Winham the 'power' and 'leadership' of major actors in the complex and uncertain context of multilateral economic negotiations.[5]

One purpose of focusing on the Cairns Group is to argue the need for a modification of this approach. While the pyramidal model was still largely evident in the Uruguay Round, particularly by the end of the

Round in 1992-3, neither the consensus agreement for a new round of negotiations that came out of the 1986 Punta del Este meeting nor the progression of the Uruguay Round beyond the midpoint of the Geneva meeting of April 1989 can be explained simply in terms of the brute power of the two major actors alone. Progress in agenda-setting and in the negotiating process, we suggest, was significantly facilitated by the activities of the Cairns Group as a constructive bridge-builder and consensus-seeker in the tense and sometimes conflictual relations not only between the major actors but also between the major actors and some of the more antagonistic developing countries.

Even though the primary purpose of this chapter is to describe the role of the Cairns Group in the early phases of the Uruguay Round, our methodological approach is consistent with the theoretical arguments set out in the first chapter. But we also seek to clarify some of the linkages between the major theoretical questions and the attributes of middle power behaviour we have laid out. More speculatively, we suggest that the activities of the Cairns Group provide us with a model of group activity that non-great powers can, under certain circumstances, use to advance their own interests. Such activities help to foster change in issue areas of importance to them in a global economic order in which the decisionmaking process is increasingly more fragmented and complex, and in which major actors need both support and coercion in moving towards a more cooperative form of global economic management in the contemporary international system.

In the first two sections of this chapter, we offer a brief analysis of the pattern of change in the international trading system in the 1970s and 1980s and examine the tensions in agricultural trade during this period. In the third section, we examine the factors that led to the formation of the Cairns Group. We also examine the roles of two of the Group's key middle powers, Australia and Canada, and contrast Australia's leadership role in the coalition with Canada's more low-profile and reticent role. In the fourth section, we focus on the Cairns Group as an actor in the international political economy of agriculture, devoting special attention to the Group's agenda for reform, its role as a political coalition, and its attempt to provide intellectual leadership in the pursuit of a more liberal agricultural trade in the Uruguay Round. We then consider the prospects for the success of this multi-member, single-issue coalition of weaker states as a vehicle for sponsoring change in an international trade regime that is no longer underwritten by a hegemonic actor.

Transformations in the International Political Economy

This chapter does not enter the broad-ranging debate over the issue of posthegemonic change in the international political economy – other than to note its importance for locating our study of agricultural trade in the contemporary international trading system. In this regard, three general points need to be made. First, the post-1970 period saw a serious erosion in the principles and norms that had been established at Bretton Woods and in the articles of GATT that formed the basis of the post-Second World War liberal international economic order.[6]

Second, the chief characteristic of change in the international economic order was a shift from hegemony to multipolarity. This is not to say that American preponderance was supplanted, nor that a system of advanced multipolar management of the global economy emerged to replace the hegemony of the United States. Rather, the United States has been joined by other major – even if still lesser – economic powers, such as Japan and the European Community, and this has complicated the power-sharing arrangements in the international political economy, the governance of which is no longer possible under the principles established in the second half of the 1940s.[7] It is, of course, possible to argue that there has been no measurable decrease in the ratio of trade to gross national product,[8] and that, by logical extension, the real impact of non-tariff barriers is, in fact, limited. The point of concern for us, however, is the degree to which perceptions both of a major shift from an earlier liberal ethos and of the pervasiveness of non-tariff barriers came to have a deleterious effect on the wider commitment to liberalism in many quarters of the global system.

Third, a major victim of these broad changes in the international economic order would appear to be the more specific principles and norms that are enshrined in GATT, and which guided the international trading system until the 1970s: multilateralism, non-discrimination, and a legal or codified approach to regulation rather than a negotiated approach, which preserves the sovereign administrative discretion of states. The codified approach represented a preferred American position to that of its European allies in the decades after the Second World War.[9] These principles and norms, however, came under increasing pressure in the 1970s and 1980s. Not only did the rise to major actor status of the EC and Japan undermine the ability of the United States to set the agenda, but it would appear that, at the same time, many in the United States no longer believed that the principles that served American interests well during its period as hegemon were still serving the national interest in the 1980s.[10] Increasingly, the major debate over the international trading system was driven by ideological and philosophical questions about the relative merits of liberalism and mercantilism. While GATT was successful in lowering tariffs, it was unable to discourage the use of non-tariff instruments, which have become the major reflection of 'illiberality' in the trading system. With the emergence of the new protectionism,[11] a panoply of government-sponsored measures (described variously as strategic trade policy or industry policy[12]) became the norm, and the international control of these measures could only be brought about by multilateral rather than bilateral decisionmaking and negotiation.

The Politics of Agriculture in the 1970s and 1980s

It is in this broad context of change that the politics of agriculture has to be understood. In the immediate post-Second World War period, the United States was the dominant actor in the international agricultural trading system. By virtue of its willingness to take on the burdens of stockholder of last resort in grains, in both commercial and concessional transactions, the United States may be said to have performed the role of manager of the international agricultural trading system. Indeed, the norms and rules of the post-1945 food regime reflected the liberal economic values championed (although not always practised) by the United States – values which included comparative advantage, specialization, and the free and open exchange of goods and technology.'[13] Under such conditions, American policymakers argued that economic growth and efficiency would be maximized on a global level. To make such an assertion is not, however, to deny a history of protectionism in American agricultural policy in the years immediately after the Second World War – which, in part, explains the weakness of GATT on the issue of agriculture. After all, in the first few years of GATT's existence, it was the United States which secured the 'temporary waiver' of certain quantitative import restrictions that conflicted with the interests of its own agricultural markets – a waiver that was still in place at the beginning of the Uruguay Round. However, the issue of United States protectionism in the post- 1945 era is one of degree. While the government in Washington was markedly less protectionist than were the European countries in agricultural trade in the 1950s, it was, nevertheless, restrictionist. However, the United States became more liberal throughout the 1960s, as its agricultural industry became more efficient and as the exchange rate of the dollar became more favourable and increased its competitive edge.[14]

But a regime directed by the United States had a number of benefits for its allies. The liberal flow of food allowed Western Europe and Japan to secure cheap and plentiful supplies of agricultural goods and, thereby, enabled them to concentrate on restructuring their industrial infrastructure. Furthermore, it allowed them to benefit from the positive effects of technological transfer, with the import of American stock, equipment, machinery, and expertise – all of which facilitated the development of new agro-industries in Japan and the EC countries.

Despite these benefits, many advanced industrialized governments remained suspicious of the principles of economic liberalism and, also, of the leadership of the United States in agricultural policy. The EC had its Common Agricultural Policy (CAP) and Japan had its Basic Agricultural Law; both imposed import quotas and other protective devices on a wide range of items, even after the 1961 liberalization of foreign trade controls. These protectionist devices also reflected the widespread belief that agriculture should enjoy a unique status in political affairs. Certainly protectionist-oriented farm lobbies had considerable political clout: in both the EC and Japan, agricultural interest groups were not only vociferous in their defence of specific interests, they were also bulwarks of support for conservative governing parties.

However, what eventually undercut the stability of the international agricultural trading system was not the internal illiberal practices of Japan and the EC. Rather, erosion came about because of a number of exogenous shocks in the early 1970s. Some of these shocks were natural: for example, crops throughout Asia, the Soviet Union, North America, and Africa failed due to drought. Some, however, were political. For example, the United States signalled, even before the crisis caused by droughts, that it was withdrawing from its commitment to the orderly international marketing of grains and that it was going to attempt to redefine the terms of trade with its allies in order to promote American exports. Through its new emphasis on national self-interest – as opposed to international obligations – the United States helped to redirect attention away from the anomalies and defects of the EC's CAP and Japan's import restrictions and towards its own declining will and capacity to maintain and defend the system.

To these indirect shocks were added the more direct shocks associated with the food crisis of 1972-4. The most publicized of these was the sudden decision of the Nixon administration to place an embargo on the export of soybeans and soybean products. To be sure, the embargo itself was short-lived, lasting only from 27 June to 2 July 1973. It was then replaced by export controls that continued through the rest of the summer. The embargo could be explained as an action designed to defend the interests of both domestic and foreign consumers during a time of reduced supplies (due largely to the vagaries of nature) and higher prices for protein. Nevertheless, the impact – both economic and psychological – of the embargo on the EC countries and Japan was profound, given the emphasis these countries traditionally placed on 'food security.' Whether the Nixon administration's decision to impose the embargo without consulting other countries was interpreted as a sign of poor crisis management, as an indication of the dominance of domestic interests, or simply as a blatant attempt to use American 'food power' in the commodity sector, the credibility of the United States as a reliable supplier of foodstuffs was seriously damaged.

The ultimate effect of these shocks, compounded by the subsequent actions of the Organization of Petroleum Producing Countries (OPEC), was to place the issues of autonomy and self-sufficiency with respect to food at the top of the political agendas in both Japan and the EC. Now that dependence on the United States for specific imports had become equated in the minds of European and Japanese opinion leaders with vulnerability and the loss of independent decisionmaking, far less emphasis was given to the idea of trying to reform illiberal trading practices. Rather, far more emphasis was placed on building and maintaining food security in keeping with a narrowly defined self-interest. If the United States was unwilling or unable to continue to provide adequate protection in terms of international food security, the industrialized countries would have to immunize themselves against unreliability of supplies. In other words, self-help was legitimized and encouraged at the expense of economic liberalism. As a leading American proponent of a market-oriented agricultural trade approach noted, 'Americans must admit that our own temporary embargo ... gave support to arguments for protectionism ... [and created] a climate that continues to be deleterious to our efforts to ensure reductions in barriers to trade in agricultural products.'[15]

The EC and Japan had a number of options available to them as part of an overall strategy of ensuring supplies of food. One was simply to raise internal support prices for basic crops while relying less on agricultural imports. To a considerable extent, this path was followed by Japan:

the government in Tokyo established an emergency stockpile of two million tons of rice and imposed restrictions on the import of meat through such measures as the 1975 beef price stabilization scheme. This inward-looking approach had the inevitable consequence of generating new bilateral conflicts with the United States and other exporting countries over access to the Japanese market. As the president of the Brookings Institution suggested with respect to the United States embargo and Japan's response, 'It is not difficult to see how a pattern of thrust and parry could thus be established in U.S.-Japanese agricultural relations, which have hitherto been relatively free of tension'.[16]

Similarly, in products covered by the CAP, the EC concentrated on increasing its internal farm production through the continuation of high prices and the expansion of open-ended intervention guarantees. While the food crisis continued, the financial cost of this approach seemed to be well justified. Even as dogmatic a critic of the CAP as the *Economist* could admit in 1974 that 'instead of the ogre it once appeared to be, the CAP is protecting the community from some of the unstabilizing effects of the price spiral.'[17] The long-term implications of such a 'food security' approach were only realized when the crisis receded in the late 1970s, for this inward-looking expansionist strategy had pushed the EC's overall agricultural production (as, indeed, it pushed American production) well beyond the requirements of immediate food security needs. By 1983, the degree of EC self-sufficiency in percentage terms was higher than 100 per cent in a wide range of products: 144 per cent in sugar; 125 per cent in wheat; 123 per cent in butter; 110 per cent in poultry; 108 per cent in cheese; 104 per cent in beef and veal; and 101 per cent in pork.[18]

The EC's shift to a net-surplus actor in a variety of agricultural products introduced new sources of tension into the international agricultural trading system. As mountains of agricultural produce accumulated in the post-crisis environment the CAP was gradually globalized, and a new EC agricultural export strategy, based on export subsidies and restitutions, emerged. The EC justified this new strategy on pragmatic grounds, arguing that it was better to subsidize consumers outside the European Community (especially those in the Third World) at a low cost than it was to subsidize the storage and preservation of stockpiles inside the EC at a high cost. Still, to the traditional defenders of the CAP, an explicit export strategy also had the significant advantage of institutionalizing the surpluses.

The EC's efforts to 'export' the CAP's problems posed a direct challenge to American leadership in international agricultural transactions. In overall commercial transactions, the United States continued to lead, with $41.7 billion of produce sold abroad in 1982 – 70 per cent more than in 1976.[19] But the EC vaulted into second place, with agricultural exports valued at $27 billion in 1982, representing a 156 per cent rise during the same six-year period. In terms of major agricultural commodities, the EC had, by the early 1980s, become the world's largest exporter of poultry, the largest market economy exporter of sugar, the supplier of three-fifths of the international market in butter and dried milk, the second largest exporter of beef (after Australia), and a major exporter of grain and flour.

The impact of this challenge was felt in a variety of ways. At the level of values, there continued to be fundamental differences between the rhetorical weight placed by the United States on a 'free market' and the emphasis placed by the EC on 'sovereignty' and the 'management' of international transactions. At the level of action, the increasingly aggressive export approach prompted a backlash from the United States. During Jimmy Carter's presidency, and in the early years of Ronald Reagan's first administration, the response from Washington centred on a concerted attempt to secure a revamped subsidy code of international trade under GATT. Dissatisfaction with the slow pace involved in changing the formal rules governing export subsidies, however, shifted American agricultural diplomacy towards 'fighting fire with fire,' particularly after the November 1982 GATT ministerial meeting. One of the first expressions of American dissatisfaction with international dispute-settlement procedures was the largely ad hoc decision of the United States, in January 1983, to openly subsidize the sale of one million tons of surplus wheat flour to Egypt, which had traditionally been supplied by the European market. With the introduction of the Export Enhancement Program (EEP), however, subsidies became not only more institutionalized but also more globalized: the program targeted traditional markets of other agricultural exporters. Through its shift in approach, the United States signalled to other actors involved in food and agricultural trade that it was willing to resort to neo-mercantilist practices in order to defend economic liberal values.

In short, while agricultural trade was always seen as an exception by the major producers, it also came to exhibit all the worst elements of the new protectionism in most nations. Thus, from the end of the Second World War until the 1970s, agriculture occupied a position of peculiar political sensitivity that made it distinct from, although not unconnected to, other sectors of global trade. Because of this, government policy in most countries – developed and developing nations, market-oriented and command economies, and major and minor powers – became geared to defending the agricultural sector, and international trade rules were moulded accordingly.

From the 1970s, agricultural policies, especially those of the major powers, were pursued in an increasingly aggressive and nationalistic manner – indeed, as an arm of foreign policy. This, in turn, led to strain and tension in relationships between the United States and Japan, the United States and the EC, and the EC and Japan.[20]

Given how deeply rooted the political interests in agriculture became, it should not be surprising that reform of the system would be so difficult. There were three areas in which reform was needed: (1) in the domestic structures of agricultural production around the globe; (2) in the international trading system generally; and (3) in the GATT system specifically. These areas of reform were, of course, interlinked, and an acceptable set of new rules could be secured without reform in all three. However, while reform of the international system of agricultural trade could not be achieved without domestic restructuring, it is the international context generally, and GATT and the actors in the Uruguay Round specifically, which are the focus of the remainder of this chapter.

The Cairns Group: A Profile of Strange Bedfellows

One should not exaggerate the role of the Cairns Group as a go-between and consensus-seeker in the early phases of the Uruguay Round. However, we would argue that the efforts of middle powers, particularly the intellectual and entrepreneurial leadership exercised by Australia, reflected the characteristics we outlined in Chapter 1. Before examining the role of both the Group and the middle power leader in particular, however, some detailed characteristics of the Group need to be outlined.

There were fourteen members of the Cairns Group: Argentina, Australia, Brazil, Canada, Chile, Colombia, Fiji, Hungary, Indonesia, Malaysia, New Zealand, the Philippines, Thailand, and Uruguay. Although the Group included several countries, besides Australia and Canada, which could be labelled as traditional middle powers on the basis of their economic capabilities or diplomatic stature (for example, Argentina, Brazil, Hungary, and Indonesia), the differences between these countries and their coalition partners with respect to their levels of economic development and the nature of their political system were marked. Moreover, the Group contained a large number of countries not generally thought of as middle powers, such as Chile, Colombia, Fiji, Malaysia, the Philippines, Thailand, and Uruguay. This unusual pattern of association can be seen most clearly when the Cairns Group is contrasted, for example, with the Group of 12 – a group of middle powers which sought to exercise collective influence during the Law of the Sea negotiations. At the United Nations Conference on the Law of the Sea (UNCLOS), Australia, Canada, and New Zealand joined with nine like-minded Western European democracies – Austria, Denmark, Finland, Iceland, Ireland, the Netherlands, Norway, Sweden, and Switzerland – to press the major powers on law of the sea issues.[21] The Cairns Group was radically different: its members might have had a commonality of interest, but they were 'like-minded' only in that one narrow objective. By its mixed composition alone, then, the Cairns Group may be regarded as a coalition unlike any other in the contemporary international political economy. Members were, in simple terms, from both sides of the East-West and North-South divides in the international order.

The Group's marked heterogeneity of structure, differing levels of development, and divergent political interests in most other domains should be contrasted with its strong commonality of interest and homogeneity of policy in the Uruguay Round and, particularly, with its members' common interest in reforming global agricultural trade. Moreover, Cairns Group states did have important structural commonalities. Each had a highly competitive export-oriented agricultural sector, with agricultural exports as a percentage of total exports ranging from 18 per cent for Canada to 73 per cent for Argentina.[22] The high percentages of the Group members can be contrasted with the percentages of the United States (17 per cent), Japan (1 per cent), Germany (7 per cent), Britain (8 per cent), Italy (9 per cent), and France (19 per cent). In addition, all of the Cairns Group states played an important role, individually or collectively, in a large proportion of the world's agricultural markets, ranging from 21 per cent of the world's sugar and honey to 92 per cent of the world's vegetable oils.[23]

Although Australia and Canada, two Western developed countries, played an important role in the Cairns Group, it should be noted that the Group was primarily made up of developing countries. In this respect, the Group represented but one major developing country perspective on global agricultural trade, an alternative to which was the perspective of the Food Importers Group, another coalition of developing countries, which also had an active, if somewhat ineffectual, voice in the MTNs.[24] In addition to this division, there were considerable manifestations of diversity among the developing countries within the Cairns Group. Along an economic axis, Argentina, Brazil, Chile, Malaysia, and Uruguay fell into the World Bank's upper middle income category, while Colombia, Fiji, Indonesia, the Philippines, and Thailand were in the lower middle and low income categories. Along a regional axis, developing country members came from Latin America, Southeast Asia, and the South Pacific.

The collective weight of the Cairns Group gave it the potential to be a significant 'third force' in the GATT negotiations. The combined gross domestic product (GDP) of the Group, at close to $1.06 trillion, was not much less than that of Japan at $1.3 trillion; moreover, the Group's share of world agricultural exports was 26 per cent, second to the EC's 31 per cent share but considerably larger than the 14 per cent share of the United States.[25] Furthermore, the amount of manufactured goods imported by the Cairns Group was roughly equal to the amount of manufactured goods exported by Japan.

Despite the competitiveness of their agricultural sectors, all members of the Group identified the 1980s as a period in which they were adversely affected by the growth of illiberality in agricultural trade in general and the policies of the United States and the EC in particular. While the problem of access to the markets of the major industrialized countries was important, the worst problem for the competitive status of Cairns Group members was the growth of the EEP and, for want of a better expression, the perceived 'globalization' of the CAP. Subsidized European expansion into 'nontraditional markets,' and subsequent American retaliation, affected the ability of Cairns Group countries to hold their own in these markets.

Given this, it is hardly surprising that the middle-sized and smaller agricultural trading countries increasingly saw themselves as the real victims of the tensions between the EC and the United States. Many of their leading exports – wheat, animal feed, rice, and meat – were being hit hard by the EEP; but they did not have the financial resources to engage in a protracted campaign of agricultural subsidization themselves. Moreover, the problem was particularly acute for the Latin American countries, saddled as they were with huge debts, since the servicing of their debts required, among other things, an expansion of sales of agricultural goods. It is hardly surprising, given these imperatives, that these middle-sized agricultural producers had considerable motivation to band together in a coalition of 'fair traders' to emphasize reforms in the global agricultural system that would reward efficiency and free market forces.

Australia and Canada: Changing Roles in Middle Power Behaviour

A distinctive feature of the Cairns initiative lay in the exercise of leadership within the Group. As we noted in Chapter 1, in the post-Second World War period, the Canadian government was traditionally out in front with respect to the thinking and practice of middle powers,[26] while the Australian government tended to adopt more of a followership role. Indeed, as one student of Canadian and Australian diplomacy has described the role of the two countries in the post-1945 era, 'Canada appeared to lead the way in directions along which Australia has moved.'[27] This source of leadership was particularly evident in the ability of Canadian diplomats to assemble coalitions and to work with other countries on the implementation of proposals.

But in the Cairns Group, these traditional roles were reversed. In a sharp departure from past behaviour, Australia assumed the pivotal intellectual and leadership position in the process of coalition-building and maintenance, while Canada's commitment to the Cairns Group was markedly nuanced and, at times, positively ambivalent.

The coalition behaviour associated with the Cairns Group emerged as a response to the increasingly intense form of competition in the international agricultural trading system previously outlined. These states were faced with a rising threat not only in terms of a denial of access to the markets of the major industrialized countries but also in terms of the intensification of competitive subsidization by the United States and the EC. But they lacked the financial resources to compete with these stronger actors. The middle-sized and smaller actors sought to win a commitment in the MTNs to agricultural reform, especially a standstill and rollback in reference to subsidization and a break in the nexus between production and administered internal pricing. To give momentum to this drive, some form of collective action directed towards improved rules of the game was thought necessary. Indeed, for the weak, the alternative to seeking safety in numbers was to continue to be victimized individually.

The role of Australia and Canada, from a political and historical viewpoint, is of particular interest with regard to the formation of the Group. These two countries, it could be argued, were the 'first followers' of the post-1945 agricultural trade regime. More even than the hegemon, Australia and Canada remained committed to the maintenance of the rules, principles, and institutions of the regime and were willing and able to make the diplomatic effort to defend it against erosion. In the late 1960s, when the United States sought to increase the sales of American produce (thereby threatening to destabilize the pricing agreement established under the International Grains Agreement), both Canada and Australia took on a greater burden of responsibility in an attempt to ward off the collapse of the system. Jean-Luc Pepin, then Canadian minister of industry, trade and commerce, told the House of Commons in 1969 that even if 'we may have lost a number of sales' in the process of trying to save the International Grains Agreement, it was 'worth the effort.'[28] Likewise, Australia showed restraint in the face of increasingly cutthroat competition during the same episode. As one Australian journalist wrote in regard to the situation, 'International cooperation was only maintained by a virtual waiving of the price provisions and agreement by some exporters, such as Australia, to compete a little less aggressively so as to allow other nations to maintain their traditional share of the world market.'[29]

Canadian and Australian interests in the agricultural order also help give more precise shape to the concept of middle powers. The different diplomatic styles displayed by these countries comes out strongly in this issue area.[30] In defending the post-1945 order, Canada always placed a greater emphasis than did Australia on mediation and compromise. Though Canada was a significant actor, its diplomatic initiatives tended to be of a reactive nature: they usually came in response to the actions of other countries, particularly the United States. In contrast, Australian diplomacy was more inclined to actively challenge the major actors (if their policies appeared to be at odds with the norms of the regime) rather than to play the role of the low-key 'helpful fixer' in multilateral fora.[31]

This is not to say that Canada was reluctant to criticize the actions of the United States or the EC. However, when it did make diplomatic protests, it did so either privately or in concert with other countries. Canada also paid a great deal of attention to confidence-building measures, in particular, seeking to build up consultative or dispute-resolution fora and mechanisms. The highly contentious issue of American techniques for disposing of agricultural surpluses, for example, triggered the establishment of the Joint United States-Canada Committee on Trade and Economic Affairs.[32] Similarly, Canada joined with the United States in various early attempts to mediate the fundamental differences on the question of restricted access to the EC market due to the implementation of the CAP. Initiatives along these lines included the formation of a special committee of the Organization for European Economic Cooperation in order to examine the problem and the arrangement for consultations in May 1960 between the EC and representatives of the major exporting nations.

These differences in diplomatic style highlight the important structural differences between Canada and Australia with respect to their relative positions in the international political economy. Canada's position is the more ambiguous of the two, especially in relations with the United States. On the one hand, Canada had a far greater dependence on a single trading partner than did Australia, since more than 75 per cent of Canada's trade is with the United States. On the other hand, in relative terms, Canada remained in a far stronger overall economic position than did Australia. Canada had a higher GNP per capita as well as a more diversified overall economy. As a result, Canada's exposure to trade tensions in the agricultural area was far less marked than was Australia's. The profile of Canadian farm exports tends to be concentrated, with grains and oilseeds dominating as the competitive sector and with dairy and poultry products remaining relatively uncompetitive and domestic-oriented sectors.[33]

The Australian position was rather different. Although Australia had more diversified trading partners, it did not have the economic strengths of Canada. Not only was Australia more dependent on its export of resources, but its vulnerability to the denial of market access and to the competitive subsidization of agricultural commodities was far greater, given the wide range of agricultural produce it exports (rice and sugar as well as grains, dairy produce, and meat). Indeed, for the so-called 'lucky country,' the 1980s were a sober period, because agricultural prices fell and Australia no longer had the cushion of strong mineral and energy exports. From 1973 to 1983, Australia slipped from being the twelfth largest trading nation to the twenty-second, and its share of the world export market dropped from 2.6 per cent to 1.2 per cent. This downturn was starkly reflected in the rise in capital debt, the fall in the currency level, and the increase in the balance-of-payment deficit on the current account. In short, Australia underwent a process of increasing marginalization in the global economy during this period.[34]

The changing positions of Canada and Australia in the international political economy also helped to give more precise shape to the foreign economic policy options available to the two countries.[35] Canada was fortunate in having a number of global, regional, and unilateral options available to it. It was able to take advantage of the manoeuvrability that its economic capabilities allowed, particularly with respect to its presence in the G-7 and other exclusive fora. At the same time, however, it could continue to place a high emphasis on securing political and economic concessions vis-à-vis the United States (albeit, it could be argued, not without trade-offs on sovereignty). Australia's options, by contrast, were much more limited. As one Australian official bluntly put it, GATT represented the only game in town: 'Despite its shortcomings, the GATT is the only rule of law applying to world trade ... Warts and all, [it] represents the best available political commitment ... in an imperfect world.'[36]

Yet, far from being successful in this global approach, Australia seemed, by the mid-1980s, to be increasingly isolated from its traditional political and ideological allies. In this respect, the emotional response by the Australian delegate at the 1982 ministerial meeting of GATT over the inability to get agriculture on the agenda served as a crucial learning experience for the Australians and exposed the futility of pursuing an abrasive diplomatic approach. When Doug Anthony, Australia's deputy prime minister, stormed out of the meeting, calling it a 'fiasco,' the action did not earn diplomatic kudos but, instead, was greeted with 'loathing and disrespect' from some of the key actors in the issue area.[37]

The coalition-building behaviour that eventually led to the formation of the Cairns Group, then, was part of a serious process of self-criticism and re-evaluation for Australia. Frustrated in its efforts to reform the agricultural trading system head on, Australian policymakers embarked on a more indirect, step-by-step approach to achieve the same end. Reform, it was realized, could only come by collective action. The Labor government of Bob Hawke, moreover, not only had an economic imperative for 'doing something' about agricultural trade, but it also had a domestic imperative for action which related specifically to the rapidly escalating 'rural crisis.' An externally oriented campaign against the illiberal practices of the United States and the EC, while not a complete answer to the Labor government's political problems at home, certainly proved a useful political palliative.

Despite its unsuccessful performance with respect to agricultural trade diplomacy in the early 1980s, Australia had certain advantages in its efforts to mobilize a broad-based international coalition for the purpose of agricultural trade reform. On one side, Australia benefited from a long-established sense of mutuality of interest and purpose with several like-minded countries on agricultural issues. For example, Australia sought closer relations with New Zealand, symbolized by the Australia New Zealand Closer Economic Relations and Trade Agreement (CER). Likewise, between 1979 and 1981, Australia and Canada (along with Argentina) made several attempts to revive the idea of an international wheat agreement as a means to halt the cutthroat competition in that sector. Later, the two countries even talked of plans for 'joint defence' against the looming wheat trade war between the European Community and the United States.[38]

On the other side, Australia could capitalize on an accumulated store of good will from the less developed countries (LDCs) for championing their causes in the past.[39] Australia's long-standing sympathy for the position of raw material exporting nations was exemplified by the country's repeated attempts in the 1950s and 1960s to introduce more equity into the international political economy. At the 1958 Common-wealth Trade and Economic Conference, for example, the Australian minister for trade, John McEwen, suggested a plan for a worldwide agreement on commodities designed to stabilize prices. The idea was then discussed in a number of fora, including a meeting of Common-wealth trade ministers in London in May 1963, a GATT ministerial meeting a few weeks later, and a United Nations Conference on Trade and Development (UNCTAD) meeting in 1964. In 1965, Australia formally applied to GATT for an exemption allowing it to accord preferential treatment to some LDCs with respect to import duties for a range of products of special interest to them. By extending an offer of this nature, despite the deeply embedded internal support for industrial protection, the Australian government stated that it hoped to 'demonstrate by positive action Australia's willingness to help overcome the trade problems of the less developed countries.'[40] Australian policy remained consistent on this score, and the country continued its support of the common fund until the early 1980s.

The harmonious connection between Australia and the South was reinforced by the links that both Fraser and Hawke developed with many of the South's major agricultural exporters in the late 1970s and the early 1980s. Functionally, the contacts with these countries were made through bodies such as the Southern Hemisphere Temperate Zone Agricultural Producers, the Wheat Exporting Group, the Association of Iron Ore Exporting Countries, and the International Bauxite Associa-tion, as well as UNCTAD and GATT. Geographically, the prime focus of the Australian foreign economic strategy was on the Asian-Pacific coun-tries. Building on the institutional base established through the South

Regional Trade and Economic Cooperation Agreement (SPARTECA), the Economic and Social Commission of Asia and the Pacific (ESCAP), the Association of Southeast Asian Nations (ASEAN), and the ASEAN Australia Economic Cooperation Program, the Australians launched a diplomatic offensive between 1983 and 1984 to make sure that the region had a coherent and integrated approach to present in the MTNs.

In acting as the driving force behind the formation of a broad-based coalition with which to make a push for the reform of agricultural trade, Australia tempered its hitherto hard line with a deft and sophisticated diplomatic approach. In the 1980s, Australia's Bureau of Agricultural Economics took the lead not only in compiling and analyzing the technical details of the costs of subsidies and protection in agriculture but also in widely publicizing this information in order to marshal the arguments against the supposed short-term gains of protectionist policies as opposed to the long-term goal of a fairer trading system.[41] Indeed, the research was used explicitly as a diplomatic tool both bilaterally and in the multilateral arena. We are not unappreciative of the fact that much of the data may have been available in the respective home markets and that political imperatives more often than not transcended the 'self-evident' advantages of economic rationality in accounting for the reception of these reports. Rather, we are suggesting that the importance of such research had less to do with the impact it may have had on domestic agricultural lobbies than it did with its impact on the members of the policymaking community charged with the task of negotiating agricultural agreements. For example, the Organization for Economic Cooperation and Development (OECD), following Australia's lead, took steps to institutionalize the concept of producer subsidy equivalents (PSEs) and to use it as the index of government support for agriculture.[42]

Furthermore, in the 'pre-negotiations' about the agenda for the Uruguay Round, Australia effectively used the escalating nature of the trade situation to transform the issue of agriculture from a low-level bureaucratic question to a high-level political question that could no longer be ignored. Specifically, Australian policymakers used Washington's decision in mid-1986 to globalize the EEP (a move highlighted by the Reagan administration's decision to negotiate sales of subsidized wheat to the Soviet Union) as a catalyst to quicken the pace of building a coalition of the 'nonsubsidizing' agriculture-exporting nations – all of which were hard hit by American actions.

Vital to this mobilization process was the leadership displayed by

Australia. The declaratory statements made by Hawke and other Australian policymakers on the theme that it was time to call a halt to the 'ridiculous world trade war' and 'subsidy madness' served as a rallying call for collective action. Moreover, the Australian government buttressed this rhetoric by efforts at agenda-setting, coalition-building, and confidence-building. Moving beyond the stage of informal discussions held in small groups or in telephone conversations between leaders (for example, between Hawke and Mulroney during the U.S.-Soviet subsidized wheat sale episode), Australia took the crucial step of formally initiating the 'creation of a group ... with common interests ... for the long term' by inviting ministerial-level representatives of fourteen carefully selected nations to a meeting at Cairns in the last week of August 1986.[43] In its justifications for this step, the Australian government argued that the external environment had become so threatening that it was only through the development of a 'co-ordinated approach to such impositions' that these targeted middle-sized and small actors might prevent 'our shared interests and concerns' from being 'bypassed.'[44]

The Agenda and Strategy of the Cairns Group

Having outlined the context and the evolution of the Cairns Group, and having explored some of the differences and common interests of its membership, we turn now to a description and analysis of the Group's agenda and strategies in the Uruguay Round. Our approach draws on the model we set out in Chapter 1, and, following our illustration of Australia's role as a catalyst in the formation of the Group, special attention is paid to Canberra's role as both facilitator and manager in the further development of the Group and its activities. We first outline the central elements of the Group's demands and approaches and then discuss its participation in the specific stages of the Uruguay Round up to the Brussels meeting at the end of 1990.

The Aims of the Cairns Group

The aims of the Group were encapsulated in two major documents: the Declaration of the Ministerial Meeting of Fair Traders in Agriculture, adopted by the Group at its 26 August 1986 meeting in Cairns, and the Comprehensive Proposal for the Reform of Agriculture, adopted by the Group at its 21-3 November 1989 meeting in Thailand and tabled at the GATT agricultural negotiation group meeting four days later. The 1986 declaration, which was more exhortatory and less detailed than was the

1989 proposal, called for the full integration of agricultural trade in a GATT process that, over ten years or less, would ensure a stronger market-oriented agricultural system with strengthened and operationally effective rules and disciplines.

The Group's long-term reform package for the Uruguay Round was intended to secure four major reforms: (1) the reduction of existing tariffs and the conversion of non-tariff barriers into tariffs that would be progressively reduced; (2) the reduction of distorting internal support measures; (3) the phasing out of existing export subsidies and the prohibition of new ones; and (4) the special and differential treatment of LDCs in accordance with their individual development needs and also in recognition of the particular concerns of the net food-importing countries.[45] It is thus clear that the Group was not just interested in the question of curbing the impact of major power subsidy policies on the agricultural system – issues of market access were also fundamental.

Such long-term goals of the Cairns Group were supported by a series of short-term recommendations geared towards confidence-building in relations between the major players. In particular, the Group attempted to formulate remedies which would have assuaged EC concerns over 'rebalancing' (such as withdrawing Dillon Round concessions on zerobindings for various commodities) and American concerns with 'tariffication' as a way of placing an easily identifiable ceiling on variable levies. The Group's short-term proposals included the following: a freeze on all new access barriers; immediate across-the-board cuts in subsidies by agreed percentages; fixed-percentage increases to improve market access; the establishment of targets for reducing support and protection over a ten-year period; and a ban on the introduction of any new non-tariff barriers and trade-distorting subsidies.

While the combined status of the Cairns Group members in global agricultural trade placed them in the position of being a potential 'third force' in the negotiations, they were careful to offer positive initiatives that built confidence in the major players with regard to the prospects for success in the Uruguay Round. As the Cairns Group negotiators – and especially the central figures in the Australian trade negotiations bureaucracy – were also well aware, without such initiatives, the prospect for a joint solution imposed by the United States and the European Communities (but geared only towards resolving their own specific differences) was likely to be greater as the Uruguay Round drew to a close.

The term confidence-building, which has been widely used in both academic and policymaking circles involved in arms control, is defined as the regulation of the negotiating environment – a regulation which is designed to improve communication and understanding, offer reassurance about the intentions of the participants, and, thereby, reduce the prospects for conflict.[46] Confidence-building measures are, thus, intended to generate predictability and to monitor deviations from the norm in state behaviour. A major problem throughout the Uruguay Round and, indeed, in the years of waning faith in the GATT system of the early 1980s, was that the major actors increasingly lacked confidence in their ability to understand the intentions of the others and in their ability to compete successfully in the absence of protectionist support mechanisms. In this regard, confidence-building measures were not a substitute for a new trade agreement but, rather, were simply a tool to smooth the way towards a new agreement.

The paths to building a climate of confidence were many and varied, and, as the chronological discussion that follows illustrates, the activities of the Cairns Group were multifaceted. Three components of Group policy are worth noting prior to this discussion: first, a commitment to a gradual, step-by-step approach to edge the major actors over potential stumbling blocks; second, a commitment to the technical improvement of the methods of transparency,[47] since transparency (like verification in arms control agreements) is assumed to enhance mutual understanding and trust; and, third, in cases in which deadlock appeared likely, a commitment to the extensive use of shuttle diplomacy and brokerage by senior Australian trade negotiators.

From Punta del Este to the Montreal mid-term review, the Cairns meeting accomplished a great deal with respect to the establishment of an informal working relationship among Group members, the identification of principles, and the development of tactics to maximize the Group's influence within the international political economy. Although the individual members may have been unclear about what they were committing themselves to at this early stage, the momentum generated by the meeting and the negotiating demands embraced at Cairns allowed the Group to move quickly to the point where it could be considered an emergent 'third force' in agricultural trade issues.[48]

In the declaration issued by the Cairns Group, primacy was given to the need for agriculture to be adequately addressed in the MTNs, with ministers seriously questioning 'the value of a new Round which failed to solve the long-standing problems in agricultural trade.' To ensure that 'their concerns regarding the negotiating objectives on agriculture' were 'adequately met,' the Cairns Group agreed to consider ongoing cooperative efforts at the bilateral, regional, and joint levels. These efforts would include 'pressure to secure early changes in current domestic farm support policies of those countries whose policies adversely affect international trade in agricultural products.'[49]

Crucial to the campaign for agricultural trade reform and liberalization was the emergence of a division of labour among Cairns Group members. Each country concentrated on what it was most involved with, was best equipped to do, or found the least sensitive to domestic political concerns. The LDCs concentrated on ensuring that the problem of agricultural trade remained high on the agenda of fora such as the Food and Agriculture Organization (FAO) and UNCTAD, while Canada focused on presenting the Cairns position at the G-7 meetings in Venice and Toronto and at the Quadrilateral meetings.

Australia, for its part, focused on institution-building and policy innovation within the Cairns Group. As a diverse agricultural exporter and also, as we will show in subsequent chapters, as a reputation-builder within the international system, the Australian government was willing to devote a considerable amount of time and resources to building up the profile and capabilities of the Group. Indeed, it is not an overstatement to say that Australia took on the burdens of managing the Group with some relish. To push the coalition forward, the Australians paid particular attention to consolidating and giving coherence to the activities of the Group's diverse members through the establishment of a loose coordinating mechanism. John Dawkins, Australia's minister for trade and the Group's first acting chair, offered his department's resources to provide a secretariat to facilitate cooperation and liaison both among Group members and with the major trading economies.[50]

Australia also came increasingly to play the role of intellectual leader of the Group. More than any of its partners, Australia was willing to continue to invest heavily in the MTNs – putting everything it had on the negotiating table – even though this approach was detrimental to certain domestic sectoral interests in the short run. The perception that GATT continued to be the 'only game in town' for Australia was well captured by Hawke in a speech given to the GATT Contracting Parties in October 1987: he committed Australia to an ambitious ten-year internal reform program as part of a broad-based multilateral strategy.[51]

It is important to note that the Cairns Group had the bureaucratic ability to compete with the major powers. As Jeffrey J. Schott reminds us, we tend to overestimate the number of GATT's ninety-six signatory states that have the bureaucratic capability to track, digest, analyze, and contribute to all facets of the negotiating processes in the diverse and complex multilateral trade negotiating rounds.[52] While the major powers may have the huge resources necessary to play an active role in all of the negotiations, most of the secondary players do not. However, as we showed in Chapter 2, both Australia and Canada developed a substantial and skilled multilateral trade bureaucracy capable of following the complexities of the GATT negotiation process, understanding the issues, and formulating appropriate technical responses. Such expertise lay not only in the specific negotiating panel on agriculture but also in other GATT fora.

With respect to the delicate negotiation process with the United States, the EC, and other actors, Australia was instrumental in shaping the incremental, step-by-step approach of the Cairns Group. The key to this approach was, as is indicated above, the adoption of confidence-building techniques (techniques traditionally associated, in the multilateral context, with Canada), which would clear the air of animosity and bilateral recriminations, convince all actors of the usefulness of the negotiations, and gain a collective commitment to a 'standstill and rollback.' The group recognized that without such a 'litmus test of the good faith of all countries,' confidence and trust between the parties would be difficult to achieve.[53]

By time the Punta del Este meeting was held in September 1986, the nationalist and protectionist tendencies in international trade had grown to severe proportions: agricultural markets were suffering from oversupply and depressed prices; there was an increasing tendency towards dumping and subsidization; and the need to stabilize the agricultural markets was, at that time, widely accepted in both the United States and Europe.[54] The timing of the Cairns Group's activities was, therefore, propitious. Facilitated by the Group's collective 26 per cent share of world agricultural exports (as well as the emotional and practical appeal of its declaration), this coalition was able to secure a central place for agriculture on the GATT agenda. There were to be no exclusion clauses or qualifications concerning the 'special' nature of agriculture. Of course, crucial to this process was the support of the United States on the one hand, and, on the other, the reluctance of the EC to oppose the proposals. As one analyst put it, 'The mighty Cairns ... succeeded in embarrassing both the European Community and the United States into serious negotiations on farm talks.'[55]

Nevertheless, as the MTNs proceeded, the Cairns Group faced serious constraints in translating this procedural victory into substantive success in securing major reform. Most crucially, the incremental and flexible approach of the Group remained at odds with the rigid American proposal for agricultural negotiations.[56] Even though it was widely seen as a bargaining chip, this proposal called for the complete phase-out of all barriers to import access and subsidies over a ten-year period. Until these long-term demands were met by the EC and other actors, the United States declared itself unwilling to address issues in relation to short-term relief.

It was also significant that tensions began to surface within the Cairns Group itself. Although the members had common objectives, they continued to have differing priorities. This was certainly the case with many of the LDCs. While 'signing on,' they were reluctant to identify themselves too explicitly with a mixed coalition of developed and developing countries. The overriding concern for most was 'special and differential' treatment for their agricultural economies. Some, such as Brazil and Argentina, went even further in their demands, hard-pressed as they were to come up with the funds needed to cope with their enormous debt problems. But Argentina, it should be noted, was, nevertheless, one of the most steadfast supporters of Group unity throughout the Uruguay Round.[57]

Pressure on unity in the Cairns Group initially emanated from a need to assuage the concerns of the members of the Food Importers Group. As discussed earlier, Egypt, Jamaica, Mexico, and Nigeria, for example, believed that the Cairns Group had a bias towards temperate producers and that acceptance of its proposals would bring about an increase in prices, which would have a negative impact on their own balances of payments as well as on their efforts to increase food self-sufficiency. Under these circumstances, the LDCs in the Cairns Group were extremely sensitive about maintaining G-77 solidarity. Indeed, the Food Importers Group members were able to secure assurances from the Latin American members of the Cairns Group that they would be consulted about initiatives on agricultural trade policy.[58] As these linkages increased, though, liaison between the Cairns Group members themselves became more difficult and the overall relationship more tense. Contrary to the assurances received at the initial Cairns meeting, for instance, Brazil, on several occasions, failed to keep the other members of the Group informed of the evolution of its agricultural policy. To promote group unity, Australia took a stand consistent with its overall foreign policies towards LDCs and argued the case for differential treatment of Southern countries vis-à-vis external markets and domestic support systems. This approach was subsequently incorporated in the Group's proposal.

From the perspective of international credibility, however, it was the ambivalent Canadian position within the Cairns Group, rather than the division between developed and less developed countries, which caused the most persistent problems. As was the case with some other important trade-related issues, the perceptual gap between Canadian rhetoric and Canadian practice was growing.[59]

Canadian policymakers persisted in talking about Canada's leadership within the Group. The minister of state for the Canadian Wheat Board, for instance, claimed that 'we have been taking the lead internationally in seeking a lasting solution to these problems.'[60] Yet, because of Canada's apparent unwillingness to accept its burden of costs for the internationalist campaign, the country was increasingly viewed by its partners as a free rider within the coalition. Members of the Group were also concerned about Canada's defection from the principle of 'standstill and rollback.' Canada did not keep strictly to the guidelines of this central confidence-building measure and moved, instead, to higher levels of subsidization of the domestic grain and oilseeds industry.[61] Most significant, of course, was the Group's concern that the bilateral Canada-United States negotiations on a free trade agreement was at odds with the spirit, if not the letter, of the MTNs. At the very least, the agreement would undermine the principle of non-discrimination, giving Canada a differential status from its Cairns Group partners with regard to American import laws. Indeed, in late 1989, Australia registered its objections to Canada's failure to grant some of its products the same access rights as those applied to products from the United States under the free trade agreement.[62]

In contrast to Canada, Australia, at that stage, had reviewed and rejected the idea of seeking a free trade agreement with the United States,[63] thereby highlighting the differences between the two major members of the Cairns Group. Australia was thus to become not only the driving force behind the Cairns Group's negotiating demands but also the mediator and stabilizer of the coalition. Above all, to preserve unity within the Group, Australia had to continue to find compromise solutions acceptable to the more assertive LDCs and to the cautious and recalcitrant Canadians. On the one hand, Australia was able to persuade a sceptical Canada that the idea of special and differential treatment for the LDCs should be entrenched in the policy statements of the Cairns

Group.[64] On the other hand, Australia was able to preserve the single-issue orientation of the coalition by defusing Brazilian pressures to broaden the Group's agenda to include nonagricultural issues. Of particular relevance here was the issue of linkage between agriculture and the services and intellectual property negotiations in the Uruguay Round – a theme picked up again by Brazil and other Latin American countries at the December 1988 GATT mid-term review.

As the Uruguay Round progressed, the issue of linkage became much more difficult to manage. Yet on both a theoretical and practical level, it attained increased importance.[65] On 'new issues,' such as services and trade in intellectual property, major agreements between supporters in the developed world and opponents in the developing world tended to be linked to significant reform of the international system of agricultural exchange, especially concerning the protectionist policies of the developed countries. This cross-issue linkage caused some problems for the unity of the Cairns Group, given that some of its members strongly opposed substantial codification of trade in services and intellectual property, whereas others strongly supported it. For example, Australia, which was keen to support United States initiatives in services and intellectual property, remained at odds over this issue with a number of Cairns members (particularly Brazil).

An even more difficult issue for Australia to manage was its step-by-step approach to the GATT negotiations. The delicate nature of this process can best be illustrated by the Australian proposal, put forward at the Bariloche meeting of the Cairns Group in February 1988, for a freeze on all farm subsidies and new import barriers to commence in 1989. The practical arguments for a freeze were strong, and the proposal was well timed to coincide with the mid-term review of the current GATT round. Representing a 'down payment' or 'advance' on a long-term agreement on agriculture, the proposal was to be yet another step in the process of confidence-building. However, the political constraints on the implementation of this 'down payment' proposal were formidable. As Michael Aho has pointed out, 'Trade negotiations are as much domestic negotiations as they are negotiations among countries.'[66] This was certainly true for Canada, which had to take into account the interests of both its competitive export-oriented and its uncompetitive domestic-oriented sectors. This profile of dual interests accounted for Canada's ambiguous role in the Cairns Group. As long as the Cairns initiative was directed at those competitive sectors, such as grains and oilseeds, in which Canadian farmers had been victimized by a high degree of subsidization by the stronger countries, Canada showed considerable enthusiasm for the internationalist approach of the Cairns Group – especially since that initiative was fully consistent with the long-standing tradition of Canadian multilateralism. However, when uncompetitive sectors – such as the dairy, egg, and poultry industries, with its 38,000 farmers – were targeted, this enthusiasm was dampened. Canada increasingly appeared to be at odds with other members of the coalition, because it was unwilling to accept measures that involved significant political and economic costs to itself.

Although Australia was expecting that all the members would be willing and capable of making the necessary 'advance' in 1989 and 1990, Canada persistently argued that, because of its internal difficulties in making structural adjustments, these 'adjustments should be phased in progressively over time and that governments should retain some flexibility in the choice of policy instruments.'[67] In the defence of its own long-term agricultural programs, Canada tried hard to establish a criterion for differentiating between government support measures per se and trade-distorting measures.

The firmness of Canadian resistance to the 'down payment' proposal was, in part, due to timing. When the Australian proposal was introduced at Bariloche, Canadian negotiations with the United States for a free trade agreement were at a critical point. In particular, negotiators were fixing on the future of Canada's agricultural marketing boards, the Canadian Wheat Board, and other institutions that substantial elements of the Canadian farming community believed to be sacrosanct. Furthermore, the Progressive Conservative government was beginning to campaign for the general election called for November 1988 – an election in which the support of regional economic interest groups (such as the western grain farmers and eastern dairy and poultry producers) was considered vital for success. Canada's resistance was also exacerbated by the rise of tensions within the Cairns Group resulting from the ascendancy of Australian leadership and the increasingly contradictory Canadian attitude towards membership in the coalition.

These differences ultimately led to serious questions about the stability of the Group. Such speculation was fuelled by a number of public controversies. In mid-1988, stories in the *Australian Financial Review* suggested that Canada was about to leave the coalition altogether because of the Australian proposal.[68] Although these stories were consistently denied by Australian and Canadian policymakers, it is important for our analysis to note that the crisis management techniques adopted by both countries indicated the seriousness of the problem. In fact, agricultural trade policy dominated the discussions when Canada's deputy prime minister, Don Mazankowski, travelled to Australia in early June 1988. Despite high-level diplomatic efforts, the rift between Canada and Australia about how the freeze was to be implemented surfaced again later in the month over the submission of a Cairns Group proposal to a GATT agricultural committee session in Geneva. Canada, although willing to agree to a freeze on further trade-distorting initiatives and prepared to accept an overall reduction of 10 per cent in subsidies over the next two years, remained adamantly opposed to any commodity-specific measures, particularly those directed towards the domestic-oriented sectors. As John Crosbie, the Canadian minister of international trade, bluntly put it, 'We're not going to accept any settlement in GATT that would endanger our farmers ... They're not part of the problem.'[69]

Confronted by this threat to its image as a progressive force in the international political economy, Australia sought to push forward with the proposal – but not at the expense of the long-term stability of the coalition. The awkward compromise Canberra subsequently settled upon was to delete the specifics with respect to the 'down payment' in the Cairns Group's 'Time for Action' proposal but to hand in a separate proposal of its own with detailed recommendations.[70] The Group approached the mid-term review of the Uruguay Round at the end of 1988 somewhat uneasily. That it did so as a unified force was, in large part, due to Australian diplomatic efforts.

From Montreal to Brussels

While the members of the Cairns Group managed to maintain considerable diplomatic unity, it was not enough to overcome the reluctance of the great powers. The Montreal mid-term review meeting demonstrated the degree to which the intransigence of the major powers affected progress in the Uruguay Round. The much-touted review foundered on the insistence of the United States on securing a commitment to its 'zero-option' on all forms of agricultural subsidy and the equally strong European refusal to countenance such an approach rather than a gradual, step-by-step method. The deadlock saw eleven Latin American GATT contracting parties, led by Argentina and including four other Cairns Group members, threaten to block progress in eleven of the other fourteen areas of negotiation in the round if there was no progress on agriculture. This action indicated to all contracting parties the degree to which success in agriculture was the central element in any successful outcome for the Uruguay Round. As noted earlier, many of the developing countries, especially India and Brazil, linked a favourable outcome on agriculture with progress on trade in intellectual property and services – agenda items becoming increasingly central to the goals of the United States. In order to overcome the Montreal deadlock, the mid-term review was set in abeyance until April 1989.

The Montreal meeting shook the contracting parties and appeared to engender a new spirit of compromise in the agricultural negotiations – at least for a while. While the softening of the American and European positions was the essential component of this new-found spirit, it can be argued that the Cairns Group played a crucial role in nudging the Uruguay Round over this particular barrier. The United States moved from an 'all or nothing' position on trade-distorting subsidies to a position of accepting a 'ratcheting down of support,' and the EC joined the United States in agreeing to the Cairns Group's demands for a minimum ten per cent reduction in 1990 and 'substantial progressive reductions in agricultural support and protection ... sustained over an agreed period of time.'[71] Contracting parties were to reach agreement on the nature of 'long-term reform' by the end of 1990.

We do have to keep the role of the Cairns Group in proper perspective, however. The Group was an important force for compromise between the major protagonists in the movement from deadlock in Montreal to breakthrough in Geneva. But we should not discount the importance of the arrival of a new administration in Washington during the interval between these meetings: the electorally induced paralysis that had hung over Clayton Yeutter as the U.S. trade representative in Montreal was removed by the time he took over as secretary for agriculture and Carla Hills replaced him at the Geneva meeting.

Yet our justification for stressing the importance of the Cairns Group activities is more than circumstantial. It was the Cairns proposal for itemized progressive reductions which offered the opportunity for the required movement of the United States government away from the 'zero option.' This movement was possible because the Group's proposal also offered a way to pressure the EC to move. Cairns Group involvement in the pre-Geneva meetings was also much greater than is commonly appreciated. While welcoming the U.S.-EC bilateral talks prior to the meetings, the Group let it be known that agreement at Geneva required real overall progress and was not simply a case of the two major conflicting parties reaching an accommodation of their own. This point was articulated at the March ministerial meeting of Group members in

New Zealand; Hawke, encouraging the adoption of greater flexibility, reiterated the same point to Bush and the European leaders. Cairns Group positions were also articulated by Australia's minister for trade negotiations, Michael Duffy, in a bout of trans-Atlantic shuttle diplomacy (with Clayton Yeutter, Willy de Clerq, and Frans Andreissen) as well as by GATT's chief executive officer, Arthur Dunkel, during informal trilateral meetings with American, European, and Australian officials representing the Cairns Group.[72] These meetings, in effect, gave the Group de facto status as the 'third force' in the agricultural negotiations.

Above all, of course, concrete evidence of the importance of the Group is found in the adoption by the major players of its proposals, especially the freeze on existing support levels, the early cutback in 1990, and the formulation of a long-term package by the end of 1990. The American proposals for the November 1989 agricultural negotiations group meeting in Geneva drew extensively on the Cairns Group's initiatives, especially on its commitment to 'tariffication' of non-tariff import access barriers and a ten-year timetable for the total prohibition of subsidies and other trade-distorting measures.'[73] This major softening of the initial American negotiating position brought the United States much closer to the Cairns Group and provided what Michael Duffy called a 'circuit breaker' in the agricultural negotiations.[74]

The position of the EC, however, continued to differ sharply from that of the United States and the Cairns Group. As outlined in its negotiating paper, the EC still defended price support intervention in order to prevent abrupt adjustments of agricultural production in cyclical crises. This position left the CAP mechanisms largely unchanged and continued agricultural surpluses through price support. The EC also adhered to its proposal for the reduction program based on the aggregation of all internal support mechanisms – a proposal that remained (up to the Brussels meeting) much too imprecise for either the United States or the Cairns Group.

A situation in which the position of one of the major players – in this case, the United States – moved towards that of the Cairns Group left open the prospect for some change in the latter's negotiating strategy. After functioning as an 'honest broker' and keeping the agenda moving along in the early stages of the Uruguay Round, the Group, in the run up to the Brussels meeting, threw its weight behind the American position in order to keep pressure on the EC to accept more substantial reform. But a negotiating shift such as this was not necessarily inevitable, had the willingness of the EC to adopt the 'tariffication' proposals and to be more flexible in other ways been forthcoming. Because of the differences of opinion between the United States and the EC, the Cairns Group established a procedure for monitoring the compliance levels of participants to the freeze and cutback measures. While Cairns Group members, especially Australian negotiators, would argue that any initiatives which created a greater transparency in contracting party behaviour were good things in their own right, the short-term issue of compliance throughout 1990 would clearly have been an important consideration in securing a favourable outcome in the Uruguay Round. Goodwill and trust in the bona fide intentions of the major actors was, in the run-up to Brussels, becoming an increasingly important question for secondary players cognizant of the growing recourse of the major players to economically nationalist activity in other domains, including the Canada-U.S. Free Trade Agreement and Europe 1992.

For a variety of reasons the Brussels meeting failed to resolve any of the agenda items in the Uruguay Round. One reason was the intrusion of the conflict in the Persian Gulf and the manner in which it limited the abilities of the United States – in need of European support for its Gulf expedition – to bring pressure to bear on the European Community in areas such as the Uruguay Round of negotiations. Thus, the EC's offer of a 30 per cent reduction in domestic subsidies from the 1986 level, rather than being seen as a breakthrough, was seen as a sign of intransigence. While the standoff between the United States and the European Community represented a failure for the Cairns Group's endeavours in the first four years of the Uruguay Round, the real significance of the Group's activities was the fact that the major powers did not cut a bilateral deal over the heads of the smaller parties to the negotiations in other areas.

Although this section of the chapter has concentrated on the process of negotiation in the Uruguay Round, our discussion of Brussels and the subsequent extension of the former into a fifth year – and then a sixth – illustrate the degree to which we are sensitive to the need not to lose sight of the larger context and of the factors that constrain the prospects for reform. Analysis cannot be quantified in a simple debit/credit fashion, since many of the factors that should dictate the imperative for successful agricultural reform are also the chief reasons why reform was so difficult to secure. This section analyzed the impact of the Cairns Group, rather than the impact of exogenous variables, on the negotiating process.

Conclusions

This chapter has sought to show that, despite the heterogeneity of the Cairns Group's membership, the Group's aims and policy approach to the Uruguay Round demonstrated a surprising degree of homogeneity and solidarity. This was because areas of potential conflict in the Group's various interests (services and intellectual property, for example) were kept firmly in a secondary position behind the goal of agricultural reform. The Group did not overplay its hand or try to push negotiating parties beyond what their own domestic political constraints would permit. Moreover, by keeping its aims sharply focused on the single issue of agricultural reform, the Group avoided ideological conflict and the dissipation of its energies in the pursuit of wider non-tangible goals.

The Group's approach was firmly anchored in the understanding that agricultural reform is not simply a technical or market-specific process but a political process and, as Henry Nau notes, primarily a domestic political process at that.[75] While informal and commodity groups have existed before in GATT, these tended to be largely comprised of officials concerned with activities related to a specific commodity, such as sugar. The Cairns Group went considerably beyond this approach. Its efforts to reform agricultural trade were underpinned by a greater recourse to the ministerial decisionmaking process than was the case in previous rounds as a way of overcoming the potential for bureaucratic inertia in the negotiating process. Australian negotiators were especially aware of the degree to which political action at various stages – but especially in the pre-negotiation phase at Punta del Este[76] – would be needed to break technical and other deadlocks. Secondary states, acting individually, would have little role in the negotiations. The formation of the Cairns Group was designed to overcome this disadvantage.

The preparation and research underpinning the Group's negotiating position were important to its performance. In particular, we have argued that the role of Australia (as intellectual leader, provider of technical support, and political convener of the Group) was instrumental in its success. Australia demonstrated considerable innovation in refining the identification and measurement of illiberality in the trading system. At the same time, we are not unaware of the long history of protection in Australia, especially of the manufacturing sector. Indeed, it is this history that makes the intellectual sea change in Australia in the 1980s so very interesting.[77] In addition, the role of the Australian multilateral trade bureaucracy in providing supporting documentation and argumentation for the Cairns Group in the Uruguay Round was widely recognized. The technical competence of Australia was of considerable importance in establishing the Group's credibility and its need to be taken seriously in the negotiations.

At the political level, Australia's acceptability to a variety of competing political and ideological interests in the current MTNs was important. Its economic profile as a commodity exporter, its regional location in the southern hemisphere, and its stand on various North-South issues over the previous decade placed it in good stead with the LDCs. At the same time, however, Australia's position as a Western country in general and as a member of the ANZUS alliance in particular – and its close economic relationship with Japan – helped convince the other major actors in the Uruguay Round of the Group's moderation and earnestness.

We should stress that we do not intend to overstate the role of the Cairns Group in the final phases of the Uruguay Round. For, towards the end of the Round, Winham's 'pyramidal model' was to assert itself once again. The final stages of the Round were marked by the desire of the major powers – the United States, the European Community, and even Japan – to come to a compromise on the vexatious issue of agriculture. But that does not detract from the importance of the Cairns Group in the earlier part of the negotiations. At our boldest, we have argued that the Cairns Group was a major force in the early phases of the Uruguay Round. It helped set the agenda and provided an important middle way for progress when negotiations between the United States and the EC appeared to be heading for deadlock – especially in Montreal. In addition, its presence as a 'third force' at Brussels ensured that the Round would not come to a sudden end as a result of strictly bilateral deals between the major powers.

An important caveat must condition our conclusion, however. Our emphasis on the Cairns Group as a 'third force' in the negotiations has inevitably been at the expense of a more detailed analysis of the negotiating positions and actions of the other major players. Our justification for this is twofold. Not only are the positions of the major players better understood, but the Cairns Group is also, we have argued, a sufficiently novel coalition of states to be of considerable interest in its own right to students of international political economy and to practitioners of multilateral economic negotiations. Thus, by viewing the Uruguay Round through the lenses of the Cairns Group, we have provided a corrective to other analyses of the multilateral trade negotiations, which have tended to focus on the major powers alone.

4

The Regional Economic Agenda: Asia-Pacific Economic Cooperation and North American Free Trade

Introduction

The changes in the international economic order in the 1980s gave a new sense of urgency to the study of international institutions, which once more became fashionable.[1] These changes included: the strains and tensions emanating from a re-emergence of economic nationalism; the growth of the new protectionism; the erosion in the international trading system associated with the weakening of GATT; and the waning of the economic and political leadership of the great powers. One of the principal manifestations of these changes was the rise of geographically defined economic regions, or blocs, in Western Europe, North America, and Asia. Another was the emergence, in the 1980s, of different forms of economic cooperation between states, such as bilateral free trade agreements or regional integrated markets. And we also saw the rise of markedly different economic outlooks, both positive, outward-looking, and trade-inducing, and negative, defensive, and trade-restricting.

This chapter does not seek to rehearse well-worn arguments about these broader tendencies in the global economic order.[2] Rather, our focus is on international economic cooperation-building and the role of Australia and Canada in that process. We examine the evolution of the Asia-Pacific Economic Cooperation (APEC) initiative of the late 1980s and Australia's role in it. But we also contrast the options open to Australia in regional economic cooperation with those available to Canada, demonstrating that Australian interests in APEC and Canadian interests in a North American Free Trade Agreement (NAFTA) had, fundamentally, the same roots.

By way of contrast to the discussion of the multilateral trading agenda, we pay particular attention to the question of leadership in the evolution of regional cooperation. Although our focus is on economic cooperation, our deeper concern is an examination of the political process by which this cooperation was achieved.

The chapter is divided into three parts. In the first part, we review the emergence of economic cooperation in the Asia-Pacific region, paying particular attention to the evolution of institutionalization in a regional context. We then provide a more detailed discussion of the impetus for the November 1989 APEC conference – a major gathering of the foreign and other senior ministers of the twelve principal market-oriented states of the Pacific.[3] This meeting is of interest in its own right. However, we argue that it is also of considerably wider theoretical interest for students of international institutions, for the evolution of cooperation in the Asia-Pacific region (seen in contrast with economic cooperation in a North American context) provides an important insight into the processes of institutionalized cooperation in the international system. We then examine Canada's role in APEC and contrast regional cooperation in the Asia-Pacific with North American cooperation, particularly in NAFTA. Finally, we examine the different types of leadership and followership evident in both APEC and NAFTA.

The evolution of cooperation – and the processes of regional institutionalization – in the Asia-Pacific region and North America in the late 1980s demonstrates the importance of alternative forms of leadership (in international economic cooperation) to those envisaged under hegemony. As we argued in Chapter 1, the essence of these forms of leadership lies less in their reliance on structural – or power-driven – bases of international leadership associated with hegemony and more with forms of persuasion that come from the development of significant technical, intellectual, and entrepreneurial skills (often by secondary actors in the system). Moreover, the secondary states have recognized that their interests demand that they exercise a more active role in the formation of coalitions than they did in the previous era, when the major, or hegemonic, powers were exercising clear leadership in the international system.

A general theme of this book is that such coalition-building was increasingly evident in the foreign policies of Australia and Canada in the late 1980s and early 1990s; the specific theme of this chapter is that, in the absence of positive leadership from the great powers, middle power diplomacy applied in a regional context fostered limited international economic cooperation – in this case in the Asia-Pacific region.

Economic Cooperation in the Asia-Pacific Region
In the late 1980s, it was fashionable to speak of a 'Pacific community' and 'Pacific cooperation.' While pleasant-sounding, such phrases obscure the fact that there is little agreement about the very notion of a 'Pacific' region. It has been subject to distortion, exaggeration, and – as in the pejorative connotations in the idea of a 'Pacific Rim' – even abuse. While the 'Pacific,' as Gerald Segal shows,[4] is much more than an ocean, it is by no means a coherent region deserving of the hyperbole associated with the oft-heralded arrival of the 'Pacific century.' If such an expression is meant to imply the privileging of a coming Pacific era, at the putative demise of an equally illusory 'Atlantic century' or 'American century,' then it is clearly premature on both counts. There is no Pacific 'community' in a linguistic, religious, cultural, political, or ideological sense; nor, historically, is there much evidence of regional consciousness.[5] And although such distinguished scholars as James Kurth would have us believe that there is a 'Pacific paradigm' standing in contrast to an Atlantic one,[6] there is little evidence that such a paradigm exists, no matter how elastic one's definition of the term. Moreover, there is no formal framework of cooperative institutions comparable to those that developed in Western Europe over the forty years after the Second World War. Despite the hyperbole about an Asian trading bloc that followed the abortive Brussels meeting of the Uruguay Round in December 1990, there is little likelihood that an Asian Community, comparable to the European Community, will emerge in the 1990s.

For all such cautionary remarks, however, developments in the Pacific region have had considerable significance for the structure of the global order in both its political and economic guises. We have witnessed considerable market integration in the region, brought about by a growing process of economic interchange.[7] Since the details of this growth are now well documented, we need to outline only the essentials. Most notable has been the growing economic stature of Japan. The Japanese economy reproduced itself in the two decades from the early 1950s until the first oil shocks of 1973-4; this growth continued at a rate in excess of its OECD partners. Japan emerged as the world's largest surplus capital-exporting nation and the world's third largest trading nation. Likewise, the four principal newly industrializing economies (NIEs) – Singapore, Hong Kong, Taiwan, and South Korea – grew at an even faster rate than did Japan, although their economic growth started somewhat later.

In aggregate terms, Pacific production grew so that between 1960 and the early 1980s its share of the global product increased from 9 per cent to 19 per cent of the total – while that of the United States declined from 40 per cent to 27 per cent of the total. In similar fashion, the Pacific area made comparable strides in its share of world trade, growing from 30 per cent to 37 per cent of the total between 1965 and 1987. Perhaps more important for our discussion, intraregional trade in this period grew from under 50 per cent to 63 per cent. As Drysdale and Garnaut point out, at 71 per cent, such a concentration of intraregional trade is not much lower than that of Western Europe.[8] They note that for most of the countries of the region, intraregional trade is almost twice as large as is their share of world trade. While it is the magnitude of such changes that laid the foundation for the current interest in greater regional economic cooperation in the Asia-Pacific region in the late 1980s and early 1990s, it is necessary to locate this within a context that takes account of both the changes in the contemporary global economic order and earlier cooperation-inducing initiatives.

Contemporary Changes
Three general factors coalesced in the mid- and late 1980s to increase the tempo of calls for some form of regional framework that would allow the closer coordination of foreign economic policies among the market-oriented states of the Asia-Pacific region. These three factors were: (1) the fear of hardening trade blocs (such as the move to a Single Integrated Market in Europe in 1992 or the emergence of both the United States-Canada Free Trade Agreement and the North American Free Trade Agreement); (2) the difficulties that attended the Uruguay Round negotiations and a further deterioration of a rules-based multilateral trading system; and (3) the oft-touted prospects of a major economic conflict between the United States and Japan.[9] There is a paradox here that is difficult to miss: increased global interdependence over the last few decades has also seen a growth of economic nationalism and renewed efforts to regain greater state autonomy in the management of economic policy. These, in turn, have seen a renewed interest in regionalism. Various writers have noted the degree to which the problem is almost circular.[10] Globalization has encouraged structural rigidities as part of a domestic political response to external competition. Thus, adherence to multilateralism, which previously had provided the environment for rapid growth and development, is, ironically, tested by the resort to protectionist policies to secure greater competitiveness. This involves not the reintroduction of higher tariffs but non-tariff measures and

'new' trade theories and policies (albeit not in a manner envisaged by the new trade theorists themselves).[11]

The message coming from Europe and North America was not lost on the rapidly growing states of the Asia-Pacific region, nor, particularly, on Japan. The implementation of either regional or bilateral strategies at the international level and the implementation of industry and strategic trade policy at the national level were intended to stem the challenge to European and North American competitiveness from the Asia-Pacific region. It is beyond the purview of this chapter to enter the debate over the degree to which the dynamic economic development of both Japan and the NIEs themselves was fostered by state-induced industrial policies that allowed them, over the last few decades, to steal an unfair march on supposedly more liberal European and North American competition in crucial strategic sectors of the global economy.[12] Rather, we need simply to note the degree to which this perception tended to prevail, particularly in North America. Indeed, it resulted in retaliatory policies that were underwritten by notions of specific (as opposed to diffuse) reciprocity in American trade policy.[13] Thus, much of United States trade policy in the late 1980s and early 1990s was driven by a grail-like quest for 'level playing fields' – a quest underwritten by what Richard Leaver of the Australian National University has somewhat irreverently characterized as 'flat earth economic theory.'

To be sure, the pursuit of such policies yielded the occasional short-term success in freeing up some sectors of the Japanese and Korean economies. However, the aggressive political rhetoric that tended to accompany these attempts also led to a long-term questioning, in the Asia-Pacific region, of the American commitment to multilateralism. Likewise, it prompted the states of the region to consider how they should best approach the problems of the relationship with the United States in particular and the reform of the international trading system in general. A widely held assumption in the Asia-Pacific region was that American policy was designed primarily to resolve its own economic problems by externalizing them rather than by making the necessary domestic adjustments. Such a view was confirmed by the financial support that the Japanese were bludgeoned into providing to the United States for its role in the Gulf conflict. The regional consensus among the market economies of the Pacific was that continued economic growth and well-being was dependent not only on stronger regional cooperation but also on the continued openness of the global trading system.

While both smaller and middle-sized states tend to be dismissed in much of the hegemonic stability literature as free riders[14] – wrongly, as we argued in Chapter 1 – it is possible to argue that free trade (or, more specifically, increasing trade liberalization) became more important to these states than it was to the traditional hegemonic provider of the 'public good' of an open multilateral system, despite all of the free trade rhetoric from the administrations of Ronald Reagan, George Bush, and Bill Clinton. This is not to suggest that free riding does not exist, nor is it to suggest that leadership per se is not important for an open system. Rather, it is to suggest that, under certain conditions – especially those of declining competitiveness – there are limitations on the attractiveness of free trade for a hegemon.[15] As one GATT review of American trade policy noted, the proportion of imports to the United States adversely affected by significant barriers doubled to nearly 25 per cent from 1980. While it remains one of the most open economies in the world, the United States has been moving against the tide of the majority of other countries that are liberalizing their trade. As our discussion of the APEC initiative demonstrates, an immediate spur to regional cooperation was the degree to which it might have facilitated the wider goal of preventing any further defection from a rules-based GATT-directed global trading order, especially by the United States and the European Community.

However justified such views may be, perceptions which developed throughout the 1980s proved to be more important than reality. Strongly held views in the United States concerning the necessary apportionment of blame for their own domestic problems and the wider crisis of the international economic system were not equally shared in the Asia-Pacific region. Similarly, third parties to the conflict between the major actors became increasingly frustrated by the seemingly self-centred nature of the debate in the United States and Europe. Moreover, they were concerned at the degree to which unilateral or bilateral problem-solving by the major actors tended to ignore third party concerns.[16] For example, traditionally pro-American sectors of the Australian community, such as the farmers, resented the manner in which Canberra's support for the United States in the Gulf was repaid with export enhanced subsidies of agricultural produce into favoured Australian markets. American policymakers regarded these as being in two different policy domains and, therefore, unconnected. Such a view, however, had little impact on growing feelings of resentment and frustration at the inability of secondary actors to have an impact on the policy behaviour of the larger players in the global economy – in either their bilateral conflicts or in the wider reform of the multilateral trading system. This, as we will demonstrate, was an important catalyst to middle power initiative and leadership in Asia-Pacific regional cooperation in the late 1980s.

Early Phases in Asia-Pacific Cooperation

The push for closer regional economic cooperation in the late 1980s was the culmination of a third stage in the Asia-Pacific cooperation 'conversation.' The evolution of the first two stages is well covered in the secondary literature and the main points can simply be highlighted here. The first phase, from 1960 to 1967, was principally Japanese-led and very much a response to the creation of the European Economic Community. At its core was the proposal, reflecting a growing Japanese recognition of the importance of the Pacific for its economic growth, for a Pacific Free Trade Area (PAFTA) involving five states (Australia, Canada, Japan, New Zealand, and the United States).[17] But PAFTA was both politically and economically unlikely. The five lacked the necessary degree of complementarity of development that would have prevented the skewing of the benefits of liberalization in favour of the United States or Japan. In addition, as Drysdale has noted, opinion in the United States was not (at least at that stage) interested in such a potentially discriminatory arrangement.[18]

The second phase, from 1967 to 1977, saw a variety of initiatives. The first Pacific Trade and Development Conference (PAFTAD) had as its theme the exploration of the Pacific free trade idea but went on to review many other economic policy issues of importance to the Asia-Pacific region. Likewise, ASEAN was formed in 1967, albeit more as a consensus-based politico-security community. However, ASEAN was destined to be fiercely protective of its subregional identity. Moreover, for the decade and a half after its founding, ASEAN resisted, just as fiercely, any push for wider Asia-Pacific economic cooperation. Also formed in 1967 was the Pacific Basin Economic Committee (PBEC), a private business-oriented organization with its roots in bilateral Australian-Japanese cooperation on commercial matters. While PBEC achieved few concrete results, it did play an important role as a vehicle for creating personal and information networks, which were so lacking in the region at the time of its inception.

In this second phase, support for PAFTA was abandoned in favour of a more issue-specific problem-solving approach. This debate moved through several stages, culminating in Drysdale and Patrick's 1979 recommendation to the United States Congress that an Organization for Pacific Trade and Development (OPTAD) be formed. Modelled after the OECD, OPTAD was intended to focus on trade and development interests and to serve as a forum for regional discussion, the airing of grievances, and the long-term understanding of economic transformation in the region. Finally, it was hoped that an organization such as OPTAD might present a forum that would contribute to the management of the increasingly complex relationship between Japan and the United States.[19]

The third phase of Asia-Pacific cooperation (corresponding loosely to the decade of the 1980s) coincided, in large part, with the activities of the Pacific Economic Cooperation Conference (PECC), which was formed in 1980 (following a meeting between the Australian prime minister, Malcolm Fraser, and his Japanese counterpart). PECC drew on the ideas in the Drysdale/Patrick OPTAD report to give impetus to a new era of tripartite (government, business, academe) regional economic cooperation, mainly by providing an informal setting for consultative meetings and specific task forces. As it turned out, PECC was successful in developing a Pacific perspective on trade and development issues and in facilitating communication and networking on issues of regional economic significance. It is also significant that ASEAN members were part of PECC, representing an important breakthrough in ASEAN's traditional aversion to wider regional participation. Likewise, China and Taiwan became full members; the Soviet Union and, subsequently, Russia participated in several task forces.[20]

Since its inception, PECC took on some of the characteristics of the OECD. It began to publish a *Pacific Economic Outlook* not dissimilar to the *OECD Outlook*. However, it did not establish a centralized bureaucracy (as did the OECD) and did not develop the capacity for the kind of multilateral surveillance that has been central to the role of the OECD. The reluctance to bureaucratize reflected a recognition that, while a trans-Atlantic organization was appropriate for industrialized countries with different decisionmaking processes and preoccupied with macroeconomic coordination, such a model would be less appropriate in the Asia-Pacific region. For most OECD members, a relatively clear line separates the state from society; by contrast, in the Asia-Pacific region, there is little such differentiation among the decisionmaking and opinion-forming elites.

The point is well made by Stuart Harris – an agricultural economics professor, a former head of the Australian Department of Foreign Affairs

and Trade, and a member of the Australian Pacific Economic Cooperation Committee (AUSPECC, the Australian arm of PECC). Commenting
on the state of economic cooperation in the Asia-Pacific, he noted

> the relatively clear line that separates government, the private sector,
> and indeed the academic world in the West is not evident in the region.
> Government systems here operate differently. Moreover, the reality of
> economic co-operation is that the business sectors and not govern-
> ments can supply much of the knowledge needed for analyzing eco-
> nomic issues. The tripartite character of PECC – with government,
> business and academic involvement – worries some who dislike mov-
> ing from known patterns and models. Those associated with it see it,
> however, to be an important institutional innovation meeting the
> special characteristics of the region – and perhaps the times.[21]

The membership lists of national PECC committees confirm the type
of representation to which Harris alludes. Although not as developed as
the trans-Atlantic linkages described by Gill,[22] the building of transregional networks and linkages in the Asia-Pacific region was given
considerable impetus by PECC and other bodies in the 1980s. Further,
there was considerable antipathy to being captured by a single international bureaucracy or the individual bureaucracies of the member states.
Such a move, it is argued, would have led to rigidity and defensive
policymaking rather than to the transparency and flexibility offered by
a leaner organization.[23]

The principal characteristic of all three historical phases was the clear
preference for an informal consultative approach to cooperation rather
than for an approach aimed at developing formal institutional frame-
works. The late 1980s saw a recognition and acceptance of the need for
some kind of region-wide forum for government-to-government interchange. In part, this was a consequence of the maturing of these earlier
initiatives; in part, it was a response to the recognized limitations and
problems of the multilateral economic system at the end of the decade;
and, in part, it was a response to the dramatic changes underway in the
global political system. Indeed, Harris argued that a stronger regional
voice (built on an improved regional data base) and a better understanding of member states' individual interests would work for enhanced
mutual trust and the greater regional good in global fora on important
trade liberalization. Moreover, it would work to the Asia-Pacific region's
advantage on other issues, such as Chinese and Russian economic

modernization and reform. The November 1989 APEC meeting in Canberra, with these imperatives at the centre of its agenda, was the culmination of the regional building-block approach to cooperation in the 1980s. The issues were principally economic in nature, but the political dynamics at work in the inaugural meeting are of comparable interest for the student of international cooperation.

The Asia-Pacific Economic Cooperation Forum
The so-called 'Hawke initiative' – contained in a speech delivered by the Australian prime minister in South Korea on 31 January 1989 – called for the establishment of a regional meeting of foreign and trade ministers which would be the launching pad for a 'more formal intergovernmental vehicle.'[24] Hawke's initial suggestion for an Asia-Pacific Economic Cooperation forum was met with much early resistance, notably because it appeared that its Western Pacific focus would exclude North American participation. The reason for this was a desire to allay the fears of middle powers about the possibility of American domination, but, following Japanese pressure, participation was quickly expanded to include both the United States and Canada. Accurate or not, this initial fear was soon dispelled, as Hawke's first suggestions were followed up by regional talks guided by the secretary of the Australian Department of Foreign Affairs and Trade and by talks in the United States by both Hawke and Gareth Evans. As a result, all of the nominated countries agreed to participate, if, in some cases, only reluctantly.

The members of ASEAN, in particular, remained suspicious of the aims of the proposed APEC forum. Not only was ASEAN concerned that its own role might be diminished in any wider regional grouping, there was also some unease, in certain member states, concerning the role of Australia as the surrogate, or stalking horse, for continued Japanese encroachment into the region. What Hawke saw as sensible and non-threatening, others saw as potentially intrusive and counter-productive to their national development strategies.

The United States was also somewhat lukewarm at the outset. To be sure, after James Baker gave a speech to the Asia Society indicating United States participation in the meeting, the *New York Times*, the *Washington Post*, and the *Wall Street Journal* – all evidently oblivious to the previous five months of Australian diplomatic activity – reported the gathering as a 'United States initiative.'

In the end, 27 ministers and 211 delegates and observers from twelve countries attended the November 1989 gathering. Because of the

Tiananmen Square massacre of June, China was not included on the final list of invitees. However, in deference to Chinese sensibilities, neither Hong Kong nor Taiwan were invited.

The Canberra meeting addressed four principal agenda items: (1) world and regional economic developments; (2) the role of the region in global trade liberalization; (3) specific opportunities for regional cooperation; and (4) future steps in the cooperation process. Emphasizing their opposition to trading blocs, the assembled ministers agreed to attempt to advance the Uruguay Round by consulting closely in its concluding phases. They also agreed that any trade liberalization among APEC economies would be consistent with GATT principles and would not work to the detriment of any other economy. The ministers also stressed that ASEAN's special relationship with its so-called 'dialogue partners' – Australia, Britain, Canada, Japan, New Zealand, and the United States – was important for the development of the APEC. Left unresolved, however, was the ultimate institutional structure of APEC. Rather than the OECD model, which was seen by many as a Western and, thus, inappropriately bureaucratic model, the clear preference of the ministers, expressed in the meeting's joint statement, was for a loose consultative process.

Elaboration on these points came in the statement of the chair, which stressed that APEC's role would complement, not detract from, the role of existing organizations, especially ASEAN, whose proposal that its own institutional mechanisms form the basis of APEC was not taken any further at the meeting.[25] In addition, a work program and a regular program of consultations was started immediately by senior government officials. Two issues were stressed: (1) the need to collect and review data on regional trade and economic developments and (2) the need to identify trade, investment, and technology transfer opportunities in the region.

The other key issue left unresolved at the meeting was that of long-term membership. Was the Asia-Pacific region to include all countries on the rim of the Pacific Ocean? Should there be a minimum size for membership? Should membership be confined to democracies alone? If so, how was that notion to be defined? Should participants be only market economies? Although most conceptions of Pacific cooperation have turned upon economic links and market orientation, it was quite clear that these questions had not been resolved. Nothing better illustrated the point than the inability to come to any conclusion on the status of the 'four Chinas' – China, Hong Kong, Macau, and Taiwan.

Likewise, there was no agreement on the proper role of the Soviet Union or its successor states in the region.[26] Evans's summary did, however, note that regional linkages, not ideology, should be the basis for deciding the question of future membership.

At first blush, the product of the first meeting seemed meagre. Yet the very fact that a meeting at such a senior level of representation had taken place, and that the groundwork for future meetings had been laid, was not without significance, given the reservations that were initially held in a variety of quarters. Informed opinion gave it a positive, albeit cautious, reception.[27]

The second meeting, held in Singapore in July 1990, consolidated the progress made at the first meeting. First, future 'vote of confidence' meetings were scheduled for Korea in 1991, for Thailand in 1992, and for the United States in 1993. Second, flowing from the general principles established in Canberra, a series of priority projects for practical cooperation was identified. Third, there was agreement on future membership: the meeting expressed the desire that China, Taiwan, and Hong Kong participate in the 1991 Seoul meeting or soon after. Finally, keeping with the strong trade policy focus of APEC, the group issued statements in support of liberalization and urged the major powers, particularly the EC, to acknowledge the crucial nature of the final stages of the Uruguay Round for the future of the global economy. Particularly important in this regard was the ability of the meeting to get the United States and Japan to agree to review their negotiating positions for the final stages of the Round. Not only did this send an unmistakable message to the EC, it also reaffirmed the notion that the members of APEC should attempt to use their collective influence in the pursuit of global liberalism.

After the second APEC meeting, a meeting of APEC trade ministers was held in Vancouver in September 1990 to discuss developments in, and strategies for, the closing stages of the Uruguay Round. The work program – aimed at practical cooperation in the areas of trade promotion, human resource development, telecommunications, tourism, fisheries, and energy questions – was started; the progress of these projects was reviewed at regular intervals by meetings of senior officials to ensure that subsequent meetings achieved tangible results. Also, there were suggestions to improve market access and to harmonize domestic legislation and regulations on quality, safety, and environmental standards.[28]

For our purposes in this chapter, the first two APEC meetings, and the subsequent activities of the organizations, are important in both a historical and a theoretical sense. The historical context has been outlined in the preceding discussion. Some of the wider theoretical questions it poses for us, especially with regard to institution-building, cooperation, and leadership, are discussed in the next section.

Institutionalization and APEC

There can be no denying that both formal cooperation and levels of institutionalization in the Asia-Pacific region are low. As Robert O. Keohane has noted, however, there is no necessary correlation between the degree of institutionalization and political importance.[29] Highly developed institutions can be of little real importance, while nascent institutions can become important at a rate faster than that of their institutional growth. Depending on how we choose to define institutions, this hypothesis is not beyond consideration in the Asia-Pacific context. At a minimum, we might start thinking about the Asia-Pacific region in the context of institutional analysis. Keohane provides us with several sets of lenses through which to consider the regional cooperative enterprise. In this section we borrow from his examination of institutionalization at the theoretical level in order to understand the processes at a practical level.

In his threefold definition of institutions, Keohane urges us not to limit our understanding to formal organizations and regimes. Rather, he suggests that we remember the importance of conventions. While they do not specify rules of behaviour, conventions provide the essence of understanding and form the basis of a shared recognition of the utility of cooperation. We cannot yet point to the existence of explicit rules – the hallmark of a regime – in APEC, but it is possible to see the evolution of a process of understanding and, much more central to the APEC agenda (in its work program for example), a considerable desire for usable information about the individual preferences, policies, and performances of APEC members. If, as Keohane argues, 'one of the major functions of institutions is to retain and transmit information',[30] then, without overstating the point, APEC is engaged in the not insignificant early stages of institution-building. The absence of readily digestible, quality information – especially concerning the domestic economic policies and strategies of regional states – is a source of uncertainty and misunderstanding in the region and a potential source of future aggravation. If the commitments expressed at the inaugural APEC meeting have any long-term meaning, then the provision of better information would be an important first step on the road to greater regional understanding.

We also need to distinguish between information and understanding. Following Keohane's analogy with banking, both information and understanding are important: just as 'lenders need to know the moral as well as the financial character of borrowers ... governments contemplating international cooperation need to *know* their partners, not merely know *about* them.'[31] Nowhere is this more important than in such a culturally heterogeneous group as that found in APEC. Thus, the successful coordination of regional policy is highly dependent on the abilities of the foreign service personnel who conduct the regional 'conversation.'

Policy coordination also depends on information and expectations. The gradually evolving role of PECC throughout the 1980s – especially with its tripartite structure – was concerned with the provision of information, the generation of consistency of regional expectations, and a growing adherence to common regional goals. The importance of this process of opening up the different states of a culturally heterogeneous region to each other cannot be overstated. Again, in Keohane's words:

Intergovernmental relationships that are characterized by ongoing communication among working-level officials, 'unauthorized' as well as authorized, are inherently more conducive to information exchange and agreements than are traditional relationships between internally coherent bureaucracies that effectively control their communications with the external world.[32]

The creation of a better specific regional information base and greater general understanding is a long way from the achievement of transparency, which, Kratochwil and Ruggie argue, is the 'core requirement' of a regime.[33] It is, however, an essential step in the process of institutionalization. It is also a step that, in the Asia-Pacific regional context, has taken considerable energy, initiative, and informal diplomacy. Numerous individuals in PECC have invested time and capital in the nurturing of this process.[34] In this regard, it is also fair to say that practices are an important part of the process of institution-building. Both at the level of first-tier multilateral economic diplomacy (through APEC) and at the level of what we might call second-tier diplomacy (through PECC) the market-oriented states of the region have laid the foundation for continued interchange throughout the 1990s. As we will attempt to demonstrate in Chapter 6, second-tier, or informal, diplomacy remains an important part of the repertoire of the technically advanced foreign policy bureaucracies of middle powers such as Australia and Canada.

Both APEC and PECC provided the opportunity to nurture, rather than to induce, closer cooperation-building, which allows us to talk of a gradual process of institutionalization taking place in the Asia-Pacific region. Beyond that, however, little progress was made. The work programs of APEC made slow and unspectacular progress. Institution-alization, such as the creation of a bureaucracy or a permanent head-quarters for APEC, remained an unresolved issue. While it will undoubtedly be important in the long run, attempts to deal with such a thorny issue at its first meetings would have been both premature and counter-productive for APEC. At the first meeting, strong ASEAN pressure for its own post-ministerial conferences to be used as the foundation of APEC was resisted, but no attempt was made to bring forward an alternative structure (because the members of ASEAN would have found almost any other formal structure unacceptable at that stage). Similarly, while the important role played by PECC in the development of the APEC initiative cannot be underestimated, it seems unlikely that its tripartite structure will form a long-term model for the institutional evolution of APEC.

Instead, the institutional arrangement embraced was one that took an 'economic summitry' approach. In other words, the designated host of an APEC conference took on the bulk of the responsibilities for that meeting. Acting as a 'shepherd,' the host government made all the necessary arrangements and directed consultations on the agenda-setting process. This type of informal approach left scope for research and administrative input from organizations such as PECC and ASEAN, while at the same time it provided a framework within which even the smallest of members felt that they had reasonable input into the organization. In that such a scheme recognized institutional format as a highly political agenda item, it avoided the issue of formalizing the structure of the organization prior to the emergence of a greater identi-fication of, and consensus on, its role. As Gareth Evans put it, such an informal approach 'suited the mood of the participants, the great majority of whom, including Australia, were well content to let these things evolve naturally rather than forcing the pace.'[35] Given the benefits of the summit approach, it is perhaps not surprising that the three meetings that followed the 1990 meeting – in Seoul in 1991, in

Thailand in 1992, and in the United States in 1993 – used more or less the same format that had operated in 1989 and 1990.

The question of future institutional structure was, thus, always contingent on successful, appropriate, and acceptable leadership in the region in the 1990s. This, too, was clearly in a process of evolution in both a specific regional context and as part of the more global 'conversation' in which the region and its members were intimately involved. It might help our understanding of the direction of this evolution if we examine the way in which it emerged in the context of the APEC initiative.

Australia and Regional Economic Cooperation: APEC

In this section we examine Australian interests in economic cooperation in the Asia-Pacific region and, in particular, Australian leadership in articulating the APEC proposal. We also examine the interests and motivations of the other actors.

The Hawke initiative that led to the APEC forum was paradoxical in several ways. Australia was an unlikely candidate to be the driving force behind an ambitious exercise in institution-building at the regional level. Far from having the leverage that comes from the possession of structural leadership assets and capabilities, Australia had undergone a process of structural marginalization in both a global and regional economic context over the previous two decades. It had been weakened in an absolute sense by its declining share of overall world trade, which, in a forty-year period, dropped from about 2.5 per cent to less than 1.2 per cent of the world total. But Australia's position had also been marginalized in a sectoral and regional sense. Growth through trade in manufactures and services was the order of the day in the post-Second World War era. While Australia was party to some of that growth in the service sector, it remained dependent on its provision of primary produce and raw materials to world markets as the major source of its wealth. Moreover, Australia was a less significant player in its own region than it had been in the past, even while the Asia-Pacific region grew in importance not only to the world economy but to Australia itself.[36]

Given this apparent contradiction, three questions can be asked about Australian leadership in the evolution of APEC. First, what factors motivated Australia to take the lead in attempts to secure the greater formalization of intergovernmental cooperation in the region? Second, what techniques were used to perform this role? Attention here must necessarily focus less on national power capabilities and more on the technical and entrepreneurial skills of brokerage and negotiation discussed in Chapter 1. Finally, was there a leadership vacuum in the Asia-Pacific region into which Australia could, and was encouraged, to move, and to what extent were other regional states prepared to follow this lead?

One way to explain Australian leadership is simply in terms of international status-seeking. According to such an interpretation, the Hawke initiative was motivated by a desire to enhance Australia's overall reputation in world politics by way of compensation for its decreased economic role and its exclusion from such fora as the G-7 and the Quadrilaterals.[37] It may have been true that Hawke made the decision to include the initiative in his speech to the Korean Business Association on the flight to Seoul, as the Australian media suggested. It may, indeed, have been a haphazard initiative, although there is considerable evidence to the contrary.[38] Yet it was hardly an unusual foreign policy initiative for Australia. We show in other chapters that the Hawke government was prone to embark upon a number of high-profile initiatives in foreign policy, going well beyond the normal expectations of a state of Australia's stature.

While the self-aggrandizement thesis may have some substance, it is not a sufficient explanation for Australia's APEC initiative. Indeed, it is unlikely that such initiatives were driven by a desire for status or crude electoral gains. Rather, it is likelier that the APEC initiative was motivated by a mix of important structural and situational factors. Like its approach to the Cairns Group, Australia's approach to APEC is a classic case of what Robert Putnam has called a two-level game.[39] At a first level, Australia was forced to come to terms with the dynamic changes taking place in the global economy in general. More particularly, it had to confront those changes that had a deleterious effect on its international position, such as increased economic conflict between its major partners: the United States, Japan, and the EC.[40] At a second level, the Hawke government was preoccupied throughout the 1980s with a highly specific domestic agenda for economic reform that entailed having to balance hard and unpopular political choices with the need to face the electorate once every three years in Australia's short electoral cycle.

For a variety reasons Australia has always been constrained from making a full-blown commitment to integration into the Asia-Pacific economy. Although aware of the market and investment opportunities in the region (opportunities that flow from proximity and complementarity), Australian sectoral interests, historically, were unwilling to pay the adjustment costs associated with such two-way trade.[41] Until the 1980s, challenges to the protectionist orthodoxy met with opposition across the spectrum of the Australian polity. The 1980s saw considerable change in the terms of the domestic debate in Australia, as the protectionist philosophy lost substantial appeal. APEC needs to be seen, in this regard, as an aspect of the external dimension of the Hawke government's economic reform agenda that focused on liberalization, rationalization, and deregulation in order to capitalize on Australia's fastest-growing markets in the Asia-Pacific region.[42]

APEC is, in short, part of a process meant both to inform the region of Australia's break with its insular and protectionist past and to express its desire for a greater regional role.[43] Given its past record, there were still some in the region who treated Australia's new-found enthusiasm for the Asia-Pacific region with suspicion. Australia's behaviour was sometimes seen as an attempt to ride on regional growth without making the necessary domestic adjustments that would provide the opportunity for reciprocity. Indeed, even within Australia this view was to be found: as the economics editor of the *Australian*, David Potts, put it, 'It is a sad commentary on our economic performance that all we can offer the Pacific Rim is a place to talk.' Given Australia's resource wealth and high levels of development and education, this might have been an incomplete, if not a misleading, view; but there was still a gap between the rhetoric and the reality of the domestic adjustment process in Australia. In addition, the wider regional audience remained to be convinced of Australia's will and ability to hold onto the structural adjustment nettle once having grasped it.

An equally important motivating factor behind the APEC initiative was the belief that such a regional grouping might make a useful contribution to Australia's manoeuvrability in international economic diplomacy. Given its commodity-oriented export profile, Australia has always placed a premium on multilateralism and a rules-based international economic order – a commitment underscored by its role in the Cairns Group during the Uruguay Round of multilateral trade negotiations. Indeed, such a commitment stems from the lack of available alternatives. Bilateralism was neither popular nor feasible once British colonial supremacy had faded. The idea of a special relationship with Japan was mooted in the 1970s but dropped because of lack of Japanese interest and fears among Australian policymakers of the implications of such a relationship. The notion of a free trade arrangement with the United States was reviewed and rejected.[44] The only viable bilateral option was the limited context of the Australia New Zealand Closer Economic Relations and Trade Agreement – or, more commonly, the CER.

To be sure, regionalism is a preferred option to bilateralism. As early as 1979, a major report on Australia's relations with what was then called, in blunt and blanket fashion, 'the Third World' indicated that some form of Asia-Pacific grouping would offer the best fall-back option for Australia in the event of a collapse in GATT and the strengthening of a tendency towards hardening regional economic blocs.[45] More important, APEC pressure was seen as a supplement to Cairns Group activity in pushing along the Uruguay Round. Indeed, it was not coincidental that the Seoul speech followed hard on the heels of the deadlocked mid-term review of the Uruguay Round in November 1988.

But it should be noted that 'political will' is also not a sufficient explanation for Australia's leadership role in the APEC forum. The bureaucratic capacity to formulate and to implement such an ambitious program is not axiomatically present in middle or smaller powers. The presence of such a capacity in the Australian foreign policy community was clearly important to the eventual outcome. The Australian government could call on a highly skilled foreign policy bureaucracy, especially since, as we saw in Chapter 2, the amalgamation of the departments of foreign affairs and trade. Moreover, as we saw in the last chapter, active participation in the Uruguay Round and managing the Cairns Group provided Australian officials with a sense of confidence with regard to coalitional diplomacy. These skills were brought into play in the implementation phase of the APEC initiative and were made considerably easier by the fact that seven out of the twelve states participating in the forum were also members of the Cairns Group. In addition, important regional networks established throughout the 1980s by the national bodies of the PECC (and, especially, by senior academic and corporate members of the AUSPECC) provided an additional informal network.

In any assessment of Australian leadership in APEC, it is important to consider the counterfactual condition: to speculate what might have happened had the Australian government not taken the initiative and shown the leadership it did. In other words, Australia's role cannot be evaluated in isolation from the action, or, perhaps more accurately in this instance, the inaction, of the other players in the region – the United States and Japan on the one hand and what we might call the followers on the other. We approach this question in two ways. First, we look at these other actors in the specific case of APEC. We then contrast the leadership of major powers with that of secondary players.

While the United States continued to exert tremendous military, diplomatic, and economic influence in the Asia-Pacific region in the late 1980s, it is not unfair to suggest that it failed to produce its own coherent or comprehensive vision of regional cooperation during this period. As James Kurth put it, 'although the United States is the primary power in the Pacific, it is not primarily a Pacific power.'[46] Not surprisingly, the Pacific policies of the United States were all too often seen, to their cost, as out-of-area contingencies, formulated as an adjunct to Cold War imperatives. In the rapidly changing environment of the late 1980s, the United States was left with an inadequate framework within which to formulate its Pacific policies. This is not only the case in the economic domain but also, as we will show in our discussion of efforts to secure a Pacific security dialogue (Chapter 6), in the politico-strategic context, where its policies came under considerable critical scrutiny in both the North and South Pacific regional contexts.

It is true that American suggestions for closer economic cooperation were put forward: for example, George Shultz's proposals for closer cooperation of 'like-minded' states in the areas of trade, investment, transport, and telecommunications; the Cranston-Lugar proposals for an annual Pacific Basin Trade Forum; and the Bradley proposal for more regularized consultation between Australia, Canada, Indonesia, Japan, Mexico, South Korea, Thailand, and the United States.[47] Yet these proposals generated little interest or debate within the United States; the regional cooperation option was, as a result, subsumed within the climate of growing economic nationalism of the second half of the 1980s, during which time aggressive reciprocity became the cornerstone of foreign economic policy – all of Washington's rhetoric in favour of multilateralism notwithstanding.

To the extent that the APEC concept was supported by the United States in the first phases, it was to represent what Baker called a framework for 'a new Pacific partnership.' For Baker, the essence of this framework was the need for a 'more creative sharing of global responsibility with Japan'[48] – a framework not unlike the American approach to greater burden-sharing in Europe. In addition, we may speculate that it was an effort to send out two other sets of signals. First, it was to signal to the other market economies of Asia, and especially ASEAN, that there was more to American economic interests in the region than its bilateral relationship with Japan. Second, it was to signal the potential of the Asia-Pacific region as a counterweight and bargaining lever for the United States in its dealings with the European Community.

Nevertheless, Washington did become increasingly self-absorbed in the latter part of the 1980s; and Japan, continuing to become more economically powerful, was thrust into a more prominent role in the push towards Asia-Pacific Economic Cooperation. Without overstating Japan's enthusiasm or abilities for regional hegemony, its growing support for greater cooperation was founded on two pillars. The first was its enhanced position as financier, as source of technology and management, and as architect of a transformed set of production relationships as well as its trade and investment linkages in the region. The second was a growing recognition that regionalism might offer the government in Tokyo a useful tool with which to offset what Japanese officials saw as an aggressive American shift to managed bilateralism. In addition, a significant Japanese interest in the idea of a 'Pacific concept' stretches back to the 1960s, as we noted earlier.

Despite a growing enthusiasm for the idea in influential Japanese political and business circles, especially during the prime ministership of Yasuhiro Nakasone, Japanese diplomacy in the region was marked by a cautious, risk-free approach. Rather than bold entrepreneurial leadership based on its structural power, Japan concentrated on leadership designed to deal with technical matters in areas such as customs clearance and transport and communications links in the region.[49]

In addition, there are two important constraints on Japanese activity in APEC. Domestically, there was a considerable divergence of opinion within the Japanese bureaucracy on the merits of the idea. While a number of departments and agencies (for example, the Economic Planning Agency and a think tank in the finance ministry) put forward proposals for a ministerial level conference of Asia-Pacific countries, the foreign ministry was much more reluctant. In part, its hesitancy was based on bureaucratic questions of 'turf,' but it was also unsure of the degree to which such a conference might send out negative signals concerning the strength of Japan's commitment to multilateralism. The Ministry of International Trade and Industry (MITI), for its part, proposed an annual meeting of trade and industry ministers but, unlike the initial Australian proposal, was careful to ensure that its definition of the region was seen to include the United States and Canada.[50] These differences continued through to the Canberra meeting, where both

MITI and the Ministry of Foreign Affairs felt constrained to have their ministers make separate opening statements emphasizing different issues.

The major Japanese constraint was, however, external. Japanese policymakers were conscious of the existence of deep concerns over Japanese intentions among many of the smaller and middle powers of the region. Given the memories of the 'Greater East Asia Co-Prosperity Sphere' of the 1940s, the worst-case scenario for ASEAN and South Korea was that regional cooperation would prove to be a euphemism for an institutionalized division of labour, in which they would be relegated to the lower levels of industrial activity. The Japanese Ministry of Foreign Affairs, in particular, did not want the impression created that Japanese regional diplomacy cared only for trade and economic issues.[51] Given these conditions, Japan preferred not to go out in front on the APEC initiative. Without a domestic consensus on the issue, and fearful of a potential rebuff abroad, Japan played a more discreet – but supportive – secondary role behind Australia. Indeed, according to two Japanese journalists, the Japanese government was not unhappy that Australia's position at centre stage on the initiative prevented the capture of the initiative by the United States.[52]

For their part, the ASEAN states had serious reservations about APEC. Despite the low Japanese profile in the APEC initiative, the ASEAN governments were clearly anxious about the prospect of economic domination by its major partners, especially Japan. They were also concerned that there would be a diminution of ASEAN's internal cohesion in the face of any greater penetration of the region brought about by increased openness and liberalization. Finally, there was a concern that APEC would compromise the non-aligned status of some of its members.[53] In hindsight, however, it is possible to argue that the APEC initiative could have increased the solidarity of the group, forcing it to redefine its interests in an era of waning strategic concerns and new economic challenges. By exerting its diplomatic weight in a well-considered and concerted fashion, ASEAN was able to have a considerable impact on the APEC agenda at both the pre-negotiation stage (pushing for the inclusion of the United States and Canada) and at the end of the Canberra meeting, when the Chair's Summary Statement contained a commitment to a looser form of institutional structure for the organization than had been envisaged in the original draft.[54]

APEC's acceptance within ASEAN was challenged by Malaysia, albeit only indirectly. The Malaysian prime minister, Bin Mohammed

Mahathir, suggested the formation of an East Asian Economic Grouping – one that pointedly excluded the non-Asian members of APEC. The
Malaysian challenge was, however, ineffectual: according to some
accounts, Mahathir took this initiative without consulting either his
own trade minister or, more important, his colleagues from the other
ASEAN states – notably Indonesia, which expressed considerable dis-
pleasure at both the initiative and at the manner of its introduction.[55]

Canada and Regional Economic Cooperation: APEC and NAFTA

Canada's attitude towards APEC was even more ambivalent than
ASEAN. Pacific cooperation, broadly defined, was the third best option
in Ottawa's foreign economic strategy. Multilateralism remained the
favoured approach, and Canada, in concert with Australia, was an active
proponent of greater liberalization and stronger disciplines and rules in
the Uruguay Round. Unlike Australia, however, Canada had a clearly
defined fall-back position in the event of a dramatic deterioration of
the multilateral system: continentalism or regional cooperation (narrowly defined). The Canada-United States Free Trade Agreement and
the North American Free Trade Agreement, involving Canada, Mexico,
and the United States, reflected Canada's second preference after
multilateralism.[56]

Thus, whereas GATT and the Free Trade Agreement received contin-
uous (and much publicized) high-level political and bureaucratic attention, the prospect of Pacific cooperation and Canada's role in it was
conducted on a low-key basis. The main thrust of Canada's approach
towards the region was to concentrate on facilitating a 'bottom up or
private sector first approach.'[57]

Although many officials in Ottawa were sceptical about excessive
regionalism,[58] Canada remained determined to be included in any talks
concerning the prospect of an emerging regional grouping. This may,
in part, be explained in reputational terms: Canada, like Australia, takes
its role as a 'good international citizen' seriously. More important,
however, Canada's interest can be explained in both a medium- and
long-term tactical way. The acquisition of a regional option provided
Canada with added manoeuvrability, while its exclusion from this
institution-building exercise would have left it potentially vulnerable if,
in the future, the initiative had moved from the goal of open economic
cooperation to the creation of a regional economic bloc (with the
attendant discriminatory trading practices). The hope was not that
Canadian involvement could, itself, prevent the rise of an Asian-centred

economic bloc in response to the growth of European and North American blocs; rather, it was hoped that the presence of the two North American countries might serve to dampen fears in the western Pacific about the rise of blocs elsewhere in the international political economy.

Consequently, Canada campaigned hard in the early stages of the Hawke initiative to ensure that it was not excluded. This was done in two ways. First, Ottawa engaged in hard lobbying at the senior ministerial level, targeting Japanese support in particular. Second, it sought a softer exercise in image-building to convince regional states, especially ASEAN, of Canada's regional bona fides.[59] A key element in this effort was the announcement in May 1989 of the 'Pacific 2000' initiative, a set of proposals designed to further Canada's linkages with the region; to raise Canada's profile in the Asia-Pacific; and to overcome the common Asian perception that 'Canada is the unimportant part of North America.'[60] As Joe Clark, the secretary of state for external affairs, put it, the Pacific 2000 initiative was designed to 'dispel the myth that we are content to put all our eggs in the North American basket.'[61]

While it wanted to be a player, Canada's enthusiasm for the substance of what, in his Pacific 2000 speech, Clark called Hawke's 'enterprising initiative' remained restrained. Specifically, Canada had serious reservations about the early Australian suggestion of creating a Pacific OECD-like organization rather than creating a gradual extension of existing informal arrangements such as PECC, PAFTAD, and PBEC. Canada was also opposed to the idea that APEC should have decisionmaking powers. Its strong preference was for a body that was consultative only.[62] As John Crosbie, the minister of international trade, argued to the OECD ministerial meeting in May 1989: 'Canada supports initiatives towards the creation of arrangements to enable the countries of the Pacific to consult on economic matters affecting the area ... Consultation among Pacific countries could provide the basis for greater co-operation on regional economic concerns and for common approaches to adjustment.'[63]

Canada's role in APEC was, in many ways, not unlike its role in the Cairns Group. Determined to be a participant, it nevertheless exhibited an ambiguity towards both enterprises. In the economic area, Canada's approach to the Pacific in the early 1980s was what Douglas A. Ross termed 'ad hoc bilateralism.'[64] Rather than interacting with the countries of the Asia-Pacific region as a group, Canada tended to deal with these countries primarily on a bilateral, and an issue-by-issue, basis. For example, it was significant that during his trip to Hong Kong and Japan in May 1991, Prime Minister Brian Mulroney focused on specific issues of mutual concern – such as refugees, immigration, trade, and invest-ment – and did not seek to use the trip to advance the wider agenda of regional cooperation. On the other hand, by the end of the decade, the government in Ottawa had shed some of this ambiguity, introducing a strong Pacific push in its diplomacy, particularly in the security dimen-sion (as we will see in Chapter 6).

The Canadian government's embrace of a North American Free Trade Agreement (NAFTA) reinforces the point that Canada occupies a mark-edly different geographical and structural location in the international economy from that of Australia. The difference of location is crucial to understanding the differences in the diplomacy of the two countries. We have noted that Canada did not attempt to play a leadership role in APEC, preferring a followership role. It demonstrated similar behaviour in the evolution of NAFTA. Deeply sceptical of the utility of extending the bilateral Canada-United States free trade arrangement to a trilateral free trade arrangement,[65] the government in Ottawa decided that 'going along' with NAFTA was tactically preferable to being excluded from a bilateral Mexican-American free trade deal, regardless of the wider effects of NAFTA on the international trading environment.[66]

Canada's difficulty in coming to terms with its neighbourhood was, in many ways, similar to the difficulties being experienced by Australia in the Asia-Pacific region. While Canada is clearly a North American country, it was far from emotionally connected to Mexico (or, indeed, any other Latin American country). Contacts were neither broad nor deep. With very different histories, cultures, political systems, and perceptions of national interests, their relations were 'modest but episodic.'[67]

If there was a lack of clear mutuality of interest between Canada and Mexico, there was a coincidence of interest shaped by their shared proximity to the United States. Historically, the priority of both govern-ments in Mexico City and Ottawa was to restrain the overweening influence of the United States, and the traditional preference was always to try to manage American influence in strictly bilateral terms. Thus, Washington's attempts to forge a North American common market were always viewed as means by which the United States could extract additional benefits by playing the two smaller countries off against each other. For example, Ronald Reagan's call for a North American 'Accord' in late 1979 was treated not as an opportunity but as a threat.[68]

At another level, Canada and Mexico made similar efforts to shift the United States away from aggressive unilateralism and towards the maintenance of the international order. Both countries sought to high-light issues on which they differed from the United States – most notably on the embargo against Cuba and on the issue of the Reagan administration's policy towards Central America in the 1980s. Both countries sought to temper American behaviour and channel it towards multilateral fora. For example, Lopez Portillo and Pierre Trudeau engaged in a joint effort to promote a North-South dialogue at Cancún in 1981.

Such a safety-first approach was challenged not by any change in Canadian attitudes but by external pressures. A crucial factor was the change in Mexican economic strategy. Mexico was hit hard by the shocks of the 1980s – tumbling oil prices, rising debt, dramatic devalu-ations, and the failure of import-substitution industrialization and statist intervention. The government of Carlos Salinas de Gortari was galvanized to embrace a vigorous and outward-looking program of reform. At the same time, the United States was also changing its thinking: American policymakers became increasingly attracted to the idea of moving from bilateral trade deals to regional economic integra-tion. At first, policymakers in Washington were attracted to bilateral and regional options, because they appeared to offer useful demonstration effects for others in the international trading system. In particular, it was believed that flirting with bilateral or regional free trade areas would show Europeans and Japanese that alternatives to the multilateralism under GATT were possible.[69] However, as the Uruguay Round bogged down, the regional approach was increasingly regarded not as a fall-back option but as a preferred first option, gaining credibility and legitimacy on its own merits.

The result of these shifts in Mexican and American thinking led to a renewed effort at creating a North American economic arrangement. But the NAFTA initiative posed a serious dilemma for Canadian foreign policymakers. Any extension of the Canada-United States Trade Agree-ment jeopardized its status as the institutionalization of the special relationship between Canada and the United States. By contrast, NAFTA raised the spectre that Canada would no longer be special. Instead, it would join Mexico as a mere spoke to an American economic hub, as Richard Lipsey and Ronald J. Wonnacott have characterized it.[70] More-over, if NAFTA, in turn, served as a prototype for a more comprehensive set of pan-American agreements, the number of those spokes would be expanded.

NAFTA also posed political problems within Canada. The Mulroney government had little to gain from its campaign to sell NAFTA to Canadians. Opponents of the Canada-United States trade agreement were given another chance to rally against the perceived costs of trade liberalization. The government was blamed for the loss of jobs due to structural adjustment; for the flight of Canadian firms to low-wage areas; and for signing an agreement with a country alleged to tolerate low environmental standards and human rights abuses.

To be sure, advocates of NAFTA argued that the status quo was not a viable option for Canada. Economically, they pointed to broader trends towards market integration in North America, necessitating further changes in the institutional and legal barriers to trade and capital movements. Canadian firms were actively responding to larger dynamics – the internationalization of production or the establishment of *maquiladoras* in Mexico, for example. Historically, Canadian commercial ties with Mexico had a strong resource component; by the late 1980s, however, a different pattern was emerging – a pattern marked by direct investment and strategic alliances in manufacturing and high-technology sectors (primarily automobiles, auto parts, and telecommunications).[71]

Advocates of NAFTA also argued that, diplomatically, Canada had little choice but to be a player in NAFTA. Regionalization created more of an imbalance in bargaining strength than did the bilateral option. Nonetheless, the protection of Canadian interests seemed to be better achieved by taking part in the expanded negotiations rather than by remaining on the sidelines. 'Being there' was deemed essential for Canadian interests, particularly if the government in Ottawa was to make its influence felt. As one Canadian official put it, 'If Canada is not at the table, it cannot make its views known – the absent party is always wrong.'[72]

But if the Mulroney government joined the NAFTA process because it felt that there were few other alternatives, it did so without enthusiasm. Ottawa adopted a cautious approach. In its declarations, the Canadian government stressed that it intended to use the NAFTA negotiations to strengthen its bilateral trade agreement with the United States, particularly the dispute-settlement mechanisms; in reality, however, the Canadian approach concentrated on 'damage containment.'[73] Far from going on the offensive to extract new benefits, Canada had to fight hard just to avoid giving away any existing benefits through NAFTA that it had resisted during the bilateral free trade negotiations. As an editorial in the *Globe and Mail* stated, 'Ottawa's, and Canada's, commitment to the

[NAFTA] negotiation has never been wholehearted and has always been defensive.'[74]

The Canadian government's emphasis was on trying to maintain the basic structure of the Canada-United States agreement, particularly in such sensitive areas as culture, agricultural marketing boards, and environmental and health standards. To be sure, Ottawa pressed for modifications in areas in which the Canada-United States free trade agreement itself needed clarification. For example, Canada wanted a clearer definition of the rules of origin regarding the production in North America of Asian automobiles, particularly in view of the Honda dispute of the last months of 1991.[75] Likewise, from the outset, Canada paid special attention to the possible extension of NAFTA to the western hemisphere as a whole. It took a distinctly minimalist line on the issue of additional members, pressing for a 'special accession' clause, which would fix the minimum concessions that other countries would be required to give before being allowed to join.[76]

By the time NAFTA was signed in December 1992, two important questions about the agreement itself, and Canadian trade policy in general, remained unresolved. The first was whether or not Canada had, indeed, discovered 'its vocation as a nation of the Americas,' as Michael Hart so succinctly put it.[77] It is true that in 1990 the Mulroney government reversed four decades of Canadian tradition and joined the Organization of American States; it is also true that it abandoned an even longer tradition in embracing continental free trade. However, it may be that, just as Australia gradually shifted its relations with its Asia-Pacific neighbours, Canada was simply coming to terms with its neighbourhood. Indeed, like the Australian government, which saw regional cooperation in Asia as a welcome alternative to bilateralism, the Canadian government came to believe that regionalism in the Americas was a viable alternative to growing American preponderance in bilateral relations. Widening hemispheric economic regionalism, in other words, was seen as preferable to deepening American penetration. Finally, there was the hope that, as Winham has noted, regional blocs incorporating GATT rules and evincing a multilateralist philosophy – such as the Canada-United States FTA – 'might improve the management of multilateral negotiations, while at the same time providing a mechanism that could effectively address uniquely regional problems.'[78]

The second question left unresolved was what such regional architecture would look like. Again, as in the case of the Asia-Pacific region, the choice was between a more positive, trade-inducing and a more negative, trade-restricting form of regionalism. The regional option ran the risk of moving in directions likely to invite aggressive responses from those outside North America concerned about the possibility that NAFTA signalled the transformation of the North American market into a closed economic bloc.[79]

Major Powers, Middle Powers, and Regional Leadership

How can order be returned to the global political economy in the absence of clear leadership? In posing this question we are not implying the necessity of hegemony for stability and the provision of the various public goods of multilateralism. Rather, we suggest that a much more complex understanding of the question of leadership needs to be introduced. Intellectual, technical, and entrepreneurial leadership needs to be seen as a necessary complement to more usual types of leadership, which have, traditionally, been based on the structural attributes of the major powers. In this section we consider some of the wider elements of the debate about leadership and cooperation in a regional context. In North America, it is clear that the United States demonstrated leadership in organizing and driving much of the regional economic cooperation that occurred in the 1980s – first the Free Trade Agreement with Canada that came into force in January 1989 and then the North American Free Trade Agreement with Canada and Mexico that was signed in December 1992. In the North American context, the middle powers, Canada and Mexico, were followers rather than leaders.

In the Asia-Pacific region, by contrast, we have suggested that, in the 1980s, comparable leadership was not in evidence. The United States was not providing the kind of leadership in the region commensurate with its structural influence; likewise, despite its dramatic increases in structural power, Japan was not exerting international leadership. In such circumstances, other forms of leadership were bound to play a more significant role – as secondary states were increasingly affected by the rapidly growing bilateral conflicts between the major actors. While the major powers seemed indifferent to the damaging effects of their quarrels on third parties (and on global welfare in general), secondary states were, not surprisingly, highly sensitive to the impact of these disputes.

In particular, the common belief in the United States that Japan and the EC were the source of many, if not most, of its problems, was a major cause of concern for all in the Asia-Pacific region. It was also one of the major constraints on Japan playing a greater role in cooperation-building in the region. There is evidence that Japan did, indeed, have a commitment to open regionalism and multilateralism.[80] Perhaps surprisingly, given the aggressive nature of American policy towards Tokyo in the late 1980s, the Japanese government was still hesitant to champion initiatives in the international economic order in advance of a clearly identified American position. In addition, Japan was perceived by many of the secondary states of the Asia-Pacific region as less of a threat to an open international system than was the United States. Even accepting such an interpretation, Japan was still constrained in the kind of leadership role (of the cooperation-inducing variety) that it might make either in the Pacific in particular or in the international economic order in general.

There are also other factors which explain the absence of greater Japanese activity. The structure of the Japanese domestic policymaking process is not, as Drysdale has argued, geared towards taking on the leadership role of either a regional or a global economic superpower.[81] It is possible to argue, as, indeed, we do in this book, that some states with a tradition of middle power internationalism have a greater institutional and attitudinal capability for the international diplomacy of coalition-building than does Japan. Many middle powers, such as Australia, Canada, and the Scandinavian countries, have engaged in activist policies that would, at first blush, appear to be beyond their capabilities – if leadership were based on structural power alone. On the other hand, Japan might have the base for an active foreign economic policy, but, as Drysdale notes, 'the reactive character of Japanese trade policy remains remarkably pronounced.'[82] This is, in large part, due to the absence of governmental structures capable of overriding entrenched groups in the Japanese polity and economy in the process of making foreign economic policy.[83]

Thus, it is not surprising that secondary actors have sought to take the lead in cooperation-building in the absence of leadership from the great powers. Such an approach should not be seen as existing in opposition to structural leadership; rather, it should be seen as an attempt, by skill and innovation, to harness the power of the major players in a more cooperative and pluralist form of leadership. This was clearly the tactic of the Cairns Group in the Uruguay Round. It can also be seen as a rationale behind the activity of a state like Australia in its attempts to foster economic cooperation and to provide a forum for greater dialogue in the Asia-Pacific. APEC was both a vehicle for the consolidation of a dialogue between Japan and its regional neighbours and for the creation of a framework within which the United States might become more attuned to the interests and needs of its Asia-Pacific partners.

In this sense, APEC also provided an important learning experience. Both the United States and Japan were in a learning period in the late 1980s and early 1990s – and not only in the Asia-Pacific region. Japan was learning its potential for international economic leadership, and the United States was learning anew the complexity of such leadership in an era of waning hegemony. It was clearly difficult for the United States to adjust, in both politico-institutional and psychological terms, to the need for a form of global economic leadership based more on consensus than on the assertion of hegemonic power. In many ways, this learning was delayed by what Samuel Huntington calls an overly pessimistic attachment to the idea of American decline.[84]

The decline thesis sparked a rush of defensive replies that needlessly polarized and over-dramatized the debate, effectively preventing a more measured understanding of the changing nature of America's role in the late 1980s. By the early 1990s, however, there were signs that the debate was becoming more nuanced. For example, in his treatise on American foreign policy for the 1990s, Nye recognized that power in the international system was increasingly diffused and pluralistic; Raymond Vernon and Debora Spar, while recognizing that the United States retains enormous residual structural power in the areas of trade, security, finance, and knowledge that still give it the 'ability to threaten,' then went on to note that the United States no longer had the 'ability to dominate.'[85] Likewise, David Abshire came to recognize that the changing circumstances of the late 1980s and early 1990s would have a profound influence on American diplomacy. As relative power declines, Abshire wrote, 'persuasion, coalition-building, and the art of the "indirect approach" become increasingly important' – an observation, it might be noted, that would hardly surprise scholars and policymakers of the system's non-great powers.[86]

For Abshire, it was critical that the United States recognize that it needed to rebuild credibility both at home and abroad. Not only was it not providing leadership by example; it was often a reluctant and late participant in initiatives from other sources. This was clearly having a constraining effect on the nature of American leadership – based as it is, Abshire would argue, on both power and 'the creation of perception.'[87] And international perceptions of the decisionmaking processes in Washington are generally sceptical, seeing the United States as fragmented and compartmentalized rather than as integrated in its approach towards the international economic order. American policy is also perceived as having little or no regard for the interests of others.

Conclusions

We have argued that the case studies of APEC and NAFTA suggest the appropriateness of a more complex conception of leadership for the changing global political and economic environment of the 1990s. In some cases, hegemonic leadership will continue to be asserted. Hegemonic leadership tends to be primarily structural in nature – power being the central means with which 'to overcome the collective action problems that impede efforts to reach agreement on the terms of constitutional contracts in social settings of the sort exemplified by international society.'[88] And, indeed, this type of leadership was clearly evident in American attempts to establish the postwar Bretton Woods and GATT systems; it was this type of leadership that underlay the evolution of North American free trade in the late 1980s and early 1990s. Structural power thus properly occupies a central position in contemporary international theory. But theories of leadership derived solely from power will be far too determinist and will leave little or no room for policy intervention derived from technical innovation or political creativity.

We have also argued that successful cooperation in the international economic order in the 1990s, more than at any time in the post-1945 era, requires a different kind of leadership – a leadership based on different attributes. Particularly in the absence of leadership from the major powers, organizational and entrepreneurial skills can be just as important as is the structural power usually associated with hegemony (as was seen in the case study of APEC).

Of course, entrepreneurial leadership is no substitute for major power accommodation, particularly across the Pacific, where there have been heightened tensions between the United States and Japan.[89] As Richard Leaver has noted, these tensions will have an impact on the broader system: 'If this relationship cannot be stabilized, then hopes of a broader pluralist solution to the problem of leadership of the world economy are simply wishful thinking.'[90]

To accept Leaver's argument is not, however, to suggest that the added dimensions of middle power innovation may not prove significant in mitigating the behaviour of the major players and in inducing a more cooperative economic regional environment. In the Asia-Pacific context, APEC clearly is not the beginning of a coalition to act as a counterweight to any serious future conflict between the United States and Japan. It is, however, a forum in which educative and constraining influences might be brought to bear in a manner that was not available prior to its inception. As such, it forms part of a wider process of organization-building in the international order, in which secondary actors cognizant of, and increasingly impatient about, the constraints on major power initiative are attempting to provide a spur to tension reduction and cooperative action.

Thus, a theory of leadership in which intellectual and entrepreneurial dimensions are incorporated offers increased explanatory power in accounting for the activities of middle powers, such as Australia, in the formation of the Cairns Group and APEC. In the absence of leadership from traditional sources – the great power of the great powers – other sources of leadership can be just as potent in shaping policy outcomes. The quality of a secondary state's diplomacy, for example, can be an important asset in such leadership attempts. Thus, as we noted Chapter 1, middle power diplomacy, which is geared towards mitigating conflict and building consensus and cooperation, can be as important as structural sources of leadership.

5
The Security Agenda: Coalition-building and the Gulf Conflict

Introduction

A distinctive characteristic of the foreign policy behaviour of middle powers, it is commonly said, is their embrace of multilateralism as the preferred means of advancing their foreign policy interests. Indeed, as the case studies of the Cairns Group and APEC in the previous chapters demonstrate, middle powers tend to seek out like-minded and comparably placed states in the international hierarchy; they tend to forge like-minded coalitions in order to encourage the growth and health of international institutions; they embrace notions of the 'general interest' and 'good international citizenship' in order to guide their diplomacy.[1] Multilateralism is favoured, we have argued, for reasons of enlightened self-interest: in order to maximize parochial national interests that could not be advanced alone. Moreover, it should not be forgotten that, in some situations, multilateralism affords smaller or middle-sized states the greater safety that comes with numbers – not so much against the predations of enemies as against the overweening embrace and dominance of great power friends.[2]

In the years immediately following the end of the Second World War, this multilateral impulse could be seen at work most clearly in the security issue area, when middle powers such as Australia and Canada sought not only to increase their own security by encouraging the development of multilateral alliances but sought to encourage world order by strengthening international institutions such as the United Nations and the United States-led alliance systems that were created in the late 1940s and early 1950s.[3]

We have argued above that the concept of middle power, as it emerged in the immediate postwar period, tended to be linked to the military-security issue area. However, as we have noted above, middle power coalitional diplomacy can be found in numerous other issue areas. Besides the cases of Cairns and Asia-Pacific explored in the previous chapters, one could also point to the role of the Group of Twelve in the Law of the Sea negotiations in the 1970s; the attempts of the Like-Minded Group to generate consensus in the North-South dialogue in the late 1970s and early 1980s; or the role of the Commonwealth in imposing sanctions against South Africa in the 1980s.[4] In short, these cases suggest that there has been a considerable continuity in the approach of middle powers,[5] even though the international agenda has shifted considerably since the days of such middle power proponents as Australia's H.V. Evatt and Canada's Lester B. Pearson.

While we argue in this book that we have seen middle powers taking an active leadership role in building coalitions on the newer agenda items, it should be noted that our perspective on middle power entrepreneurial and technical leadership is primarily agenda-based. In other words, we should not expect to see the same approach to coalition-building, for example, across all agendas.

This is particularly true in the case of the security agenda, where the scope for middle power leadership is more highly restricted than it is in other issue areas. Despite the changes in the power relations of the major powers since the mid-1980s, particularly in the dominant position of the United States, the importance of military capabilities in a range of issues in world politics remains undiminished. In this sphere, the system's secondary states, particularly middle powers like Australia and Canada, with their limited military capabilities, cannot (and, indeed, do not) expect to wield significant influence.

However, it is precisely in the security issue area that we can gain a more nuanced appreciation of the dynamics of the role of middle powers in coalition-building. For, to this point, our discussion of middle power leadership has stressed the essentially activist nature of its role in coalition-building. We have painted a portrait of middle powers as active 'doers,' engaging in the positive role of cooperation-building in international politics: middle powers seek out other like-minded states with which to work; middle powers work out positions that reflect consensus and compromise to press on the broader international community; middle powers carefully work to build like-minded coalitions.

Middle powers have indubitably shown themselves to be active builders of coalitions. But by stressing the activism of middle powers and their emerging leadership roles, we should not forget that the pursuit of multilateralism leads these middle powers to be international 'joiners' rather than just 'coalition-builders.' Moreover, with our focus on activism, we should keep in mind that this propensity for 'joining' can take markedly different forms: 'joiners' can, by exercising a leadership role, actively 'join' others, stitching them together in a coherent coalition; but 'joiners' can also take a more passive role, allowing themselves to be 'joined' to someone else's enterprise.

Thus, we should not ignore the fact that the middle power coalition-building associated with multilateralism has another side. This is the passive, and largely reactive, role of follower that is the necessary concomitant to the active role of leader. Middle powers may be active leaders in coalition-building, but they are just as willing to have multilateral coalitions 'built on them,' if it can be put in such terms. For joiners will always understand that multilateralism and coalition-building can only work if there are more states willing agree to join coalitions as followers than there are states seeking to play a leadership role.

This more passive role is the other side of coalition-building; it has several facets. First, the passive role of followership tends to be overlooked in discussions of middle power leadership, and it is useful to remind ourselves that, while middle powers may demonstrate leadership in some issue areas, they play the equally important role of follower in other issue areas. Moreover, although being a passive follower, merely 'tagging along,' is commonly seen as less glamorous, less exciting, or less soothing to the national ego than is being an active leader, 'on the cutting edge,' and 'out in front of the curve,' we should not forget the necessary part that passivity and followership play in coalition-building.

An examination of a case study from the security agenda also reminds us that the coalition-building exercises so eagerly embraced by middle powers can have less desirable consequences than do those usually associated with the active side of coalition-building. For followership in coalition-building creates a dynamic for the followers that, once they have joined, binds them tightly to the preferences of the coalition's leader. Once the leader has gathered a coalition around itself, it can radically alter the preferences of the coalition as a whole, relying on its superordinate power to keep its junior members with it, regardless of their own preferences. Like a rider on a roller coaster, the junior coalition partner, once aboard, has few options: there is no stopping the ride; getting off may be theoretically possible but, in practice, involves such massive costs as to make such an option impractical; and, most important, it makes no difference whether or not the rider actually enjoys the ride.

The case of Australian and Canadian participation in the international coalition formed in response to the Iraqi invasion of Kuwait on 2 August 1990[6] demonstrates the dynamic of coalition-building's other side at work. When one examines the process of the Australian and Canadian decisions within the context of United States policy, it can be argued that these middle powers joined the coalition for classical middle power reasons: using a multilateral coalition to advance conceptions of world order by imposing a non-offensive blockade against the violating state. We will see, however, that the purposes of the coalition shifted over the course of the conflict, pulling the coalition into a situation that had only been dimly anticipated by both governments in August 1990.

Building the Coalition: United States Policy

It is clear, in retrospect, that the policy of the Bush administration towards the Iraqi invasion of Kuwait on 2 August was set in the first hours of the crisis. From the meeting of the National Security Council convened on the morning of 2 August, Bush demonstrated a marked – and intensely personal – disinclination to simply accept the new status quo that had been fashioned by Iraq. Various factors led Bush to adopt a hard line from the outset, including a push from Margaret Thatcher. Moreover, the ratcheting-up effects of his own rhetoric prompted a harder line – a dynamic that was particularly evident during a press conference on 5 August, when Bush became visibly more heated the more that questions were put to him, leading to his angry, and apparently unrehearsed, declaration that 'I view very seriously our determination to reverse out [sic] this aggression ... This will not stand. This will not stand, this aggression against Kuwait.'[7]

While Bush's goals coalesced early in the crisis, the means to achieve those goals took somewhat longer to take shape. The American strategy to secure an Iraqi withdrawal proceeded along a number of tracks. First, the administration sought to move Iraq by economic strangulation – freezing assets and imposing economic sanctions. Second, it attempted, diplomatically, to widen international condemnation of the Iraqi move and to secure international support for the sanctions net. Third, it ordered the Central Intelligence Agency to begin a campaign of subversion against Hussein. The fourth, and most important, was the military track. Early in the crisis, Bush decided to seek to deploy ground, air, and naval forces to the Gulf region. The role of these forces, even in the planning phase, was always ambiguous. Once they were in position, these forces could be used for numerous purposes: to deter a possible

Iraqi attack on Saudi Arabia; to aid in imposing a blockade on Iraq in order to make sanctions as leak-proof as possible; to stage a demonstration of American power designed to coerce Baghdad into withdrawing; and, of course, to actually secure a withdrawal by force.

The success of the diplomatic, economic, and military tracks depended heavily on coalition-building.[8] In the first instance, other governments had to be convinced to refuse to accept the takeover of Kuwait as a fait accompli that could not be reversed. Likewise, a policy of economic strangulation depended on casting the sanctions net as widely, and as tightly, as possible. Finally, and most important, Washington's plan to deploy military forces in the Gulf depended on multilateral support. While, technically, the United States could have deployed its forces with the cooperation of but one state – Saudi Arabia, where American forces would be based – the Bush administration recognized that a military deployment would be most effective if it had a broad base, ideally including other Arab states.

The administration thus embarked on a concerted effort to secure support for economic sanctions and contributions to the military deployment. Bush conducted much of this diplomacy himself, mostly by telephone. Other senior officials, including the secretary of state, James A. Baker III, the secretary of defense, Dick Cheney, and the permanent representative at the UN, Thomas Pickering, also were active in rallying international support.

By the end of the first week, there were two distinct coalitions of states ranged against Iraq. One had taken only five days to emerge – that large group of states (including all members of the Security Council but Yemen and Cuba) participating in sanctions against Iraq. Some of these states had moved to impose sanctions bilaterally immediately after 2 August; others came under the auspices of UN Security Council Resolution 661, passed on 6 August.

The other coalition was in a more nascent form by the end of the first week. It consisted of those states contributing military units to an emergent coalition being built around the initial deployment of American and British naval units to the Gulf. Both Britain and France had indicated their willingness to use naval forces to blockade Iraq, and, indeed, on 6 August, Thatcher committed British naval forces for that purpose. By 8 August, Saudi Arabia had issued its 'request' for American military assistance.[9] The night Saudi approval was secured, Bush announced his decision to send air and ground forces to Saudi Arabia. This action served to catalyze the growth of this second coalition: it triggered numerous commitments of forces from other states, including the commitment of ground troops by members of the Arab League and naval forces by members of NATO. It should be noted, however, that at this stage, the publicly stated purpose of the military coalition was to deter an Iraqi attack on Saudi Arabia. In his announcement, Bush was at pains to deny that these troops were designed to attack Iraq; rather, he stressed that 'The mission of our troops is wholly defensive' – a justification he invoked no less than nine times in his address and the news conference that followed it.[10] Likewise, the publicly stated purpose of the naval forces was to aid in enforcing the UN sanctions.

Joining the Coalition: Australian and Canadian Reactions
The Australian and Canadian policy responses in the first ten days after the invasion reflected the rapid evolution of international reactions. Both governments began cautiously, with a rhetorical condemnation, which escalated three days later to unilateral and limited sanctions and, two days after that, to multilateral and comprehensive sanctions. And, within eight days of the invasion, both middle powers had committed themselves to the military coalition.

Given that there was no clear indication of how other states would react to the invasion, it is hardly surprising that the initial response from both Canberra and Ottawa was limited to rhetorical condemnation. Both foreign ministers happened to be travelling abroad at the time, but both condemned the invasion in comparable terms on 2 August. Returning to Canada from a visit to the Asia-Pacific region, the secretary of state for external affairs, Joe Clark, termed the aggression against Kuwait 'totally unacceptable'; from India, the minister for foreign affairs, Gareth Evans, called the invasion 'just indefensible.' In both capitals, the Iraqi ambassadors were summoned to the foreign ministries to receive formal protests.[11]

Neither Australia nor Canada rushed to embrace sanctions, however, even though the United States had immediately indicated its intention to do so. Indeed, Bush signed the executive orders freezing all Kuwaiti and Iraqi assets in the United States merely nine hours after Iraqi troops began crossing the Kuwaiti border. While Canada took measures to achieve similar results, the process took somewhat longer, for Canadian law does not grant the kind of sweeping powers over foreign assets granted to the president under American law. The only way to control assets in the immediate term was to ask Canada's chartered banks to ensure that the estimated CDN$3 billion in Kuwaiti investment would not be moved out of the country without the authorization of Kuwait's government-in-exile. By 3 August, Clark indicated that the government had 'made an arrangement' with the Canadian Bankers Association to effectively protect Kuwaiti assets.[12] Although it was no less concerned about protecting the estimated AUD$1 billion in Kuwaiti assets in Australia, Canberra adopted a different approach: what to do with these assets was tied to the broader question of trade sanctions, and so it was not until other sanctions were imposed that Kuwait's assets in Australia were frozen.[13]

Although the United States had also placed an immediate trade embargo on Iraq, both the Australian and Canadian governments moved more slowly on the trade front. Government officials in both Canberra and Ottawa did make a point of indicating that their countries would abide by any decision on trade sanctions taken by the Security Council (on which Canada was sitting as a non-permanent member), particularly if it employed 'Chapter VII language.'[14] It is clear, however, that the initial preference of these governments was not to adopt trade sanctions ahead of a wider international decision. This was, in large part, because of the nature of Canadian and Australian trade with Iraq, which not only ran heavily in their favour but was also dominated by sales of primary products. In 1989, for example, Australian trade with Iraq amounted to AUD$340 million, a full $327 million of which was in wheat sales. Total imports from Iraq were valued at a minuscule AUD$199,000, none of which was for petroleum. For Australia imported no oil from Iraq; and its oil purchases from Kuwait accounted for no more than 2 per cent of Australian consumption. Likewise, the live sheep trade with Kuwait was worth AUD$81.6 million in 1989. The Canadian picture was similar. Farmers sold CDN$245 million in wheat and barley to Iraq, which accounted for 95 per cent of Canada's exports to Iraq. By contrast, Canadian imports from Iraq in 1989 totalled CDN$61.8 million, mostly in petroleum-related products.[15]

By that first weekend, when the United States began its diplomatic push for a wider sanctions net, both Australia and Canada had moved somewhat closer to embracing sanctions. On Saturday, 4 August, Mulroney had a long telephone conversation with Bush 'to review efforts to bring collective international pressure on Iraq to end its occupation of Kuwait.'[16] By Sunday, Canada had imposed the following sanctions on Iraq: oil imports were banned; controls on exports were strengthened; most-favoured-nation status and Export Development Corporation coverage of new business ventures were terminated; trade, academic, cultural, and trade promotion activities were suspended. However, notably absent from the list was any disruption of Canada's lucrative grain trade.

Australian officials also met through the weekend to consider what sanctions might be adopted in response to the United States request; indeed, Evans indicated to reporters in Islamabad on Saturday that he fully expected a decision by the end of the weekend. However, according to one account,[17] officials were unable to agree on a course of action to recommend to Cabinet. Instead, when ministers met on Sunday, 5 August, they were presented with little more than lists of options on sanctions. Moreover, there was a split within Cabinet. On the one side were those ministers with responsibility for foreign affairs – Hawke; the attorney-general, Michael Duffy, who was acting minister for foreign affairs in Evans's absence; Robert Ray, the minister for defence; and, participating from Asia by fax machine and telephone, Evans himself. On the other side were those ministers with economic portfolios – John Kerin, the minister for primary industries and energy; Paul Keating, the treasurer; and John Button, the minister for industry, technology and commerce.[18] Given the lack of agreement at the official level and the lack of enthusiasm from some ministers, Cabinet eventually decided to postpone a decision until it was clearer what others were planning to do. As one Australian official said, 'It's pretty pointless to go through with work to invoke sanctions if there is no international support. We have to measure our own policy by what others do.'[19]

As it became clearer to the Hawke government, in the twenty-four hours after the Sunday postponement, that the UN was likely to move on the sanctions question, it, like the Mulroney government in Ottawa, did not wait for the UN before making its own move on sanctions. Meeting in the early evening of Monday, 6 August (which was before dawn on the same day in New York), Cabinet took but twenty-five minutes to decide to impose a series of sanctions against Iraq. Included in these sanctions were: a freeze on all Kuwaiti assets in Australia; the imposition of an embargo on oil imports from Kuwait and Iraq; the imposition of an embargo on sales of defence related equipment to Iraq; and, for good measure, the rejection of an Iraqi Airways request to open an office in Sydney.[20] Like Canada, Australia did not include a ban on grain in these sanctions. Speaking to reporters later, Kerin was blunt about the reasons for Canberra's reluctance: Iraq owed Australian vendors a total of AUD$600 million from previous wheat sales, including US$380 million in credits insured by the government and AUD$123 million owed directly to the Australian Wheat Board, and there was a fear that a wheat ban would not only jeopardize future sales but might prompt Iraq to default on this $600 million.[21]

Whatever reluctance both governments might have been displaying in their sanctions policies disappeared completely when firm international action was taken by the UN on Monday, 6 August. By a vote of 13-0, with Cuba and Yemen abstaining, the Security Council adopted Resolution 661, which invoked the enforcement provisions of Chapter VII of the Charter and established a comprehensive ban on all but humanitarian economic intercourse with Iraq and occupied Kuwait. Both governments, having previously asserted that they would be bound by UN decisions, moved to embrace a stiff sanctions policy: the day after the UN vote, formal announcements were issued, extending sanctions to bring them into line with Resolution 661.[22] In particular, both governments adopted a restrictive interpretation on the issue of food exports to Iraq in Resolution 661[23] – much to the chagrin of the wheat boards in both countries.[24]

However, no sooner had Australia and Canada joined the sanctions coalition than the focus of American coalition-building had already shifted, fixing, instead, on the deployment of military force to the region. By Friday, 10 August, both Australia and Canada had also shifted their Gulf policies again: both governments announced that they were each despatching two warships and a supply ship to the Gulf.

In Australia, the first public indication that the government was considering moving beyond a passive sanctions policy came on Wednesday, 8 August. Amid reports that Washington was planning a multinational naval force to enforce a blockade against Iraq, the minister for defence, Robert Ray, who was in Townsville, Queensland, on a tour of defence facilities, was asked by a reporter whether or not Australian forces were also preparing for action. Ray responded that the government was 'looking at all contingencies' and suggested that he could not imagine Cabinet saying no to a request for a military contribution, particularly if it were organized as a 'United Nations action.' The minister's comments prompted officials in Canberra to issue a hasty 'clarification': the United States had not asked for a contribution, and no units of the Australian Defence Force were preparing for action. However, the government would 'seriously consider' a request from the United States to participate in a multinational force.[25] At 7:15 on Friday morning, 10 August, Bush called Hawke at the prime minister's residence, The Lodge; they spoke to each other for twenty minutes. At 10:30,

Hawke announced at a news conference that Australia would 'join with the rest of the world in saying that we will not tolerate, will not stand idly by while any member of the international community purports to break the rules of civilised conduct.' He announced that he had authorized the despatch of two guided-missile frigates, HMAS *Adelaide* and HMAS *Darwin*, and a supply ship, HMAS *Success*, to the Gulf region to join the multinational force. In his comments to reporters, Hawke intimated that the decision to participate in the coalition came as a result of an American request:

> The matter was raised with us initially in the United States, and we therefore responded. We had discussions with them and it was out of those preliminary discussions that were initiated from the United States that the president rang me today and that out of those discussions we agreed that this Australian naval asset would be provided.[26]

However, according to later reconstructions of the decision,[27] Hawke's description was, as one columnist put it, 'a somewhat generous approximation of the facts.'[28] The sequence of events suggested that the process by which Australia joined the coalition was no less complex than was the process by which the Saudi 'request' had been secured. When it appeared likely that the international response would go beyond passive sanctions, and that both the United States and Britain were preparing for a naval role, Australian officials in Defence, DFAT, the Department of the Prime Minister and Cabinet had all been quick to conclude that Australia should seek to be a member. Ray himself favoured sending two warships and a supply ship – indeed, Grigson suggests that after 7 August, 'no real consideration was being given to other options.'

Officials at the embassy in Washington had raised the possibility of a contribution with American officials. In addition, Hawke had talked to Mel Sembler, the American ambassador in Canberra, about a military contribution on 8 August.[29] Because of the international dateline, it was Thursday morning, 9 August, when Bush made his announcement about the deployment of forces. Immediately after that speech, Hawke moved to firm up the Australian commitment. He phoned Evans, who was in Dacca; Ray, who was by this time in Cairns; and John Button, the government leader in the Senate, who was in Melbourne, to get their views on an Australian naval contribution. He then met over lunch in his office with the treasurer, Paul Keating, and the acting minister for foreign affairs and trade, Michael Duffy, together with several officials.

At this meeting, Hawke reported that Evans, Ray, and Button had indicated that they favoured a naval contribution; Keating and Duffy were also in favour.[30] The deployment decision was finalized; Michael Cook, the Australian ambassador in Washington, was ordered to arrange a phone call from George Bush. While Hawke portrayed this call as an American request which needed a positive response, American officials were characterizing it to Bush as a thank you call for a contribution already made.

It is clear that, although the naval contribution was very much 'Mr Hawke's decision' (as a critical *Canberra Times* editorial put it on 15 August), it seems to have been taken on the assumption that the purpose of the multinational force was not offensive but, rather, was intended to deter an attack on Saudi Arabia and to coerce Iraq into withdrawing from Kuwait by enforcing a blockade. Although Hawke was committed to sending warships as the Australian contribution to a multinational coalition, he nonetheless had persistent concerns that Australia might become involved in something more than a blockade. These concerns were 'set to rest' by Bush's public promise not to use the forces gathering in the Gulf to retake Kuwait.

A further indication that Hawke believed that the purpose of the coalition would be essentially peaceful is that he moved without recalling Parliament, which was not due to begin its spring session until 21 August. To be sure, Hawke had no desire to do anything (such as recalling Parliament) that would slow the bandwagoning that was seen as important to the coalition-building process. Thus, he readily agreed to Bush's suggestion that the announcement be made immediately in order to create a 'bow wave' effect – in other words, to push others into joining. Indeed, the eagerness to create such a bandwagon effect was reflected in the speed with which the State Department in Washington put the story about Australian involvement out to the wire services: the Australian decision was announced by the United States government immediately after the phone call – a full three hours before Hawke made his announcement. For his part, Hawke was so eager to make a speedy announcement that he did not manage to consult John Hewson, the leader of the opposition, prior to making the announcement, although he had fully intended to do so.[31]

It is true that a recall of Parliament would have brought with it a risk of exposing deep differences within the various factions of the Australian Labor Party on the issue of Australian support of the American-led coalition. Traditionally, the ALP had always evinced a generalized opposition to military deployments overseas and, in particular, had strongly opposed Australia's involvement in Vietnam in the late 1960s and early 1970s. This dislike of overseas deployments was deeply embedded in party practice and party dogma.[32] The fact that Hawke was willing to make the commitment of forces to the coalition strongly suggests that he believed it to be a 'safe' decision as far as his backbench was concerned. As it turned out, he was wrong: before Parliament resumed in August, intense cross-factional negotiations between the Left, Centre Left, and Right factions were necessary in order to deal with the unhappiness of many in the Left with the prime minister's decision. The Left faction was planning to ask the full ALP Caucus on 20 August to approve a motion calling for putting the Australian ships under UN command and also for the Caucus to be given authority over further Australian involvement. Hawke and Cabinet strongly objected, and the meeting had to be delayed for a day while a compromise was negotiated. Not until the afternoon of 21 August, shortly before Hawke's ministerial statement and motion to the House, was a compromise reached: the Left would withdraw their planned motion, Hawke would acknowledge to Caucus that greater consultation was needed, and the government would agree to insert a call for placing the blockade under UN auspices into the government's motion.[33]

A final indication that the Australian government viewed the purpose of the naval deployment as primarily blockade-related was the degree to which Canberra saw its commitment as a crucial concomitant to the decision to stop its lucrative grain sales to Iraq. Without a blockade, grain sanctions were unenforceable; shipments slipped onto the high seas could make their way to Iraq with relative impunity. One Australian official was quoted as saying that the blockade was a useful means of making sure that 'no other bastard takes over the trade.'[34]

The 'other bastard' Australian officials clearly had in mind was Canada, which, like Australia, had been reluctant to embrace full wheat sanctions. Of the large Iraqi purchases of Canadian wheat in mid-1990 – 500,000 tonnes from April to July alone (well above the traditional levels of 400,000 tonnes annually) – approximately 200,000 tonnes were in transit at the time of the invasion: 25,000 tonnes of Ontario wheat was already on the high seas; a further 100,000 tonnes of Ontario wheat was being shipped through the St Lawrence Seaway; and 60,000 tonnes of western Canadian wheat and barley was due to be loaded in Vancouver.[35]

According to Grigson's account, some Australian officials were concerned that this grain would be allowed to slip out of port before the sanctions took effect. Australian officials in Ottawa called Canberra on 8 August to alert DFAT about the possibility that the grain still in Canada would be slipped onto the high seas and beyond the reach of sanctions. The Canadian government moved that day to stop these shipments.[36] Whether it was out of concern over Canada's fidelity to the UN sanctions – as the story put out to the Australian media suggests – or simply to compare notes, Hawke called Mulroney on 9 August to tell him of the Australian deployment.[37]

By the time that Hawke and Mulroney talked, however, Canada had already made a similar commitment and was merely waiting for an appropriate moment to announce it publicly. Although at the outset of the crisis participation in a military operation had seemed unthinkable to officials,[38] by 6 August it was more plausible. That evening, Mulroney flew to Washington to have dinner with George Bush; consideration of a Canadian military commitment began the next day. While the official line afterwards was that Bush had asked for no commitment from Canada and that Mulroney had offered none,[39] it has been suggested that Mulroney, unilaterally, gave Bush a commitment for a Canadian naval contribution that evening, without discussing it with his Cabinet.[40] It does seem improbable that the two leaders did not at least discuss the issue of a multinational naval blockade, particularly since that very afternoon Thatcher had dropped by the White House on her way back to London from Aspen and had been in the Oval Office when Bush received the call from Cheney indicating that King Fahd ibn Abdul Aziz of Saudi Arabia had approved an American deployment; following this meeting, Thatcher had announced the despatch of two more British frigates to the Gulf and had declared that Britain was considering imposing a blockade on Iraq.

On his return to Ottawa, Mulroney himself started the process of developing military options at the bureaucratic level, since William McKnight, the minister of national defence, was abroad and Clark was in his riding in Alberta. Cabinet met on Wednesday, 8 August, by which time both Clark and McKnight were back in Ottawa. Discussion focused on possible responses to the emergence of a multinational blockade headed by the United States. As in Australia, there was general agreement at both the bureaucratic and ministerial levels that the most appropriate contribution would be the kind of limited naval deployment that Britain had announced and that France, Australia, and other European allies were considering. But because Bush had yet to make an announcement regarding American plans, it was decided to take no decision on a naval deployment in advance of other states. Rather, Cabinet decided to wait until after a meeting of NATO foreign ministers scheduled for Friday, 10 August, in Brussels.

In Brussels, Baker appealed to the NATO allies to contribute forces to defend the Gulf states, asking that each ally contribute 'in its own way.' At the conclusion of the meeting, numerous NATO countries announced their participation: Belgium and the Netherlands committed naval vessels; Germany, which was constitutionally bound to keep its armed forces within the NATO perimeter, pledged four minesweepers and a supply vessel for the Mediterranean to take the place of American vessels sent to the Gulf; Spain, Portugal, and Italy promised to allow American forces to use air bases on their soil.[41]

The Canadian decision to participate in the multinational coalition was announced by the prime minister at a press conference in Ottawa following the NATO foreign minister's meeting. The justifications offered by Mulroney indicated that he, like Hawke, saw the purposes of the multinational coalition as defensive: to deter a further Iraqi advance. Noting the reports of atrocities coming out of Kuwait, Mulroney called Hussein 'a criminal of historic proportions' and invoked 'the lessons of history' about responding to aggression: 'Turning a blind eye to aggression only encourages further aggression ... If a clear warning is not sent to Iraq now, it will only be emboldened to find new victims.'[42] Like Bush, Mulroney often allowed his public rhetoric on the Gulf to escalate, with the result that some of his claims sounded exaggerated and extravagant. For example, he argued that the move to participate in the coalition was taken to fulfil obligations to NATO and the UN, when, patently, the Gulf lay outside the NATO area; and the impetus for the multinational coalition was coming from the United States, not the UN. Likewise, he argued that Ottawa had a responsibility to respond to attacks and threats 'on friends and allies of Canada,' but none of the states under threat was an ally. Moreover, as Martin Rudner has pointed out, relations between Canada and the Gulf region were 'fairly remote';[43] to call these states 'friends' was stretching the definition somewhat.

Mulroney stressed that Canada's contribution was intended to convey disapproval of the invasion – but, he added, 'not in an aggressive manner.' The contribution consisted of what was fast becoming a standard contribution from smaller states – two warships accompanied by a supply ship: the destroyer HMCS *Athabaskan*, the destroyer escort

HMCS *Terra Nova*, and the supply ship HMCS *Protecteur*, all based in Halifax. These ships ranged from eighteen to thirty-one years old; none of the new frigates being acquired by the Canadian forces was ready for deployment. The ships were reconfigured for anti-submarine duty, and, thus, they had to be modernized and refitted. By the time they left Halifax on 24 August, additional forces were despatched along with them: a squadron of Sea King helicopters and units of the Royal Canadian Artillery (to work the close-in weapons systems installed in the refit).

As in Australia, Parliament was not recalled to debate this decision. In part this was because the government was expecting to be called on at the NATO meeting on Friday to announce its contribution. Had Parliament been recalled, it would not even have started its debate by the time the NATO meeting was held; and the government had little desire to have to tell its other allies that the issue of a Canadian contribution was still being debated.

But there was another disincentive: Cabinet had just sent Canadian forces units to Oka, Quebec, in response to an armed confrontation there between Native people and the Quebec provincial police. On 11 July, Mohawks in Oka, opposed to the expansion of a golf course on lands they regarded as sacred, had erected a barricade on the main road into town. The Quebec provincial police force, the Sûreté du Québec (SQ), had been sent to dismantle it. A gunfight had broken out, and a police officer was killed. On the same day, Mohawks in neighbouring Kahnawake had set up a sympathy blockade of the Mercier Bridge, one of the main commuter bridges across the St Lawrence River into Montreal. Because 1,500 members of the SQ – fully one third of the force – were being maintained at the two blockades, the Quebec government of Robert Bourassa had requested the assistance of federal troops. There was little doubt that the use of federal troops against Native people was a contentious domestic issue, and the government in Ottawa did not particularly want to recall Parliament to discuss the Gulf crisis, only to find itself having to face queries and criticisms of its handling of the Oka crisis.

As a result, the government structured its Gulf decisions to avoid having to recall Parliament before it was due to reconvene on 24 September. Because the National Defence Act requires that if Canadian forces units are put on 'active service' or combat status Parliament must be recalled within ten days, the task force could not be put on active service before 14 September if the government wanted to avoid recalling

Parliament. The government thus announced that the task force would not be put on active service until it arrived in the Gulf region. Even then, the ships steamed too rapidly across the Atlantic and had to be slowed down by arranging a special port call in Sicily for degaussing. On 15 September, these units were put on active service;[44] the following day, in what a Department of National Defence (DND) official, his tongue firmly in his cheek, termed 'a happy coincidence,' the flotilla arrived in the Red Sea.[45]

Changing the Coalition: From Blockade to War

The multinational coalition that Australia and Canada joined on 10 August 1990 changed dramatically over the six and a half months that Iraqi forces occupied Kuwait. Usually resulting from policy decisions taken in Washington, these changes altered the purposes of the coalition as a whole and, thus, of the individual members.

Indeed, the United States was changing the coalition even as it was being formed. While ministers in Australia and Canada were considering what contributions they might make to what they thought was going to be a multinational naval coalition to enforce sanctions, the United States had completed negotiations with Saudi Arabia for the deployment of ground and air forces. As governments of smaller and middle-sized states were announcing their naval flotillas at the end of the week, American military units were being flown into Saudi Arabia, altering the dynamics of the conflict and, therefore, the nature of the coalition.

In the next three months, the focus of the international community was fixed on the UN. In a series of resolutions, the Security Council moved to tighten existing coercive measures and to respond to new developments in the Gulf. With virtual unanimity among the permanent members, the Security Council declared itself on such issues as: the formal Iraqi annexation of Kuwait (Resolution 662, 9 August 1990); foreign nationals being forcibly held in Kuwait and Iraq (664, 18 August 1990; 674, 29 October 1990); violation of diplomatic missions (667, 16 September 1990); and the destruction of Kuwait's population records by Iraqi forces (677, 28 November 1990). It also moved to tighten the embargo by allowing states to interdict shipping to and from Iraq and Kuwait (665, 25 August 1990), more rigorously defining humanitarian exemptions (666, 13 September 1990), and extending the embargo to aircraft (670, 25 September 1990).

However, over this period, the focus of the Bush administration remained fixed on the military option, even though it was still an active participant in UN diplomacy. American troop levels continued to rise until, by early October, they had reached the pre-arranged level of approximately 200,000[46] – enough to repulse an Iraqi attack on Saudi Arabia. These troops may have been a successful deterrent, but their very success posed a dilemma for the Bush administration. Once in Saudi Arabia, these troops could not be withdrawn unless Iraq withdrew from Kuwait – not only because the original threat that had prompted their deployment had not diminished, but also because Bush, who had publicly vowed to see the invasion reversed, would have suffered an unacceptable loss of face. Because of their (large) numbers, the financial and, particularly, the political costs of maintaining these troops indefinitely in Saudi Arabia were exceedingly high.[47] But because of their (small) numbers, they could not be used to forcibly remove the 400,000 Iraqi troops believed to be in Kuwait. So on 31 October, Bush gave his approval for another change in American policy: he redoubled United States forces in Saudi Arabia (a decision not announced until after the 6 November mid-term elections). It is important to note that Bush's announcement on 8 November also shifted the posture of American forces from a defensive deterrent against an Iraqi attack on Saudi Arabia to an offensive threat designed to pressure Iraq into withdrawing from Kuwait. This change, though made unilaterally,[48] had, inexorably, multilateral implications: all states in the coalition were also committed to the offensive option as of 8 November.

To be sure, this decision was subsequently ratified by Resolution 678, which authorized the use of 'all necessary means' to 'uphold Resolution 660 ... and to restore international peace and security in the area.' This resolution, passed on 29 November 1990 by a vote of 12 to 2, with China abstaining, provided for a 'pause of goodwill' until 15 January 1991 before action would be taken. But Resolution 678 also represented the logical end of UN input into the process: arming the United States with the authority of the Security Council put the final decision in Washington's hands. From that point on, all of the final stages of the conflict were driven by American decisions, from the smallest, such as deciding exactly when the UN deadline expired,[49] to the most important, such as deciding to launch the air attacks on 17 January 1991, to open the ground war on 23 February, and to declare a cease-fire four days later.

Australian and Canadian Gulf policy faithfully mirrored these changes being embraced by the United States. In the months between

10 August 1990, when they joined the coalition, and the 27 February 1991 cease-fire, both governments moved more or less in step with the coalition and, particularly, with the United States. Both leaders maintained consistent rhetorical support for the coalition,[50] even though both governments were facing increasingly strident domestic opposition as the coalition's purposes shifted over the course of the conflict.[51]

In both countries, opposition came from similar sources: a newly revitalized peace movement, some church leaders, and some members of the Arab-Australian and Arab-Canadian communities. In both countries, the pattern of opposition was also similar, with the emphasis placed on street demonstrations (frequently in front of the closest United States diplomatic mission) and public meetings, reaching a crescendo in the days before the war broke out. Even the language of protest – most of it, ironically, imported from the United States – was the same: Australian and Canadian protestors alike chanted the catchphrase 'no blood for oil' and sang the refrain from John Lennon's 'Give Peace a Chance.'

Only in the parliamentary sphere did the pattern of opposition differ. In Australia, both the Liberal and National parties supported the government's Gulf policy throughout the crisis; some members of the Left faction of the ALP were unhappy with Hawke's Gulf policy, but most either acquiesced or stayed away. This resulted in virtual unanimity in the lower house: Ted Mack, the independent member for North Sydney, was a lone voice of protest.[52] In the Senate, the Australian Democrats (who were not represented in the House of Representatives) and an independent member – Jo Vallentine of Western Australia – strongly opposed Hawke throughout the conflict.

In Canada, by contrast, the House of Commons was more divided. As J.L. Granatstein put it, the opposition parties went through 'conniptions' over Canada's Gulf policies.[53] The Liberal party opposed the government throughout most of the conflict, altering their position only after war had broken out. During the emergency debate on 15 and 16 January, the Liberals were arguing that if force were used, the government should withdraw Canada's forces from the Gulf immediately. These arguments so embarrassed the party's former leader, John Turner, that, much to the chagrin of his erstwhile colleagues, he rose to methodically pick apart all the Liberal arguments against participation, concluding that all of them were 'in the end invalid.'[54] Once war broke out, however, the Liberals abruptly changed direction: as Jean Chrétien, the leader of the opposition, put it: 'We are at war and we have to be united because Canadians are fighting right now.'[55] The New Democratic Party (NDP) consistently opposed the government's approach. It is true that after war had broken out, the NDP did feel compelled to add that they, too, 'supported the forces,' but they argued that the government should find a 'humanitarian' role for them. However, when the party's leader, Audrey McLaughlin, tried to verbalize how one assigns a 'humanitarian' role to a CF-18 fighter aircraft, her speech became increasingly incomprehensible as she attempted to reconcile supporting the forces on the one hand and opposing what the CF-18s were actually doing in the Gulf on the other.[56] For its part, the Bloc Québécois (BQ) (the political party formed from the ranks of Quebec Progressive Conservative MPs who quit the party after the failure of the Meech Lake Accord in June 1990) did not take a formal position in the Gulf debate. While several of its members supported the government on Gulf votes, most BQ members, including its leader, Lucien Bouchard, did not vote.

Despite the stridency of the opposition, participation in the coalition continued to enjoy broad support in both countries. Editorial opinion generally approved not only the initial naval deployment but also the subsequent decisions; likewise, polls showed that 60 per cent or more of Australian and Canadian respondents approved of the Gulf policies of their respective governments.[57] No doubt this was one reason why both governments felt comfortable increasing their original contributions to the coalition as it began to shift in purpose.

The Australian government both expanded the role its ships played in the Gulf and augmented the units it was deploying. Once the UN Security Council approved Resolution 665 on 26 August, giving states authority to impose a blockade, Canberra agreed to expand the rules of engagement for its ships; the changes were announced on 11 September, following a naval conference in Bahrain, which included all of the countries engaged in the blockade. The new rules allowed the use of 'minimum force short of sinking,' and specified a graduated series of steps that could be used in interdictions, from shots across the bow to shots into the steering gear.[58] Likewise, the Australian response to the public appeal by the United States to its NATO allies for more contributions to the coalition expanded its contribution: on 16 September Ray announced the decision to send a twenty-member naval medical team,[59] which would eventually be deployed on the United States hospital ship *Comfort*. After the passage of Resolution 678, the government announced that the task force would be available to participate in whatever action arose out of the interpretation of that resolution.[60] By war's end, other augmentations in the Australian commitment included the doubling of the medical contingent to forty and the despatch of twenty-three Navy divers for mine disposal. An almost unnoticed Australian contribution to the coalition's war efforts were the joint facilities at Pine Gap and Nurrungar, which played a critical role in providing the United States with early warning of Iraqi missile attacks.[61]

The Canadians also augmented the original commitment of three ships and responded positively to Baker's appeal: on 14 September, Mulroney announced that Canada would commit a squadron of eighteen CF-18 fighters from Germany to fly air cover for the Canadian ships.[62] In addition to the 450 pilots and ground crew, units of the Royal Canadian Regiment and the 22nd Canadian Regiment (the 'Van Doos') were deployed to protect 'Canada Dry,' the air base that was established in Qatar and shared with an American squadron of F-16s. A Canadian headquarters to coordinate the naval and air operations was established in Bahrain in mid-October, necessitating the deployment of a signals squadron. In the new year, it was decided by the coalition to give Canada responsibility for arranging logistics for all the naval contingents in the Gulf. As the UN deadline approached, an additional six CF-18s were flown in to Qatar to bring the squadron up to normal strength; a Boeing 707 refueller was also deployed.[63] In response to a British request, a 100-bed field hospital was set up in Jubayl in Saudi Arabia after the war had broken out. A team from the Royal Canadian Engineers was also sent to the Gulf to assist in mine clearance and bomb disposal. The role of the fighters also underwent a transformation: when they were first deployed in October, they were assigned a defensive role, providing air cover for coalition shipping; after 17 January, they were ordered to fly 'sweep and escort' missions, accompanying allied planes on attack missions. On 20 February, the role of the CF-18s was altered again, this time to allow pilots to engage in combat attacks on Iraqi targets.[64]

Analyzing the Coalition
To this point, we have explored the initial decisions that Australia and Canada took in response to the Gulf crisis and the premises that underlay them. We have also sketched the changes initiated by the United States and have demonstrated that the governments in both Canberra and Ottawa moved in step with the coalition and its shifting purposes over the remainder of the conflict. To what extent does the

middle power argument outlined at the outset of this chapter accurately describe the Australian and Canadian approach to the Gulf coalition?

The process by which Australia and Canada joined the coalition was examined in considerable detail, because the account strongly suggests that both countries *joined* the coalition for the kind of middle power reasons outlined in the introduction. The reasons why they *stayed* in the coalition are more problematic.

First, it is clear from the sequence of events that, in this case, both middle powers were, indeed, as their domestic critics so frequently asserted,[65] following the lead of the United States. American preferences drove much of the international community's response to the invasion of Kuwait, and Australia and Canada were no exception. Neither middle power sought an activist leadership role, no doubt because the room for middle power initiative-mongering in this instance was slim or non-existent. However, if both Australia and Canada willingly accepted the role of follower in this case, the followership was more complex than simply toadying to Bush. Rather, it can be argued that both middle powers responded positively to the idea of participating in a coalition – when it appeared that a coalition was possible. In other words, both states participated in a classical bandwagon dynamic: left to their own devices, and in the absence of negative reaction from other states, both Australia and Canada might have been concerned about the violation of the principle of territorial integrity, but neither would have moved unilaterally to disrupt their profitable relations with Iraq. However, as it became apparent that numerous other states were prepared to join a sanctioning coalition, Australia and Canada quickly moved to join, regardless of the damage it would do to their agricultural interests. Likewise, as it became apparent that numerous other states would join a multinational blockading force, Australia and Canada again moved to join. It should be stressed that the account above makes clear that both states were not simply agreeing to join at another state's behest – both Canberra and Ottawa actively sought to join.

Second, the account here suggests that both Australia and Canada actively sought to join these coalitions for a complex admixture of reasons,[66] the most important of which were world order concerns. Both middle powers were concerned over the violation of territorial integrity by Iraq, more because of its implications for order than because of any abiding concern for the fate of the al-Sabah emirate. Both governments believed that one of the ways of deeply entrenching the norm of territorial integrity in contemporary international politics was to ensure that as many states as possible reacted negatively to the Iraqi invasion.[67]

To be sure, this concern resonated in different ways in both countries. In Australia, the concern over the maintenance of territorial integrity was not just abstract and symbolic. Rather, the fear that Australia's territorial integrity could actually be violated was concrete and instrumental – a fear persistently reflected in official Australian defence policy in the 1980s.[68] In particular, the Australian experience in the Second World War, which left a widespread belief that conquest by Japan had only been staved off by American intervention, continued to linger in the collective memory.[69] A frequently sounded theme during the Gulf debate was that support for the coalition was necessary for Australia's own security. It was likely, the argument tended to run, that the United States would withdraw its protection from the South Pacific in the future, and that Australia would have to rely on international norms to defend itself from threats to its territorial integrity; if the international community acted in concert to uphold the sanctity of borders, would-be violators of the territorial integrity of others would be deterred, and Australia would be the safer for it.[70]

For Canada, by contrast, the concern expressed for the sanctity of territorial integrity was entirely symbolic. Since Canadians have not worried about being invaded for over a century, it is not surprising that the instrumental deterrent argument was never made in the Canadian Gulf debate.

A related world-order desire was to capture the moment presented by the unprecedented Soviet-American cooperation that emerged immediately after the invasion to build up the UN as an effective means of channelling interstate conflicts and imposing a particular order on the state system. Moreover, both governments were genuinely impressed by the multilateral impulses the Bush administration displayed from the outset of the crisis – a happy departure from the more unilateral tendencies of the Reagan administration. It was clear that Bush and Baker were devoting considerable energy to consulting friends and allies and working within a multilateral framework. There was, thus, a desire in both Canberra and Ottawa to encourage this behaviour.

It should be noted that, in the past, Canadian governments have regarded such multilateral linkages as exceedingly important for restraining the more unilateral impulses of American administrations;

in both the Korean and Vietnam wars, Canadian diplomacy was concerned to constrain what officials in Ottawa worried would be the more hawkish predilections of the United States.[71] In the Gulf conflict, there was some evidence of comparable fears at work and of comparable Canadian reactions. At the outset of the crisis, for example, a number of members of the Security Council, including Canada's permanent representative, Yves Fortier, successfully pressed the United States to take a multilateral route and to seek UN authorization for its proposed interdiction of ships in the Gulf.[72] Likewise, later in the crisis, there were anxieties in the Department of National Defence that the United States would escalate the conflict prematurely. Part of the calculus of remaining as part of the coalition was that one could only exercise restraining influence from inside the coalition.

Likewise, both Australia and Canada were concerned about the effects of future Iraqi behaviour on the international economic order. Given the interest of Western industrialized states in keeping control over oil supplies as divided as possible, there was a fear that Iraqi expansionism, particularly an attack on Saudi Arabia and the smaller Gulf states, would have profoundly negative consequences for the supply and price of oil, which, in turn, would have a negative effect on the international economy and, by extension, on Australia and Canada.

Finally, the account here suggests that the deployments cannot be attributed to the personal relationship between the American president and the prime ministers. This was a common explanation, with numerous variants on essentially the same theme. Mulroney and Hawke were portrayed as eager to please their good friend George Bush;[73] or eager to please the United States;[74] or eager to be 'stroked' by the powerful.[75] It was commonly asserted that Hawke or Mulroney were just fawning or toadying to the Americans; the analogy of choice on both sides of the Pacific was the servile canine, with both prime ministers referred to as lap dogs, puppy dogs, and presidential poodles.[76] Such interpretations were dismissed by Australia's minister for defence, Robert Ray, as having 'all the intellectual depth of a yabby's brain,'[77] but they were nonetheless pervasive among critics.

In fact, Bush's 'telephone diplomacy' played no part in Australia's Gulf decision: Hawke had no contact with Bush until after the Australian decision was made. By contrast, Bush and Mulroney had two long conversations before the Canadian decision, one by phone and another over dinner. But it can be argued that the president's personal relationship with Mulroney had no impact on *whether* Canada would contribute to the coalition, only an impact on *when* Canada would make the commitment to deploy. In other words, had there been no personal contact between Bush and Mulroney, a commitment might not have been given on 6 August, but it would eventually have been made by Friday, 10 August.

If the process by which Australia and Canada joined the coalition is a good example of middle power coalition-building – albeit of the passive rather than of the active kind – what happened after 10 August 1990 is a good example of the more negative aspect of coalition-building, where the coalition follower, like the queasy roller coaster rider, has little desire to continue the ride but has no option but to hang on tightly until the end.

To arrive at such a conclusion one must take a somewhat circuitous route. One should begin by asking whether or not both these middle powers were happy with the changes being imposed on the coalition by the United States, for it is possible that roller coaster riders who are put through such delights as a 30-metre vertical drop or triple corkscrews will discover that they actually enjoy the experience. We would argue, however, that neither government was fully comfortable with where the United States was taking the coalition. This may at first appear hugely presumptuous, since both governments were at pains to insist that they were entirely happy with the shift to an offensive posture and the use of force: both were unstinting in their rhetorical support for each of the steps taken by the United States and the UN that moved the coalition to a war posture; and both put their own forces in the Gulf in harm's way by committing themselves to offensive action once the war started.

However, we would argue that, in this case, it would not be inappropriate to question whether or not the Australian and Canadian governments were in fact as comfortable as they claimed to be. One key measure was the gap between the rhetoric of both governments on the one hand and what they actually committed to the coalition on the other. For example, both governments claimed unflagging commitment to the cause: Mulroney was to assert that Canada 'must do everything it can' to restore Iraqi respect for international law;[78] Gareth Evans was to declare that 'We must remain committed to ... doing everything we can as a nation – paying whatever price is necessary.'[79] But it was clear from their behaviour that both governments were unconvinced that 'everything' should be committed to this conflict.

For if they really had been convinced that force rather than economic strangulation should be used to expel Iraq from Kuwait, both governments might have embraced a more force-oriented posture – a posture that would have tried to match, at least in relative terms, the mounting commitments of the United States, Britain, and France. Indeed, had Australia and Canada matched the British ground contribution on a per capita basis, 12,000 Australians and 20,000 Canadians would have been committed to the Gulf conflict. Another measure might have been the commitment of ground combat troops to Saudi Arabia at any one of six points in the conflict: at the outset, along with American and British forces; or in September, when the full extent of the initial American deployment became clear; or in early November, when Bush doubled the United States forces and put them on the offensive; or in December, in anticipation of the implementation of Resolution 678; or in January, when the UN deadline expired; or in February, when the ground war began. That ground forces were not committed suggests that neither government was convinced that it was really necessary for the national interest to commit Australians or Canadians to fight a war against Iraq – a lack of conviction that stands in telling contrast to their behaviour in August, when the enthusiasm for a blockading coalition demonstrated clear conviction that such a coalition was a good idea.

At the same time, both governments recognized that the structure of the game was such that there was always a possibility that the military situation could change. We noted above the anxieties about a pre-emptive attack by the United States or the possibility that a conflict with Iraq would involve the use of nuclear or chemical weapons, possibly over the involvement of Israel. There was also the fear that the United States might ask its coalition allies for ground troops. In Canada, the government laid the ground for such an eventuality by signalling, shortly after the United States shifted its forces to an offensive posture, that it was not ruling out the use of Canadian ground forces. Mulroney indicated that the government would 'reflect on' a request by 'the United Nations or the allies' for 'another commitment.'[80]

In Australia, by contrast, the government moved to head off the possibility of such a request by signalling its desire to limit its involvement. Canberra's response to Bush's 8 November announcement was to note that there were no plans to send ground troops, though it would consider committing the three ships in the task force to an offensive action. Hawke clarified this position during the parliamentary debate after the passage of Resolution 678: having announced the deployment of the ships from the Gulf of Oman into the Persian Gulf, and the despatch of a further two medical teams, he then stated: 'It is not proposed to make any other contribution of naval, air or ground forces.'[81] This commitment to make no further contribution emerged from negotiations between Cabinet and the ALP factions. By this time, the divisions within the ALP on the Gulf issue had multiplied, and some state politicians were publicly urging their federal counterparts to bring back the ships; a meeting of the National Left faction (which included parliamentary and extraparliamentary members) was split between the 'hard Left,' which opposed the government, and the 'pragmatic Left,' which took a position of 'understanding opposition' to any escalation in Australia's role. Within the federal caucus, however, there was widespread agreement – even in Hawke's own faction, the Right – on one issue: there were to be no 'boots in the sand'; even the medical team had to be aboard a ship.[82]

While it can be argued that such reluctance to commit themselves to a fully offensive posture indicated that neither government was fully comfortable with the war option, it is also clear that neither government was in a position to leave the coalition at any of the points at which the United States changed the operating assumptions. The option of pulling out after 10 August was, quite simply, unthinkable, as the costs of defection would have been too high: all other coalition members, and the United States in particular, had too much at stake to countenance an open crack in the unity of the coalition with equanimity. (The only viable option for those states which were opposed to the change in the coalition's direction was to try to make their contribution as invisible as possible – as some Muslim governments, facing strong domestic opposition, tried to do.) In the Australian and Canadian cases, moreover, there would also have been considerable domestic costs: a withdrawal would surely have brought down on both governments more trenchant criticism, and from a wider segment of the population, than what they were receiving for their continued participation.

It is important to stress, however, that in both the Australian and Canadian cases, the decision to stay the course was not simply driven by a recognition of the huge costs, internationally and domestically, that would have come with a decision to defect. It is clear from their behaviour that both states wanted to remain as members of the coalition, even though they would be bit players in the larger game, and even though they might not have been comfortable with the idea of committing their own forces to battle. Evans nicely captured the mixture of resignation and willing acceptance that characterized the Australian and Canadian view when he said, in September 1990, that 'the general assumption is that we are in for the long haul and we had better prepare ourselves both physically and psychologically for that.'[83] Likewise, Clark resignedly acknowledged, in October, that war would mean 'thousands of casualties,' but that if war came, Canada would still be there: 'We should not rule out the possibility that young Canadian soldiers will not return to this country for celebration but will stay there for burial.'[84] While this grim sentence was widely interpreted as war-mongering by the opposition – who took to calling Clark 'Rambo Joe' and 'G.I. Joe' – this speech makes more sense when read as an expression of Clark's opposition to a too-hasty embrace of the war option.

Conclusions: Coalition-Building's Other Side

As it turned out, the Gulf conflict did not drag on as many had expected: the allied side quickly achieved air superiority; the threat of Iraqi chemical or poison gas attacks never materialized and neither, therefore, did the spectre of nuclear or chemical war; the ground war was unexpectedly short-lived; and on the coalition side, at least, the loss of life was relatively light. For all the middle power contingents, Australia and Canada included, the war was surprisingly painless: at the end of hostilities, one Italian pilot was listed as missing in action; apart from this, there were no combat casualties among any of the middle power contingents (with the exception of damage to Italian fighters, all of the middle power assets despatched to the Gulf survived undamaged); and the call for ground forces never came.

Despite this happier-than-expected outcome, Australia's and Canada's participation in the Gulf conflict nonetheless provides a good example of the other side of coalition-building at work. We have argued that Australian and Canadian decisions to join the coalition can best be accounted for by a middle power explanation; but their subsequent decisions cannot be fully explained by reference to this argument. This is because what began as an exercise in classical middle power coalition diplomacy was transformed by the coalition leader, the United States, into an exercise driven largely by that country. We have also argued that, while the great power explanation so heavily favoured by critics of Australian and Canadian participation in the Gulf coalition does not explain the decision to join, it also does not fully do justice to the position of these middle powers as it emerged over the course of the crisis. However, it is clear that once the decision to join had been made on 10 August, both governments were tied tightly to the preferences of the coalition leader. This case thus confirms that, while coalition-building tends to be celebrated as an integral part of middle power statecraft, certain kinds of coalition diplomacy can create a dynamic that tightly binds its middle power members in its embrace, pulling them into a vortex that may not, at the outset, be anticipated.

6
Addressing the Widening Global Agenda: Australian and Canadian Perspectives

Introduction

The previous chapters have examined four important case studies in Australian and Canadian foreign policy; by focusing on the changing nature of leadership in contemporary international politics and its impact on coalition diplomacy, we sought to explore the opportunities and constraints that middle powers face in an era of waning hegemony. Central to our argument about the nature of middle power leadership has been the contention that leadership and coalition-building is highly issue-specific: the conditions that allowed Australia to exercise a leadership role in the Cairns Group, for example, were simply not present during the Gulf conflict. As we showed in the Gulf case, a rather different leadership-followership dynamic obtained under those conditions.

In this chapter, we seek to extend our analysis by examining a number of other issues on what some have called the new, or widening, agenda of international politics in the 1990s.[1] To be sure, some of the 'new' issues are, in fact, old issues being addressed in renewed, revitalized, or revised form; others are indeed new, making their appearance on the international agenda for the first time. However, all of these issues, whether recirculated or new, have in common one important feature: they are being addressed by the system's secondary states in ways that conform to the theoretical expectations that we laid out in Chapter 1. That is, many of the players of this size and rank, Australia and Canada included, are demonstrating a relative autonomy from the dominant idea-systems of the major players, engaging in a particular brand of diplomacy that places a premium on technical and entrepreneurial initiatives aimed at advancing international coalitions along a path to greater institutionalization in the international system. It also involves 'niche diplomacy' – a decision to concentrate bureaucratic resources in a small range of issue areas likely to yield most results.[2]

In setting out the following issues for consideration, we are not proposing that what we are seeing represents a complete break with the past. Many of these issues have been deeply woven into the discourse and practice of international politics for generations. For illustrative purposes only, we single out for consideration issues that have a substantial pedigree in both Australian and Canadian diplomacy and which further demonstrate the utility of the approach outlined in Chapter 1. While the policies adopted by Canberra and Ottawa on these issues were entirely consistent with the traditional pattern of Australian and Canadian mediatory approaches to diplomacy in the post-Second World War period, they also represent a reformulated approach in the process of evolution. Thus, in the following sections we demonstrate the continual interplay of the traditional reactive diplomacy of the 'first followers' of the Cold War era on the one hand and the technical and entrepreneurial activities exhibited by both Australia and Canada in different issue-specific fora on the other.

Middle Powers and Arms Control

In the late 1980s, both Australia and Canada continued to pursue a traditional middle power course, seeking to contribute to reform on a wide variety of arms control issues. An examination of Australian policies on non-proliferation and Canadian policies towards both confidence-building measures in the European theatre and arms exports to the Middle East reveal indications of the entrepreneurial and technical leadership we identified in the preceding chapters.

Australian Initiatives

Australia's contributions to non-proliferation regimes in the 1980s provide one example of such entrepreneurial and technical leadership. In the area of nuclear weapons, Canberra's activities during the Comprehensive Nuclear Test Ban Treaty negotiations at both the 1985 and 1990 review conferences demonstrated a not unusual middle power commitment of bureaucratic expertise and diplomatic energy for the long-term global objectives of nuclear arms control. Likewise, Australia's active and long-standing participation in the G-10+1, a group of like-minded pro-Non-Proliferation Treaty (NPT) states that excludes the United States – is indicative of this general commitment to good international citizenship on nuclear questions. Sometimes referred to as the

'White Angels,' this group was keen to press for full-scope safeguards. Chairing this group allowed Australia to have a major input into the development of proposals on these safeguards. But the Australian government also played more specifically mediatory roles in this issue area. For example, at the 1985 conference, Australia successfully mediated in the dispute between Iran and Iraq on the question of nuclear testing.

Such skills were also exhibited in Australia's contribution to efforts to secure a treaty ban on chemical weapons. In 1985, the Australian government had organized, at its embassy in Paris, a meeting of fifteen states interested in the control of chemical weapons. The 'Australia Group' – which grew to twenty-two states by the early 1990s[3] – sought to identify lists of chemical ingredients necessary for chemical weapons production and to incorporate these 'precursors' into export control lists.

Building on its position as co-chair of this group, the government in Canberra hosted the first Joint Government-Industry Conference against Chemical Weapons in September 1989. With the intent of providing new impetus for the Geneva negotiations, which had been in progress for nineteen years, this conference was attended by senior government and chemical industry representatives from over sixty countries.[4] With Canberra taking a leading role, and forging close working relationships with a range of other countries,[5] agreement was sought on the basis of practical proposals and programs (such as the drafting of chemical weapons precursor export warning lists) rather than on the attainment of political consensus.[6] By March 1992, Evans, the minister for foreign affairs and trade, had submitted a complete draft of the Chemical Weapons Convention – an initiative that had the effect of shifting the negotiating climate from an issue-by-issue discussion to a comprehensive approach for the completion of the treaty text.[7]

It is clear that much of the success of such activities was due to more traditional middle power attributes such as location and reputation. As the Australian ambassador for disarmament, Richard Butler, put it, one of the reasons for Australia's effectiveness in helping to mediate the Iran-Iraq issue was how the parties to the dispute perceived Australia: 'It was very important who we ... were not. We were not NATO, we were not the Americans, we were not Warsaw Pact. Oh, and we weren't Sweden.'[8]

However, in addition to these traditional aspects of middle power activity, we can see elements of the entrepreneurial and technical leadership we ascribe to contemporary middle power activity. For example, the appointment of Australian officials to a variety of high-profile technical positions suggests that there was a wider international recognition of the importance of the expertise to be found in the Australian bureaucracy. John Gee, of the Australian Department of Foreign Affairs and Trade, was appointed as coordinator of the United Nations Special Commission Working Group charged with designing a plan to implement the Security Council requirement that Iraq reveal its holdings of chemical weapons as a condition of a permanent cease-fire in the Gulf War. The UN inspection team sent to investigate Iraq's inventory of chemical weapons in 1992 was led by another Australian, Peter Dunn. John Bardsley, from the Australian Safeguards Office, was assigned to the International Atomic Energy Agency's (IAEA) inspection team for Iraq's nuclear facilities after the war. And increasing numbers of Australian defence personnel, including analysts, technicians, and ordnance disposal experts, were assigned to other roles.[9]

At first glance, the global orientation of Australian initiatives on non-proliferation, particularly in chemical weapons, seems to be an exception to the strong regional bias in Australian diplomacy. On closer examination, however, we can see other characteristics of the Australian diplomatic style evident in this activity. On the one hand, the Australian motivation for taking the initiative on chemical weapons can be attributed to a genuine desire to be – and to be seen to be – a good international citizen pursuing a conception of 'good' that is more globally defined. On the other hand, Australian policy was also driven by a healthy concern for more narrow interests: notably, to keep its own regions – Southeast Asia and the Southwest Pacific – free from chemical weapons.

Such a regional motivation underlying Australia's global approach can be seen in the initiative by Gareth Evans in hosting a major regional seminar against chemical weapons in November 1990. It can further be seen in Canberra's support for the decision by the United States government to destroy its stockpiles of chemical weapons on Johnston Atoll in the South Pacific. To be sure, the Hawke government was widely criticized by many of the island governments in the South Pacific region for supporting the local destruction of these weapons (rather than having them shipped back to the United States for destruction). However, Australia's support was predicated on the assumption that the Johnston Atoll Chemical Agent Disposal System (JACADS) would be closed at the end of the incineration process; moreover, the Hawke government was confident that the means for the verification of American safety procedures would be found.[10]

In both style and application, the development of a chemical weapons policy echoed the Asia-Pacific Economic Cooperation initiative. Knowledge and experience from sectors other than government, especially industry, were brought to bear to improve the technical capacity of Australian officials in the regional context specifically and in the Geneva negotiations generally. Considerable diplomatic capital was invested in putting together a broad base of support for limited and incremental moves.

Canadian Initiatives

The Canadian government also played the role of mediator traditionally ascribed to middle powers in the arms control issue area. In the 'Open Skies' initiative, Canada acted as go-between at the first verification meeting between NATO and the Warsaw Treaty Organization member states in Ottawa on 12-14 February 1990.[11] However, the Canadian role was more than that of the traditional 'go-between.' At the technical and entrepreneurial level, for example, Canada pushed the issue forward in the two weeks of technical talks that followed the formal conference itself. Canadian activity also extended to chairing a working group on the subject at the UN Disarmament Commission. This international activity was given an additional fillip by the specialized work being conducted in Canada by the Verification Research Unit of External Affairs and International Trade Canada, in cooperation with a number of academic bodies. Symposia (such as the one on space surveillance for arms control and verification options held under the auspices of the McGill University Centre for Research in Air and Space Law) were conducted, and data collection and interpretation techniques (in areas such as synthetic aperture radar and aerial surveillance) were refined. At the same time, the government in Ottawa was instrumental in operationalizing several practical verification programs. Indeed, as part of the development of this confidence-building measure, a Canadian Hercules aircraft had conducted the first trial overflight of a Warsaw Pact country (Hungary) by a Western military aircraft in January 1990, which was to be followed by a Soviet or East European aircraft overflying Canada.[12]

Perhaps more ambitiously, Canada displayed some of the same diplomatic characteristics on arms exports, particularly to the Middle East. Prompted by the experience of the Gulf War, Canada pushed hard for a global summit on the instruments of war and weapons of mass destruction, with the goal of controlling the spread of conventional and non-conventional arms and creating some form of public accounting of all future arms sales. In keeping with the concept of confidence-building, Canada emphasized that it was not pushing for an immediate resolution but, rather, for an expression of political will on the need for restraint and transparency.[13] The idea was immediately rebuffed by the United States and other major powers; it was also criticized by some domestic critics, with one columnist calling it 'an idea of airy inconsequence.'[14] Despite such rebuffs, however, Clark garnered enough support from secondary powers to build up momentum for the proposal at the Conference on Security and Cooperation in Europe (CSCE) and other fora.

The eventual fate of the Canadian proposals is instructive. Unlike Trudeau's peace crusade of the early 1980s, this initiative was not marked by a great deal of prime ministerial publicity. Rather, as one analyst put it, the initiative was put forward 'quietly, persistently, collegially.'[15] Even in the midst of the Gulf crisis, Joe Clark sounded out a wide variety of countries on this idea and managed to gather a group of like-minded countries to press it in multilateral fora.

Regional Security Initiatives

In Chapter 4 we focused on the Australian interest in fostering regional economic cooperation. By way of balancing that discussion, we look briefly in this section at attempts to foster a more cooperative environment on the security agenda of the Asia-Pacific region, particularly Australian initiatives in Cambodia and Australian and Canadian approaches to Pacific security.

Australia and Cambodia

In many ways, regional security was an even more difficult task for Australia than was securing economic reform. If Australia was seen as a free rider in the economic sense in some parts of the wider Asia-Pacific region, in the security domain it tended to be treated with even greater suspicion. There were two principal reasons for this. The first was the lingering hostility to the racially determined immigration policies that had for so long been a part of Australia's political culture. The second factor was the long-standing tradition of the search for 'threats' and 'protectors' in Australian foreign policy and, particularly, its identification of various states of the region at various times as the principal threats to its security.[16]

From its election in 1983, the Hawke government worked hard to dispel many of these lingering antagonisms towards an Australian presence in the Asia-Pacific community. The legacy of the war in Vietnam reinforced in Australia a sense of obligation to intervene in a more positive fashion in the resolution of regional conflicts, particularly those lingering from the colonial period. It was an article of faith in Australian policy circles that successful diplomacy in the security domain would be an important complement to the growth of stronger economic cooperation between the states of the region. It was, thus, widely believed in Canberra that it would be vital for Australia, given the recognition that it is *of* Asia, not simply *in* Asia, that it be party to important cooperative developments in the domains of both security and economics.[17] Successful diplomacy in these domains was also believed to have important implications for the resolution of the regional refugee problem, which spilled over into the entire Asia-Pacific region in the wake of the Vietnam War.

As early as 1983, the government in Canberra was espousing a traditional middle power role of mediator in Cambodia. The Hawke government saw itself having the potential to act, as Bill Hayden (the minister for foreign affairs at the time) put it, as a 'regional honest broker.' While this was clearly part of Australia's long-term desire to build up its credibility in 'its region,' it was also an instrumentally discrete exercise. As Hawke noted, it was 'one of the areas in which my government believes that an Australian initiative can be of genuine value ... The obligation we feel and the special opportunity we have in this matter flow from the soundness of our relations with China and the ASEAN member nations, [and] the U.S., and our capacity to talk to Vietnam.'[18]

Yet, as the process of Australian involvement in the complex politics of Indochina developed over the 1980s, Australia's attempt to define a peace proposal for Cambodia took on a technical and entrepreneurial approach, which was not dissimilar in pattern to its role in the Cairns Group or in its policies on chemical weapons containment. Canberra's aim was not to develop another 'initiative' but to develop 'a possible alternative approach'[19] to break the diplomatic impasse that had emerged after the 1989 Paris International Conference on Cambodia (PICC). It attempted to do this by producing a technical blueprint, which it hoped that the parties to the dispute would adopt – the 'Red Book' of Working Papers entitled *Cambodia: An Australian Peace*

Proposal – prepared for the Jakarta Informal Meeting on Cambodia of 26-8 February 1990.[20]

The detail and technical innovation that went into this document was of the same technical level as that achieved in many of the Cairns Group papers on the Uruguay Round. Yet, in preparing the document, the Australian government was well aware that it was not a 'party principal' to the dispute; nor did it have the power to prompt the numerous parties to abandon their stances in favour of a compromise position. Indeed, the government in Canberra never saw itself as an arbiter but as a facilitator. Gareth Evans characterized Australia as a 'map maker.' To this end, the 'Red Book' was to be the map. The proposals in the Red Book stressed an enhanced role for the UN as a way around the power-sharing impasse. In particular, they were geared towards confidence-building among the parties to the dispute, offering 'step-by-step' approaches to progress. In addition, a senior Foreign Affairs and Trade officer was assigned the role of 'godfather' to the Cambodia peace initiative. Mike Costello, one of only five deputy secretaries in DFAT, was to be Australia's emissary and trouble-shooter in Cambodia.[21]

The Red Book was a painstaking outline of the role that the United Nations could and should play in civil administration, organizing and conducting elections and maintaining an environment in which those elections could be conducted fairly. It also set out procedures for the verification and monitoring of all aspects of the cease-fires and military withdrawals necessary to ensure the security components of the Comprehensive Settlement. The Red Book even went so far as to detail the cost of the operations. In fact, the UN Security Council Framework Document on Cambodia is largely a précis of the Red Book's Executive Summary.

The Australian initiative faced numerous difficulties. First, there was the intrinsic problem of securing a successful peace process within Cambodia itself, rent by intransigent factions with great power backers. The proposals were, like many other items on the international agenda, sidetracked by the Gulf War. Moreover, two of the great powers, the United States and France, had major reservations. Despite these considerable hurdles, the Australian initiative stands as an important example of the kind of technical contribution middle powers can make in the 1990s. Another important dimension of this kind of initiative is staying power. Australian diplomacy was clearly aimed at the long term. For example, considerable time and effort was invested in getting the diplomatic process back on track in the aftermath of the Gulf War. Australia's decision, in July 1991, to give diplomatic status to the Cambodian Supreme National Council (SNC) was seen by some as hasty decisionmaking and by others as leadership. The Australian position appeared to be gathering support: by late July 1991, ASEAN was actively encouraging international support for the SNC.[22]

The willingness to move out ahead of great power opinion illustrates another important component of middle power leadership: that it should very often be pursued in the face of the opposition of larger powers – and irrespective of whether or not those larger powers are allies. While initiatives that support the position of larger allies are not inimical to the definition of middle power behaviour, initiative in the face of opposition could, in fact, be seen as but another test of this definition.

Australia, Canada, and Pacific Security

We showed, in Chapter 4, that Australia, as part of its overall foreign policy concerns, focused considerable energy on attempting to foster regional economic cooperation in the Asia-Pacific. In the late 1980s, both Australia and Canada sought to extend regional cooperation in the Pacific to the security sphere. Following on the heels of the 1989 Hawke initiative on APEC, Australia embarked on an ambitious effort to move towards a comparable security dialogue in the region; for its part, the Canadian government launched a no less ambitious proposal for the creation of a North Pacific dialogue in July 1990.

The Australian government took its cue from a variety of sources, including a set of earlier Australian proposals[23] and the common security concept that was evolving in Europe and articulated by CSCE. Confidence and security-building measures (CSBMs) in the Asia-Pacific region enjoyed considerable popularity in the foreign policy community in Australia.[24] It was particularly important that the minister for foreign affairs himself was an enthusiast. Gareth Evans articulated his own conception of common security:

> The central idea of common security is that lasting security does not lie in the upward spiral of arms development, fuelled by mutual suspicion, but in a commitment to joint survival, to taking into account the legitimate security anxieties of others, to building step-by-step military confidence between nations, to working to maximise the degree of

interdependence between nations; to put it shortly, to achieving security with others, not against others.[25]

Guided by this view, Evans articulated a suggestion for a Conference on Security and Cooperation in Asia (CSCA), modelled along the lines of the CSCE. Four assumptions lay behind the proposal: (1) Canberra assumed that while the risk of regional conflict was high, it was not inevitable; (2) the Australian government assumed that the United States was bound to reduce its military commitment to the region over time, particularly as Cold War tensions diminished; (3) it was assumed that if a regional dialogue mitigated mistrust in Europe, such a technique should work in the Asia-Pacific region; and (4) the Australian government wondered whether, as Stuart Harris put it, the United States was capable of defining the security environment in the Asia-Pacific region unilaterally in the post-Cold War era. Harris wondered if Washington, as a result, was 'failing to see where its own long-term interest, and that of its allies, lies.'[26]

Such doubts marked somewhat of a departure for Australia, a junior alliance partner. Indeed, the idea of an 'Asian Helsinki' coming from a close ally was greeted with strong opposition by the United States. A series of letters from the United States secretary of state, James Baker, to Evans, expressing American concerns over the CSCA idea, was leaked to the press in November 1990. Washington's position did not change much: just as the United States prefers a hub-and-spoke approach to hemispheric economic relations (as we saw in Chapter 4), so, too, did it prefer a hub-and-spoke system of bilateral security agreements in the Asia-Pacific as the way to maintain American interests in the region.[27] Common security proposals, from Australia or elsewhere, were regarded in Washington as undermining American strategic superiority in the region; collective discussions could too easily turn into a forum in which smaller states in the region could press for such confidence-building measures as naval arms control.[28] As the American ambassador to Canberra suggested to Australian audiences, policy in the Asia-Pacific should be guided by the dictum that 'if it ain't broke, don't fix it.'[29]

While Australia quickly dropped the CSCA label, it did not drop its calls for an enhanced regional dialogue. The disjuncture between the two ANZUS partners over the Asia-Pacific security questions stemmed from different perceptions of regional problems. The United States tended to see existing regional structures, underwritten by American strategic pre-eminence and bilateral relationships, as a reason for resisting change in the region. Australia, on the other hand, looked at the Asia-Pacific through the lenses of a regional state and tended to see the need for a new policy framework that would allow Asia-Pacific input in a way that would enable that region to bypass its existing bilateral structures with the United States. By contrast, a multilateral security framework in the Asia-Pacific was seen by the United States to have two disadvantages. It would not only have inhibited unilateral action on its part; more important, it would also have offered the Soviet Union an expanded voice in regional security affairs. Indeed, at first United States officials argued that the Australian initiatives for a CSCA had been 'captured' by the Soviet Union,[30] though it was an argument that was heard less often after the collapse of the Soviet Union and the weakening of Russia as a Pacific power.[31]

Given the importance of the region to Australia, a long-term consultative process on regional security is still seen to be an essential stratagem. Australian policy sought to establish an institutional framework for a security dialogue comparable to that being mooted for APEC, but it was never central to Canberra's approach. Rather, Australia was more interested in advancing the regional conversation on the security agenda through the process of extensive second-track diplomacy. Because Australian officials were conscious of the degree to which they could influence and develop the regional agenda – at least under some circumstances – they were more than willing to take another tack. The abandonment of the CSCA label, in the face of American objections, to pursue the issue using different terminology is an excellent example of this.[32]

The Canadian proposal for the institutionalization of regional security suffered a similar fate – and for similar reasons. Like Australia, Canada was increasingly conscious of the need for the development, in the Asia-Pacific region, of a security structure that would evolve with the waning of the Cold War in the region. And, like Australia, Canada floated a proposal for the creation of a process for increased security in the Pacific area. Ottawa, however, decided to focus the Canadian initiative on the one area of the Pacific Rim which did not have the beginnings of institutionalization comparable to the South Pacific Forum in the South Pacific, ASEAN in South East Asia, or the South Asia Association for Regional Cooperation (SAARC) in South Asia. The focus of the Canadian initiative was on the North Pacific, involving Canada, the United States, the Soviet Union, China, Japan, and the two Koreas.

The secretary of state for external affairs, Joe Clark, outlined his initiative in three speeches delivered in Victoria, BC, Tokyo, and Jakarta in July 1990.[33] The essence of Clark's initiative for a North Pacific Cooperative Security Dialogue (NPCSD) was a call for a 'process' of confidence-building in the North Pacific area through the establishment of regional multilateral dialogue.

Creating what Clark called a 'habit of dialogue' in the North Pacific involved a 'two-track' strategy. One track was the normal channels of interstate diplomacy. The other track would be a nongovernmental process, involving individuals and experts from the North Pacific countries who would be brought together, mainly through international workshops and conferences, to 'build informational bases and to promote more sophisticated understanding of national attitudes and perceptions regarding security issues.'[34] This second nongovernmental track was established at York University and conducted by Paul M. Evans, the director of the University of Toronto/York University Joint Centre for Asia Pacific Studies, and David B. Dewitt, the director of York's Centre for International and Strategic Studies. The main work of the nongovernmental track of the NPCSD has been the holding of conferences in most of the North Pacific countries and the establishment of a working papers series.

The government in Ottawa tried hard to avoid Australia's fate.[35] It was, for example, quick to assert that Clark's notion of a regional dialogue was not simply the adaptation of the CSCE structure to the North Pacific region. However, the NPCSD was commonly seen by other players in the region as little more than an inappropriate attempt to use the European model in an Asian context. For example, in a speech to an academic conference on the United States, Japan, and Canada in October 1990, Hiroshi Kitamura, the Japanese ambassador to Canada, sought to put some distance between his government and the Canadian proposal, arguing that the conditions in the Asia-Pacific region were so different from those of Europe that a multilateral dialogue would 'become more realistic once a favourable atmosphere has been created and major issues have been resolved through bilateral dialogue.'[36]

Despite the initial objections to these middle power initiatives from the region's major players, the efforts of the multilateralists bore some fruit. The idea of a security dialogue for the Pacific became firmly entrenched on the regional agenda. Indeed, nowhere is this better illustrated than in the annual Asia Pacific Roundtable on Confidence-Building and Conflict Reduction in the Pacific (held in Kuala Lumpur since 1988) or the growing number of ad hoc gatherings of regional officials and academics to discuss various technical contributions to the confidence-building process. Indeed, by late 1990, even the United States had softened its outright opposition to the proposal of new security arrangements in the region. At the 1991 Post-Ministerial Conference of ASEAN, the United States under-secretary of state for East Asian affairs indicated that alliances needed to adjust to new strategic realities in a more reciprocal manner than had been the case in the past.[37]

The changes in American policy bear out, to a degree at least, the theoretical arguments that we develop with regard to the technical and entrepreneurial role of middle powers. Despite the initial setbacks, the differing regional state interests, and the foot-dragging by the major powers, the security dialogue was moved ahead by the persistence of the middle powers.

Human Rights Initiatives

Throughout the 1980s, Canadian diplomacy continued to exhibit a traditionally strong mediatory element,[38] particularly in the area of human rights.[39] In this section, we examine two instances in which the Canadian government's approaches to a traditional foreign policy issue – human rights – were transformed in the 1980s and the post-Cold War era.

South Africa

One of the signal examples of this type of high-profile 'helpful fixer' or 'go-between' diplomacy for Canada in the 1980s was the continuing quarrel within the Commonwealth over South Africa. The evident rancour between Margaret Thatcher and all other members of the Commonwealth on the issue of sanctions on South Africa prompted a renewal of Canadian activism. The activities of Brian Mulroney at the Nassau Commonwealth Heads of Government Meetings (CHOGM) in 1985, the London review meeting in 1986, and the Vancouver CHOGM in 1987 carried forward an approach to Canadian foreign policy that dated back to John Diefenbaker's responses to the departure of South Africa from the Commonwealth in 1961, Lester B. Pearson's responses to the Unilateral Declaration of Independence by Rhodesia in 1966, Pierre Elliott Trudeau's responses to the British sale of arms to South Africa in 1971, and Joe Clark's mediatory role at the time of the Lusaka settlement of the Zimbabwe question in 1979.[40]

As constructive as were these mediatory activities on the issue of Commonwealth policy towards South Africa, it would be misleading to suggest that Canadian diplomacy was restricted merely to that of an *interlocuteur valable*. Canadian diplomacy was, in large part, directed towards advancing the agenda for action. That the Canadian government intended to remain engaged was underscored by the series of forceful statements made by Joe Clark, the secretary of state for external affairs; Stephen Lewis, Canada's permanent representative to the UN; and, indeed, Mulroney himself. For his part, Mulroney declared that 'Canada is ready, if there are no fundamental changes in South Africa, to invoke total sanctions against that country and its repressive regime. More than that, if there is no progress in the dismantling of apartheid relations with South Africa may have to be severed absolutely.'[42]

The hard line on South Africa adopted by the Mulroney government can be explained in a number of ways. On the one hand, the Canadian government's behaviour fits well with the notion of a two-level game. Mulroney's rhetoric, and his attempts to assume a leadership role on the South African issue within the Commonwealth,[43] can be interpreted as an obvious attempt to mitigate domestic pressure from Canada's strong anti-apartheid lobby groups. On the other hand, the considerable shift in Ottawa's attitude towards South Africa under the Mulroney government can also be explained as a result of the change in leadership that occurred in September 1984.[44]

More important for our analysis, the Canadian hard line on South Africa can also be explained as an exercise in diplomatic signalling. The Canadians understood full well that only Britain and the United States had the capacity to successfully coerce the regime in Pretoria; the sanctions imposed by other states would have little more than symbolic value as long as Britain, Japan, and the United States remained committed to economic links with South Africa. Indeed, it can be argued that the willingness of the Canadian government to move out well in front of its G-7 partners was designed to move these states into adopting a more coercive policy towards South Africa.

In this regard, the response of the major industrialized powers to Canadian initiatives on South Africa[45] was not dissimilar to the response of the United States to Australian initiatives on Pacific security. And the Canadian reaction to the rebuff at the G-7 was not at all dissimilar to the Australian response to United States opposition to its Pacific security initiative. Specifically, Canada was prepared to back up its rhetoric by embarking on new functional middle power initiatives.[46] At the

Vancouver CHOGM in 1987, Mulroney put forward the so-called Okanagan Statement and a draft Program of Action on Southern Africa. The Canadian government also proposed the establishment of a Committee of Foreign Ministers on Southern Africa (CFMSA) to oversee the program's implementation – an idea that originated in Canada's Department of External Affairs and International Trade. The committee was chaired by Joe Clark; its members included Clark's counterparts from Australia, Guyana, India, Nigeria, Tanzania, Zambia, and Zimbabwe. Managerially, the effort was buttressed by the establishment of a Southern African Task Force within DEA; moreover, Brian Mulroney appointed Bernard Wood, executive director of the North-South Institute (an Ottawa think-tank), as his personal emissary for southern Africa.

These activities meant that Canada was not only out in front of Japan, the major Western European countries, and the executive branch (though not the legislative branch) in the United States; it was even out in front of the Commonwealth Secretariat. Being out in front of the curve, however, meant that Canada had to assume the role of facilitator and de facto manager of these initiatives. Indeed, one of the unstated goals of Canada's Southern African policy initiatives was to offer moderating, but technical, proposals that Thatcher would find difficult to use as an excuse for Britain going its own way. Likewise, in a manner not dissimilar to the role envisaged by Australia for APEC, the purpose of CFMSA was to provide a forum for dialogue not only within the Commonwealth but also between the Commonwealth and the parties principal – including groups suspicious of Canada over its economic involvement in South Africa and Namibia.

In addition to such entrepreneurial leadership, Canada devoted a great deal of time and resources to confidence-building. This took the form of keeping the process going by working incrementally towards a goal, building the credibility of that goal, maintaining communication with other actors, dealing with misunderstandings and misperceptions, and keeping the issue before the public. On the South Africa initiative, this activity centred not only on attempting to alter the behaviour of the South African government – by steadily increasing the pressure on Pretoria through measures such as the prohibition on the transfer of technology – it also included measures designed to assist change within South Africa (for example, the provision of aid for the victims of apartheid and the opening of new forms of dialogue between people from South Africa's different racial groups). Also, Canadian confidence-building focused on the Commonwealth itself, reaffirming the sense of solidarity and downplaying differences.[47]

Finally, Canada also provided technical leadership on the South Africa issue. Specifically, it took the lead on a number of practical questions: preparing a strategy paper on how best to fight censorship in South Africa;[48] providing technical support to the security needs of the Front Line States through Canada's Military Training Assistance Program;[49] and assisting in planning for the transition to post-apartheid democracy. The post-apartheid assistance was an initiative undertaken by the International Centre for Human Rights and Democratic Development, a new arm's-length agency created by the Mulroney government to concentrate expertise on human rights issues.[50]

These Canadian initiatives, it might be noted, were mirrored by technical initiatives pursued by other Commonwealth middle powers, including Australia. For example, Canberra's role in the Commonwealth towards South Africa underwent a radical shift over the 1970s and 1980s. Initial responses to South Africa's apartheid policies were of a fiercely rhetorical and hectoring variety, culminating in Gough Whitlam's suggestion that the South African prime minister 'was as bad as Hitler.' But, in keeping with the stylistic changes that are central to the theoretical argument of our analysis, we can see a sharp change in the direction of Australian policy. The second half of the 1980s saw Australia playing both a mediatory and a technical role in Commonwealth policy towards South Africa. Among its technical contributions was a detailed research study, commissioned by the CFMSA, into the linkages between apartheid and the international financial system.[51] While not as high profile as the mediatory efforts classically associated with middle power behaviour, this kind of technical support, more often than not of a behind-the-scenes and 'non-public character,'[52] nevertheless provided invaluable practical assistance in periods of transition.

Women's and Children's Rights

Frequently the domestic political agenda was the salient factor in shifting Canadian diplomacy on certain human rights issues from a reactive to a more activist stance. In the past, Canadian foreign policy on human rights tended to be episodic and unsystematic, as violations drifted in and out of public consciousness.[53] In the 1980s, the importance of the universalist nature of the political and social dimensions of human rights set an agenda that transcended territorial barriers. This process was pushed along by the growing influence of nongovernmental organizations and lobby groups, many of which, in the Canadian case, were suspicious and sceptical of Canada's own record. In addition, these groups also developed transnational dimensions to their activities and networks.

Nowhere was this more activist dimension to Canadian diplomacy better illustrated than in the area of women's rights. As with its tactics in the Commonwealth context for attempting to institute sanctions against South Africa, there was a strong mediatory element in Canada's diplomacy on the women's rights issue. At the United Nations Decade of Women's Conference in Nairobi in July 1985, Canada sought to broker an agreement that would mitigate the antagonisms between the United States and the Third World in the Reagan era. This activity was important in the traditional mediatory sense, but only because it showed considerable entrepreneurial flair in navigating what one journalist called the 'procedural rocks' on which the conference was in danger of foundering.[54] Another commentator, not noted for his sympathy for Progressive Conservatives, allowed that Ottawa's efforts to secure a compromise solution was in the best traditions of Canadian statecraft: 'Lester Pearson would have been proud.'[55]

Here, as in its activity in Commonwealth politics, Canada's role was not simply that of the helpful fixer. In addition, advancing the agenda of reform was also important. At the declaratory level, Stephen Lewis, Canada's permanent representative to the UN, argued that the Mulroney government was 'compulsively propelled' to make some changes in women's equality at the global level by the year 2000.[56] At the policy level, Canada supported this rhetoric by embarking on new functional initiatives. For example, at the Forty-Third General Assembly, the Canadian delegation worked for the passage of a number of resolutions related to the advancement of women. These included the development of a 'Forward-Looking Strategy for Women' on a global level, a concrete commitment to achieving better representation of women in United Nations secretariats, and a push for a Convention on the Elimination of All Forms of Discrimination Against Women (CEDAW). Canada also backed up its commitment with solid bureaucratic and expert support, with its special adviser on international women's programs, officials at the Commonwealth Bureau, the International Organizations Bureau, the International Women's Equality Division at the Department of External Affairs, and the Canadian International Development Agency (CIDA) making contributions.

Much of the expertise for this Canadian initiative came from women in the domestic arena. Most significantly, it was Maureen O'Neil, the director of the federal Status of Women Bureau, who served as deputy chair of the Canadian delegation and as the head of the Western Group of Nations in the preparatory meetings prior to Nairobi (as well as being a key player in that conference's successful resolution).[57]

The focus of Canadian policy was on implementing the Nairobi forward-looking strategy for the advancement of women and strengthening the UN Commission on the Status of Women (UNCSW). To give one illustration of this Canadian activity: at a meeting held in Vienna in March 1988, which Canada chaired, a number of important steps were taken to ensure that the progress of the forward-looking strategy would continue to be monitored and appraised in a comprehensive fashion. In a parallel manner, Canada sought to improve and rationalize the work of the committee overseeing the implementation of CEDAW.[58] Because the overall Canadian diplomatic approach concentrated on unspectacular 'patient, plodding, bureaucratic work,' Ottawa was often criticized by many in the women's movement for its slowness in the delivery of dramatic change. Yet not all members of the movement saw it this way. As one well-known feminist noted, 'without Canada's persistence' it seemed likely that 'women's equality might [remain] ... entombed in dusty resolutions.'[59]

From a technical perspective, Canada moved to link the forward-looking strategy to education, environment, and population issues. As a demonstration of how women's needs and interests could be effectively 'delivered' in development programs, CIDA institutionalized a process by which all Canadian official development assistance (ODA) took into account these goals; moreover, Canadian support for organizations such as the United Nations International Children's Emergency Fund (UNICEF) and the United Nations Development Fund for Women (UNIFEM) (to the directorship of which a Canadian was appointed in 1988) was increased.

Comparable Canadian diplomatic behaviour may also be emerging in other issue areas. An interesting example of a spillover effect taking place from Canada's activist role in other spheres of international development is its growing international involvement with respect to children's rights – which are emerging as an increasingly important item on the social agenda of international relations in the 1990s. Pushed by growing public interest in the issue, especially in the emergent children's lobbies of numerous advanced industrial countries, Brian Mulroney took the opportunity to play a personal and prominent role (as co-chair) at the September 1990 New York World Summit for Children. In keeping with the overall Canadian diplomatic approach, the prime minister empha- sized the usefulness of this gathering as a catalyst, claiming that 'the summit has the potential to put children's issues on the top of the international agenda' in the same way that the UN Conference on the Human Environment in Stockholm in 1972 put environmental prob- lems on that agenda. The summit was also seen as a facilitator for further technical/specialist work by public officials. As Mulroney stated, 'Sum- mits do what nothing else can do. Put leaders face to face with each other and raise public awareness of issues. There is nothing like [that] for galvanizing a bureaucracy.'[60]

Canadian activity at this summit was, in the end, overshadowed by criticism at the domestic level. A common argument was that Canada was hardly well positioned to press for children's welfare at the global level given the condition of children in Canada. As an editorial in the *Globe and Mail* bluntly put it, Ottawa should lead by example: 'Brian Mulroney can show leadership at the summit by pledging money to fight disease and hunger at home, a shameful item of unfinished business that Canadian activists who have travelled to New York for the meeting will not let him (or the other delegates) forget.'[61] International activism is, thus, a two-edged sword. While it might well serve the international reputation of Canada and, by extension, its leaders, it also serves to intensify the process of domestic scrutiny.

Environmental Initiatives: Antarctica and Atmospheric Protection

Of all of the new items that appeared on the agenda of international relations in the 1980s, none was more salient than concern for the environment. A widening definition of security meant an expansion of the more traditional foreign policy focus on territorial integrity and physical security; it sought to include not only economic well-being but also environmental well-being – concerns about 'the protection of val- ues and the institutions that guard and enshrine those values.'[62] As with our discussion of human rights in the preceding section, it is possible to consider only two examples that illustrate the wider themes of this study: the roles that Australia and Canada played in the processes of cooperation-building and regime-making in selected areas of interna- tional environmental concern. As with our argument about the role of Australia and Canada in the Cairns Group and Australia in APEC, we suggest that these middle powers exhibited certain technical and entre-preneurial skills that helped to foster cooperation in the development of a wider set of international environmental rules.

It should be noted at the outset that we recognize that, while both Australia and Canada were genuinely concerned players in several aspects of the international environmental debate, there was a considerable degree of symbolism in Australian and Canadian policy on environmental issues. In part, the environmental policies of these middle powers were driven by the domestic logic of a two-level game. These environmental issues may have been on the international agenda in one form or another for over two decades, but the global policy debate moved dramatically from initial macro discussions, such as the 1972 Stockholm Conference, to the policy debates of the late 1980s, which were framed in a more discrete and specific context.[63] This contemporary approach is clearly to be seen in Australia's policy towards Antarctica and Canadian policy towards the problems of the depletion of the ozone layer and climate change.

Australia and Antarctica

Australia's Antarctic initiative involved a two-year process of attempting to alter the international regime's attitude towards mining on the continent. At first blush, this initiative appears to involve behaviour wholly antithetical to traditional middle power diplomacy, which, as we noted in Chapter 1, tends to stress a firm commitment to multilateralism and an emphasis on coalition-building through consensus and compromise. The Australian government's decision on Antarctica, announced on 22 May 1989, was hardly in this vein: it announced that it was going to refuse to sign the Convention on the Regulation of Antarctic Mineral Resource Activities (CRAMRA), an international agreement that had been agreed to a year earlier.[64] Citing environmental concerns as the reason for its change of position, the Hawke government announced that, instead, it was going to press to have Antarctica declared a wilderness park. Although the French government had also indicated that it had serious reservations about the convention, there was little denying the significance of the Australian decision. In one stroke, the government in Canberra had defected from a coalition of thirty-three states, which had taken six years to negotiate a convention on Antarctic mining. And because the draft convention had provided a veto to all states that had territorial claims to the continent, the decision also effectively brought the 1988 regime to an end – even though

Canberra could use the French hesitation to provide itself with some cover against charges that it alone was responsible for scuttling the agreement.

The significance of this case of unilateralism is that Australia moved from a firm position of followership, with an emphasis on being a 'team player' with its traditional allies, the United States and Britain, to a position of more risk-prone activism, in which it was attempting to firmly insert new values onto the international agenda. Australia was not challenging the validity of the Antarctic treaty system or attempting to free ride on the leadership of others. Rather, in a strange alliance with France (and in the face of strong opposition from a variety of quarters), the Australian government was attempting to widen the ambit of the treaty system to incorporate a total ban on mining for fifty years. In particular, it was anticipating changing international opinion and attempting to make explicit certain environmentalist principles.[65]

It is true that one could interpret this shift in approach as a none-too-subtle exercise in self-interest on either economic or electoral grounds. First, it was not overly vocal about this, but Australia's own mining industry clearly had a vested interest in a long-term ban on mining in Antarctica.[66] The 1988 regime, if enacted, would expand potential alternative areas of mineral exploration and would lead to the growth of state-subsidized mining, both of which had the potential to damage the Australian mining sector (already hard hit by a slump in world prices in the 1980s). The mining industry was, thus, not unhappy with a decision that was clearly in their interests.[67]

Second, the Antarctic decision can also be interpreted as having domestic political purposes. As the last great wilderness left on the planet, Antarctica is seen by many in symbolic, almost 'magical' and/or 'metaphysical,' terms;[68] indeed, it is no coincidence that the heavily forensic word 'pristine' is the favoured modifier to describe the continent in public discourse. Moreover, the strong concern over Antarctica within Australia was augmented by transnational links with environmental groups abroad. The domestic profile of the issue was, thus, inexorably raised when Hawke and Jacques Cousteau exchanged correspondence on the matter, and it culminated in a televised discussion between them in November 1989. Hawke was no doubt pleased when Cousteau praised Australian leadership on the Antarctic environment.

One can also see the Antarctic decision in even more narrow domestic political terms – as part of a larger attempt by the Hawke government to 'green' itself over the antipodean winter of 1989 and, thereby, to woo a growing number of voters with Green sympathies. The May decision on Antarctica was followed shortly thereafter by Hawke's announcement in June of a major domestic initiative on the environment. It can be argued that the turning point in the Labor government's opinion on the importance of the Green movement came in the wake of the Tasmanian state election of May 1989, when the Greens captured the balance of power in the Tasmanian House of Representatives. In the face of evidence of mounting Green support, even hard-nosed pro-mining politicians, such as Senator Grahame Richardson, minister for the environment, became what one opposition critic caustically termed 'a reborn lover of penguins.'[69] Moreover, it would appear that the environmental lobby played an important role in the re-election of the Labor government in the 1990 federal elections,[70] suggesting that the Antarctic decision was not unimportant in shifting voter preferences.

This, of course, is the cynical interpretation. However, as Lorraine Elliott makes clear, one should put the Antarctic decision into a broader context. For, in fact, Australia exhibited a long-standing tradition of pushing for stronger international standards in general, and an umbrella agreement for Antarctica in particular, that would provide for more comprehensive conservation and environmental protection. Moreover, the decision reflected a growing consensus within the scientific and legal community concerning the need for stronger forms of environmental protection with regard to Antarctica.

In suggesting that there was a strongly symbolic element in Australian policy, we are not attempting to diminish its significance. As Gareth Evans was wont to remind his critics, the Australian initiative was designed for the real world: 'In the diplomatic marketplace, where realism is the currency of trade, it is unusual to seek to redefine upwards the definition of what is possible. But that is what is required and it is what our initiative sets out to do.'[71]

As with its efforts to foster a peace proposal for Cambodia, Australia's activities concerning Antarctica were considerably ahead of opinion in all other claimant states except France. Even though the initiative broke ranks with traditional partners, it was eventually successful in moving the United States towards approval of an Antarctic Protection Act, banning American involvement in mineral exploitation on the continent. What must be reiterated here are the benefits to be gained by states pursuing long-term approaches geared towards building support for their positions.[72]

Canada and Atmospheric Protection

Canadian diplomacy regarding the ozone layer and climate change exhibited a similar degree of activism to that evidenced by Australian diplomacy regarding the protection of Antarctica. It is true that, like the Australian government's Antarctic policies, Canadian policies on the atmosphere also had a political, and often self-interested, impetus. While the Greens in Canada did not have the electoral strength that their counterparts in Australia enjoyed, the Mulroney government was no less sensitive to the popularity of environmental concerns. Like the Hawke government, the Progressive Conservative government quickly sought to convince groups in Canada of its bona fide interest in environmental questions.

Thus, it can be argued that Canadian global activism on atmospheric questions had a local, and clearly self-interested, impetus. Even though the putative threats to Canada from such phenomena as global warming and ozone depletion are long-term, the Canadian government had an abiding interest in advancing regimes on atmospheric protection on a global level in order to create spillover effects within North America, where the damage from acid rain is both immediate and visible.

On the other hand, Canadian diplomatic initiatives in this issue area also displayed elements of entrepreneurial and technical leadership – again in a fashion not dissimilar to what was illustrated by the Australian example.[73] In the late 1980s, the Canadian government sought to move the international agenda on atmospheric protection ahead, mainly by hosting a number of international conferences on the environment designed to focus attention on atmospheric pollution. This began in September 1987, with a conference in Montreal on the ozone layer, organized by the United Nations Environment Program (UNEP) and attended by forty-six states. The conference ended with the adoption of the Montreal Protocol on Substances that Deplete the Ozone Layer, which called for a 50 per cent reduction in chlorofluorocarbons (CFCs) over the following decade.[74] In June 1988, Canada hosted a further conference on the atmosphere sponsored by UNEP, Environment Canada, and the World Meteorological Organization (WMO). The conference, called The Changing Atmosphere: Implications for Global Security, drew over 300 policymakers and scientists to Toronto to draft the elements of an international regime that would address the problems of global warming and climate change.

Besides offering Canadian loci for international meetings, the Canadian government also engaged in the kind of technical and entrepreneurial leadership outlined in Chapter 1. For example, in February 1989, the Canadian government convened what Fen Osler Hampson has called a 'ground-breaking' conference of experts to discuss atmospheric protection.[75] The Ottawa Meeting of Legal and Policy Experts on Protection of the Atmosphere worked out a framework for atmospheric protection, embodied in the Ottawa Declaration. Likewise, Ottawa sent both government representatives and bureaucratic experts to Globe '90, a nongovernmental conference on the environment held in Vancouver in March 1990.

Despite these concerted efforts in the international arena, however, there was a marked disjuncture between the Canadian government's international activity and its domestic environmental policies. As Hampson has noted, 'Canada has been extremely active in advancing international co-operation to devise global solutions to these problems, though it has done little as yet to match its activity on the international front by cleaning up its own front yard.'[76] Such a gap did not escape the notice of Canadian environmental groups, which tended to be less than laudatory in their response to Canada's international environmental diplomacy. In the main, these groups tended to criticize the government for not moving faster and more effectively on internal reform. The coordinator of Pollution Probe warned that 'our international reputation as environmental advocates far exceeds our accomplishments at home.'[77] Maurice Strong sounded a similar, though more tempered, note in his remarks to the opening plenary session of the Globe '90 conference. Strong asserted that: 'International leadership must be undergirded by example. Canada must be an exemplary nation.'[78]

Contrast and Convergence in Australian and Canadian Diplomacy

An examination of issues in which Australia and Canada attempted to take an initiatory role demonstrates clearly the differences and similarities in the approaches adopted by these middle powers.[79] The 'heroic' element of Australian diplomacy, as noted in Chapter 1, was highlighted by its Cairns Group activity. Its heavily accentuated regional focus was revealed clearly in the Hawke initiative on APEC, in the attempt to find a solution to the Cambodia dispute, in the instigation of a security dialogue in the Pacific, and in the strengthening of an environmental regime for Antarctica. None of these activities, we have demonstrated, was risk-free in the context of Australia's wider international political and economic relationships. Yet, in a period of growing vulnerability to exogenous economic influences (with the concomitant negative effects on Australia's economic sovereignty and well-being), policymakers in Canberra clearly decided that the necessity of pursing innovative policy reform outweighs any contingent risks.

The essence of this brand of internationalism was its basically instrumental nature. It was heavily egoistic in orientation, issue-specific in nature, and concentrated and focused in policy application. In other words, Australia's commitment to the role of what the minister for foreign affairs, Gareth Evans, calls being a 'good international citizen' is genuinely held. But it is invariably pursued with a generous dose of enlightened self-interest.[80]

By contrast, Canadian diplomatic initiatives were more 'routine.' Moreover, Canada was also constrained in the pursuit of its foreign policies. However, the nature of these constraints differed from those faced by Australia. In the economic context, the principal factor for Canada was not a growing marginalization in the global economy, as it was for Australia, but, rather, a question of institutionalizing its special relationship with the United States (based on a range of formal and informal contacts), culminating in the two key regional economic agreements – the Canada-U.S. Free Trade Agreement that came into force in January 1989 and the North American Free Trade Agreement signed in December 1992.

Likewise, the Canadian government was also constrained in the late 1980s and early 1990s by a preoccupation with constitutional reform, in particular a series of efforts to renegotiate the constitution, to redistribute federal powers, and to settle the special status of Quebec. A great deal of energy was devoted to trying to secure approval for the Meech Lake Accord of 1987 and, later, the constitutional package negotiated at Charlottetown in August 1992. The failure of the Charlottetown Accord in the national referendum of 26 October 1992 may have marked the end of this round in the constitutional negotiating process, but it did not eliminate the root causes of the on-going constitutional quarrels.[81]

Despite these constraints, Canada exhibited creative aspects to its foreign policy in the 1980s well in keeping with the traditional characteristics of middle power behaviour. In these instances, Canadian efforts invariably eschewed the 'spectacular'; Ottawa's preference was to focus on the day-to-day bureaucratic and organizational processes so important to the gradual evolution of aspects of the international reform agenda.[82] Canadian policy is exemplified, we have argued, in its efforts to speed up the process of reform in South Africa and to advance the international status of women.

While Australian initiatives tended to focus on the second, or economic, agenda, most of Canada's initiatives concentrated on the third, or social, agenda in international politics. This meant that Canadian initiatives, even if innovative, were not in the same high-risk category as were those of Australia. They tended, however, to be extremely politically sensitive, especially to highly articulate Canadian domestic interest groups such as the women's movement and the environmental lobby.

Canada's internationalism was, thus, even more diffuse than was Australia's. First, given the domestic and international constraints highlighted above, Canada is understandably fearful of excessive regionalism. Their close economic ties to the United States notwithstanding, Canadians have always sought to demarcate differences between themselves and their southern neighbours on social policy and/or third agenda items. This is not to suggest that policy in Ottawa is formulated solely in order to exhibit differentiation from the United States. Cultural and social differences are inevitably the principal factors dictating competing policy stances. But proximity to the United States should never be underestimated in helping to explain the strongly internationalist flavour to much Canadian policy. Second, there was also a strong tradition of functionalism in Canadian foreign policy. Stemming, in part, from a strong diplomatic bureaucratic capability, Canada was able to exhibit significant initiatory skills across a wide range of issue areas.

Indeed, the Canadian experience at the United Nations Conference on Environment and Development (UNCED) held in Rio de Janeiro in June 1992 reinforces this impression of the pattern of Canadian diplomacy. One of the main goals of the Canadian approach to international environmental policy was to reinforce the perception that Canada was both able and willing to distance itself from the American position on many of the key issues addressed by the conference. While President George Bush did not attend the UNCED summit, Mulroney made a point of being there and of using the forum to signal that the free trade agreements with the United States had not impaired Canada's autonomy in world affairs. As Mulroney told the summit, 'We don't subcontract our rights and obligations to the United States in any way.'[83]

The other marked feature of Canadian diplomacy at Rio was its issue-specific and low-key form of constructive internationalism.

Although Canadian representatives took a variety of initiatives during the Rio negotiations, leading to a perception of an 'active and constructive role,'[84] the Canadian government did not pursue them in a bold way, self-consciously avoiding the mediatory role of helpful fixer that it had played, for example, at the United Nations Conference on the Human Environment in Stockholm in 1972. At the Stockholm conference, Canadian diplomats had produced a compromise solution to the issue of compensation for losses in trade suffered as a result of the establishment of higher environmental standards.[85] At Rio, by contrast, such a brokerage function was left to other countries.

To note that Canada's environmental diplomacy at Rio lacked some of the boldness that it had at Stockholm is not, however, to suggest that there was a fundamental change in the overall style of Canadian diplomacy in the environmental issue area.[86] At Rio, Canadian statecraft continued to demonstrate a traditional concern for consensus and a historical orientation that sought safety in numbers. Coalition diplomacy was no less important either: Canadian efforts to secure a convention on high seas fishing depended on working through the so-called CANZ group (Canada-Australia-New Zealand). Likewise, at Rio no less than at Stockholm, Canadians placed an emphasis on detailed technical legal statecraft in the negotiation of the Rio Declaration.

However, while these national differences are significant, one should not overlook the considerable commonalities displayed by Australia and Canada on the issues in which they took a lead. While there are clear variations in style, the leadership process in all of the case studies shows remarkable similarities in pattern. Australia and Canada, like many other middle powers, may pursue their own specific foreign policy objectives, but in attempting to be initiators or leaders, the type and content of leadership roles unites rather than divides them. While Australia had a historical reputation for 'over-zealous' diplomacy, Canberra increasingly developed a sophisticated, agenda-based, results-oriented foreign policy as the stakes of success or failure became more apparent. Likewise, Canada was no longer the quintessential middle power it was often seen to be in the so-called 'golden age' of the 1950s and 1960s; it certainly was not the 'principal power' to which some tried to elevate it in the 1980s.[87] However, Ottawa's contribution to the processes of international cooperation was still substantial.

Conclusions

The typology of middle power leadership developed in Chapter 1 focused on the ability of some states to use their diplomatic capabilities to act as catalysts, facilitators, or managers capable of providing various aspects of entrepreneurial and technical leadership in issue-specific aspects of contemporary international relations. Our case study of the amalgamation of the foreign and trade ministries in both Canada and Australia demonstrated the importance of developing the necessary bureaucratic infrastructure to support these initiatives. In the case studies of Cairns and APEC, we sought to apply this typology, showing its value in examining leadership. In the case study of the Gulf conflict, by contrast, we showed the limitations of middle power coalitional leadership. In this chapter, we have demonstrated that, as the Australian and Canadian governments addressed items on the widening agenda of contemporary international politics, they continued to exhibit technical and entrepreneurial leadership as middle powers.

Conclusion

Australia and Canada are frequently held up as exemplars of middle powers in contemporary international politics. We argued at the outset of this book that traditional perspectives on middle powers tend to emphasize such characteristics as size, capacity, or geographical location; analyses of middle powers frequently have a celebratory rather than an analytical tenor. The case studies we have presented suggest the appropriateness of a 'relocation' of middle powers. It is, we have suggested, a relocation in two senses.

First, the case studies suggest that both of the middle powers we examine, Australia and Canada, underwent a process of relocation in the international economy. During the 1980s, both states faced economic problems as they sought to negotiate their way in a changing international economy. American decline was occurring at the same time as was the rise of new economic powers, particularly the European Community and the dynamic economies of the Asia-Pacific region. These developments prompted a growth in international economic tensions, which neither Canada nor Australia could avoid. Both states had to redefine their location in the international system and, particularly, to give primacy to economic statecraft. We argued that the emphasis these middle powers gave to multilateral and regional economic diplomacy reflected this concern.

Second, while we recognize the difficulties inherent in the concept of the 'middle power,' the case studies in this book suggest that we can appropriately 'relocate' middle powers as a useful category of states in the contemporary international system. In particular, we offer several generalizations about the nature of leadership and followership in an era of declining hegemony. Focusing on middle powers like Australia and Canada, we explore the role of initiative and coalition-building in

Australian and Canadian foreign policy. We suggest that the technical and entrepreneurial dimensions of leadership can be an indispensable supplement to traditional, power-driven conceptions.

Our argument is based mainly on empirical case studies from the closing stages of the Cold War and the first and uncertain blushes of the post-Cold War environment. In particular, the case studies demonstrate that states with a tradition of middle power internationalism had substantial and largely untapped institutional capabilities for international coalition-building for the management of global problems. We showed that these capabilities were particularly evident in the absence of initiatives from the United States (the traditional source of leadership in the post-1945 international system) and Japan (a potential source of future structural leadership).

Australian and Canadian diplomacy in the late 1980s and early 1990s suggests that a central aim of secondary states was to bring about a change in the nature of leadership and cooperation-building in the post-Cold War era. Such an approach should not be seen as supplanting structural leadership but as an attempt, by skill and innovation, to harness the power of major players in the interests of more pluralist and cooperative forms of leadership. This was most clearly the tactic of the Cairns Group in the Uruguay Round. It also underlay Australia's attempts to speed up the pace of economic cooperation in the Asia-Pacific region, where APEC provided a forum for greater Japanese involvement in the region and for the creation of a framework within which the United States might become more attuned to the interests and needs of its Asia-Pacific partners.

Such diplomatic efforts occurred at a time when both the United States and Japan were in a learning period in an evolving post-Cold War international system: Japan was learning its potential for international economic leadership and the United States was learning anew the complexity of leadership and, especially, the importance of coalition-building. This is not to say that pluralist solutions to the problem of leadership in the world economy were possible in the absence of accommodation between the major players, whether they be Atlantic or Pacific powers. Rather, it is to suggest that small and middle-sized states played an important role in advancing both their own national interests and some conception of a wider international interest.

Middle power behaviour, therefore, is not defined in this work either by the more traditional process of identifying structural characteristics or by geostrategic location; it is defined as an approach to diplomacy geared to mitigating conflict and building consensus and cooperation. We have argued that this kind of activity can be an important antidote to rigidity in the international system in the face of major power inertia. If our argument has substance, then we should expect that middle power diplomacy will fix on mediatory and consensus-building activities, especially such activities as building reformist coalitions like the Cairns Group to bring about change within existing regimes or creating 'foundational coalitions' to establish new regimes.[1]

Our emphasis on Australian leadership within the Cairns Group is not without wider analytic importance for more general efforts to secure economic reform. As Oran Young argued, leadership in regime formation is not simply a function of hegemony. It also involves entrepreneurship, 'a combination of imagination in inventing institutional options and skill in brokering the interests of numerous actors to line up support for such options.'[2] Our case study of Australian activity in the Cairns Group provides some empirical support not only for this argument but also for Young's more general observation that the two principal models or explanations for regime formation – that regimes are formed either by rational utility-maximizing or by power-maximizing – are inadequate when treated as mutually exclusive. Following Young, we would argue that elements of both of these are necessary to understand the formation of the Cairns Group. Members of the Group were clearly egoistic actors, seeking to maximize the economic benefits of a freer and more open agricultural regime – prospects that were unlikely to be realized in the absence of major institutional reform. In this respect, Cairns Group states were clearly utility-maximizers. But this is not a sufficient explanation. Asserting its aggregate strength in a variety of major agricultural markets meant that the Cairns Group was also engaged in power-maximizing. Yet the activities of the Group cannot be fully explained by these two sets of factors. We have offered the role of entrepreneurial and technical leadership as a vital additional dimension that explains why the Group managed to hold together in the face of both external and internal disintegrative pressures.

Any explanation of Australia's leadership role, therefore, must look beyond the self-interest of an egoistic actor engaged in economic welfare maximization. Self-perception was very important to Australia's role. It is not simply that Australia, in Young's words, was 'an ethically motivated actor ... [seeking] to fashion a workable institutional arrangement as a contribution to the common good.'[3] It was also that a central goal of Australian foreign policy under the Hawke government in the late 1980s and early 1990s was the pursuit of 'good international citizenship.'

Australia's commitment to leadership, a significant share of global agricultural trade, and a common interest in reform were three of the factors accounting for the Cairns Group's strength as a coalition. A further factor in the Group's influence, with wider implications for coalition-building in the 1990s, was the innovativeness of its ideas and the persuasiveness with which these ideas were pressed in the negotiations. This factor cemented the Group's position in the negotiations and gained it the reputation of being not only an 'agenda-moving coalition' but also a 'proposal-making coalition.'[4]

As we demonstrated in Chapter 3, the Group's ideas and initiatives provided a 'middle way' between the two major protagonists without simply being exercises in 'difference splitting.' Specifically, they recognized the degree to which procedure tends to be a central factor in the success of any reform process. The Group's initiatives were, thus, geared towards generating confidence in the procedures. Second, the ideas of the Group represented a substantive contribution to the debate, in both its technical and political guises, over how to advance the process of agricultural reform. The Group not only offered proposals geared towards securing immediate short-term relief but also made suggestions for long-term goals that, if adopted, would have provided for rational reform in international trade in agriculture. No other actor in the Uruguay Round provided a comparable contribution to the resolution of differences between the major powers in the early part of the Round.

The influence of the Cairns Group stemmed less from the fact that it bargained away concessions to the other negotiating parties in return for support for its position than from the fact that it provided a genuine alternative middle ground upon which the major actors could meet. The Group used the threat of sanctions sparingly, refusing to act as a 'blocking coalition.' The closest it came to such activity was at the mid-term review, when the Latin American members of the Group threatened to block progress in other negotiating panels if reform on agriculture was not forthcoming. However, it can be argued that this was merely a variant of the well-known 'good cop/bad cop' routine. But despite the uncoordinated nature of the action, it was not without success.

Lest the performance of the Cairns Group appear overstated in our analysis, we can compare it briefly with the coalition of states that attempted to secure a New International Economic Order in the 1970s.

The coalition's conceptual framework for a NIEO was broad and poorly defined, with its aims appearing to be more a 'wish list' than a set of specific and tightly articulated proposals (and, further, the research that underlay the call for a NIEO was weak and unfocused). In addition, the coalition's tactics to secure NIEO reforms outstripped what could realistically be regarded as likely to secure negotiating success in any North-South stand-off. Not only was political conflict within the Southern camp frequently ideological in nature and invariably unrestrained, but the political commitment required from member states was greater than was the control that their own domestic polities would allow them.[5] Conflicts did exist within the Cairns Group, especially between Australia and Canada; and domestic political pressures did run against Group policy in Canada. But our account illustrates the degree to which these conflicts and difficulties were largely contained by processes of compromise and mediation.

Ultimately, the Cairns Group was not the major catalyst for the compromise on agricultural trade eventually brokered between the major powers in December 1992. Rather, that compromise was a product of negotiations and trade-offs between the system's major actors. The history of GATT, in particular, and the international trade regime, in general, over the last few decades illustrates the degree to which major actors were able to determine negotiations. In this regard, it is less important that the Cairns Group tried to impel the major protagonists to accept its positions either by the force of its collective economic weight or by the force of rational argument – strong as both may be – than that the Group attempted to build confidence and to provide a middle way for the major players to move beyond positions of intransigence when they decided, for whatever reason (e.g., a change of domestic leadership or administration), that the timing was right. In this way, the Cairns Group provided an important contribution to our general understanding of efforts at confidence-building in international economic relations – efforts that have been the focus of little analysis to date.

That there have been relatively few studies of confidence-building in the international economy is perhaps not altogether surprising. Confidence-building is a definitionally elusive concept, and it is not an activity that those engaged in its practice have been prone to write about. Moreover, the psychology of international economic relations has not been subjected to the same sophisticated scrutiny as has the psychology of international security, which has been analyzed by such scholars as Robert Jervis and others.[6] Yet it is clear that economic relations between the major economic actors (especially American relations with both the EC and Japan) and that perceptions of mistrust and misunderstanding were as significant in the potential for conflict between states as was the reality of fiercer economic competition in a more globally interdependent era. Such concerns clearly galvanized those states in the global political economy which would be adversely affected by increased conflict between the great powers. In its attempts to bridge gaps and to build confidence in the relationship between the major players in the Uruguay Round, the Cairns Group represented a concerted response by these middle powers.

In short, we have suggested that the Uruguay Round provides a useful illustration of the degree to which the Cairns Group of Fair Trading Nations sought to create an environment that would minimize the proclivities for rigidity and conflict and maximize the prospects for greater collaboration towards the goal of agricultural reform. The diplomacy of the Cairns Group demonstrated both the strengths and the weaknesses of coalitions in the transformation of international regimes. It did not make or break a regime of its own accord. On the other hand, the role of the Cairns Group suggests that, in specific cases, a well-organized coalition practising the politics of brokerage and constraint can play a major role in providing intellectual leadership, diplomacy, and assistance to the other principal actors.

In Chapter 4, we examined the lessons of regional economic cooperation, focusing on both the Asia-Pacific region and free trade in North America. The evolution of regionalism in the Asia-Pacific area, we argued, involved a substantially different process from other forms of regional cooperation that emerged in the post-1945 era. Although an exercise in closer economic cooperation, it was underwritten by a diversity of national political interests and levels of development not found, for example, in the European context or in North America (as we show in our discussion of North American Free Trade Agreement signed in December 1992). Greater economic or political integration in the Asia-Pacific region was always unlikely. More probable was an evolutionary model, based on a region-wide recognition of a substantial and growing mutuality of interest, which saw an emerging institutional structure that allowed for the continued expansion of communication on matters of regional economic and political interest. Among the interests we identified were strong regional desires to provide a forum for the mitigation of tension between the economic superpowers of the region, the United States and Japan; improved dialogue between ASEAN and the other members of the region; and, finally, the presentation of a regional view on broader questions of import in the global economy.

The smaller members of APEC were sensitive to the importance of collective positions for improving their potential bargaining abilities in the wider economic context. Although some of the participants at the Canberra meeting had real reservations about the enterprise, all of those present recognized the potential utility and leverage that the group could have in the face of a declining commitment to multilateralism.

As with the Cairns Group, the theoretically interesting aspects of the evolution of APEC are the insights it offers into the evolving nature of the question of leadership in the cooperation-building process. While the APEC initiative needs to be seen in a wider context, we stressed the problematic nature of coalition-building as a concept in international relations and the limited degree of success that some coalitions have had in securing their goals. If not over-extended, however, both concepts can provide useful insights into the behaviour of secondary states in international relations in the 1990s. Further, the continuing evolution of APEC, not destined to be a smooth or uneventful process, will, nevertheless, provide invaluable empirical material for the student of international cooperation throughout the 1990s.

Our discussion of the involvement of these middle powers in the Gulf coalition was intended to provide an offsetting case study on the question of leadership and followership. We showed that the manoeuvrability of states such as Australia and Canada is considerably constrained under certain conditions. The most evident of these is the continuing importance of the security problematic and post-Second World War alliance structures, of which both states are a part. Yet, notwithstanding the bilateral security relationships that both states share with the United States, Australian and Canadian involvement in the Gulf coalition was couched in multilateral sentiments. But in this instance, the pursuit of multilateralism put them in the role of 'coalition-joiners' rather than of 'coalition-builders.'

The discussion of the Gulf conflict in Chapter 5 is not meant to imply, however, that Australia and Canada are always constrained in the security domain. Indeed, we demonstrate, in our discussion of the widening agenda of international relations in Chapter 6, that, as the security problematic undergoes a process of broadening and deepening, the agenda-setting activities of these middle powers intensifies. These activities identify some of the differences of style between the two states.

For example, Australia's deep involvement in efforts to bring about a peaceful resolution of the Cambodian conflict and its attempts to generate an Asia-Pacific security dialogue demonstrate that the government in Canberra clearly opted for a more focused, or instrumental and discrete, approach. Canada, on the other hand, opted for a more globalist, or diffused, approach on such issues as arms control and verification.

As Chapter 6 indicates, neither category is exclusive. Our investigation of a variety of environmental and social issues illustrates that both regional and global elements are to be found in the policy positions of both states. The major stylistic difference between the contemporary approaches of the two states would appear to be the degree to which Canada emphasized consensus-seeking, while Australia exhibited greater mobilizing capacities in its foreign policy. But for all the stylistic differences, both middle powers were sometimes accused of 'initiative-mongering' on different international issues.

Likewise, neither approach avoided bringing the two states into conflict with their major alliance partner, the United States. However, challenging Washington occasionally yielded a success. The examples discussed in chapters 4 and 6 suggest that, in response to Australian and Canadian diplomacy, initial American opposition to initiatives on occasion gave way to a more accommodationist position. This was particularly true in the cases of APEC, Antarctica, human rights, and Pacific security questions.

Thus, the similarities and differences in Australian and Canadian foreign policy in the 1980s and early 1990s highlight the importance of comparative research on the two countries. Such research offers us insights not only into what kinds of approaches to policy might be available but also into what the limitations of such options might be. Practitioners and scholars alike – and not only in Australia and Canada – might learn from closer attention to this sort of activity.

With the end of the Cold War, the rules of the international economic and political systems have been opened to rethinking and remaking in the 1990s. The issues at stake for such countries as Australia and Canada are too important to be left to the major players alone. In particular, with the disappearance of bipolar rivalry, there are no longer any guarantees that larger allies will always take care of a junior partner's interests. In the case of Australia and Canada, there is the distinct possibility that the United States, the protector of the interests of these two middle powers for much of the twentieth century, will continue to retrench its global security reach in the 1990s, though this would have more profound implications for the former than for the latter.

To offset the negative effects of American withdrawal, it will be necessary for the system's small and middle powers to engage in more creative diplomacy to fill the obvious gaps left by the waning of 'tests of will.' The case studies in this book suggest that the 1990s will be an era in which the technical innovation and entrepreneurship in the international diplomacy of middle powers could, if effectively coordinated, play an important role in shaping the future. To be sure, the major powers will continue to play the principal role in the structuring of the global order in the 1990s; we have not tried to suggest otherwise in this work. Yet, Australia and Canada are two states, differences notwithstanding, that have sufficient common interests and international status and credit to make an important contribution to shaping that future.

Notes

Introduction

1 Henry Albinski, *Canadian and Australian Politics in Comparative Perspective* (New York: Oxford University Press 1973); B.W. Hodgson, John Eddy, SJ, Shelagh D. Grant, and James Struthers, eds., *Federalism in Canada and Australia: Historical Perspectives, 1920-88* (Peterborough: Frost Centre for Canadian Heritage and Development Studies, Trent University 1990); Malcolm Alexander and Brian Galligan, eds., *Comparative Political Studies: Australia and Canada* (Melbourne: Longman Cheshire 1992). For the rare example of the comparative study of Australian and Canadian foreign policy see Annette Baker Fox, *The Politics of Attraction: Four Middle Powers and the United States* (New York: Columbia University Press 1977). See also Robert O. Keohane and Joseph S. Nye, Jr., *Power and Interdependence: World Politics in Transition* (Boston: Little, Brown 1977), 165-98.

2 P.J. Boyce, 'Introduction,' in P.J. Boyce and J.R. Angel, eds., *Diplomacy in the Marketplace: Australia in World Affairs, 1981-90* (Melbourne: Longman Cheshire 1992), 9-11.

3 Stanley Hoffmann, 'What Should We Do in the World,' *Atlantic Monthly* (October 1989):84-6.

4 One of the best collections of essays to address this question is David P. Rapkin, ed., *World Leadership and Hegemony, International Political Economy Yearbook*, vol. 5 (Boulder: Lynne Reinner 1990). See especially Rapkin's introductory chapter, 'The Contested Concept of Hegemonic Leadership,' 1-21.

5 Perhaps the quintessential work of this genre is David Vital, *The Inequality of States: A Study of the Small Power in International Relations* (Oxford: Clarendon Press 1967).

6 Bernard Wood, *World Order and Double Standards: Peace and Security 1990-91, Director's Annual Statement* (Ottawa: Canadian Institute for International Peace and Security 1991), 32.

7 Alexander Wendt, 'Anarchy Is What States Make of It,' *International Organization* 46 (Spring 1992):391-425.

Chapter 1: Leadership, Followership, and Middle Powers

1 Declinists are said to include David Calleo, *Beyond American Hegemony: The Future of the American Alliance* (New York: Basic Books 1987); Paul Kennedy, *The Rise*

and Fall of the Great Powers: Economic Change and Military Conflict from 1500 to 2000 (New York: Random House 1987). 'Renewalists' take their name from Samuel P. Huntington's article, 'The U.S. – Decline or Renewal?' *Foreign Affairs* 67 (Winter 1988-9):75-96. They include Henry Nau, *The Myth of America's Decline: Leading the World Economy into the 1990s* (New York: Oxford University Press 1990) and Joseph S. Nye, Jr., *Bound to Lead: The Changing Nature of American Power* (New York: Basic Books 1990).

2 See, for example, Robert O. Keohane, *After Hegemony: Co-operation and Discord in the World Political Economy* (Princeton: Princeton University Press 1984), esp 39.

3 J.E. Garten, *A Cold Peace: America, Japan and the Quest for Supremacy* (New York: Twentieth Century Fund 1992); Carnegie Endowment for International Peace, *Changing Our Ways: America and the New World* (Washington 1992).

4 John G. Ruggie, 'Multilateralism: Anatomy of an Institution,' *International Organization* 46 (Summer 1992):593.

5 Oran Young, 'The Politics of International Regime Formation: Managing Natural Resources and the Environment,' *International Organization* 43 (Summer 1989):349-75; and 'Political Leadership and Regime Reform: The Emergence of Institutions in International Society,' International Studies Association, Washington, DC, 10-14 April 1989.

6 Alexander Wendt, 'The Agent-Structure Problem in International Relations Theory,' *International Organization* 41 (Summer 1987):335-70.

7 Stanley Hoffmann, 'What Should We Do in the World?' *Atlantic* (October 1989):84-96.

8 Susan Strange, *States and Markets* (London: Frances Pinter 1988); and Nye, *Bound to Lead*.

9 Nye, *Bound to Lead*, 234-6.

10 R.A. Higgott, 'Towards a Non-Hegemonic International Political Economy,' in Craig Murphy and Roger Tooze, eds., *The New International Political Economy* (Boulder: Lynne Reiner 1991), 178-219.

11 Alexander Wendt, 'Anarchy is What States Make of It,' *International Organization* 46 (Spring 1992):391-425.

12 As Stephen D. Krasner put it so tellingly to a panel of the 1990 American Political Science Association meetings in San Francisco, 'Sure people in Luxembourg have good ideas. But who gives a damn? Luxembourg ain't hegemonic.'

13 G. John Ikenberry and Charles A. Kupchan, 'Socialization and Hegemonic Power,' *International Organization* 44 (Summer 1990):288-315.

14 Robert W. Cox, *Production, Power and World Order: Social Forces in the Making of History* (New York: Columbia University Press 1987), 7; see also Cox, 'Gramsci, Hegemony and International Relations: An Essay in Method,' *Millennium: A Journal of International Studies* 12 (Summer 1983):162-75.

15 For a good discussion of what he calls the ironies of hegemony's second coming, see Richard Leaver, 'Restructuring in the Global Economy: From Pax Americana to Pax Nipponica?' *Alternatives* 14 (October 1989):429-62, esp. 439ff.

16 See, for example, Robert Gilpin, *War and Change in World Politics* (Cambridge: Cambridge University Press 1981), 29-38; George Modelski, *Long Cycles in World Politics* (Seattle: University of Washington Press 1987), 12-18; Charles P. Kindleberger, 'Dominance and Leadership in the International Economy:

Exploitation, Public Goods, and Free Rides,' in Kindleberger, *Economic Order: Essays on Financial Crisis and International Public Goods* (Cambridge: MIT Press 1988), 185-95. For an excellent critique of the mythological nature of these assumptions, see Isabelle Grunberg, 'Exploring the "Myth" of Hegemonic Stability,' *International Organization* 44 (Autumn 1990):431-77.

17 Keohane, *After Hegemony*, esp. 39, argues that we should be as interested in 'why secondary states defer to the leadership of the hegemon' as we are in how the hegemon imposes its power on the international system. See also David A. Lake, 'International Economic Structures and American Foreign Economic Policy, 1887-1934,' *World Politics* 35 (July 1983):517-43; Michael K. Hawes, 'Structural Change and Hegemonic Decline: Implications for National Governments,' in David G. Haglund and Michael K. Hawes, eds., *World Politics: Power, Interdependence and Dependence* (Toronto: Harcourt Brace Jovanovich 1990), 197-223.

18 Indeed, this is precisely how Nye determines that the United States is 'bound to lead' for the foreseeable future: see *Bound to Lead*, chs. 4-5.

19 C.A. Gibb, 'The Principles and Traits of Leadership,' in Gibb, ed., *Leadership: Selected Readings* (Harmondsworth: Penguin 1969), 213; James MacGregor Burns, *Leadership* (New York: Harper and Row 1978).

20 For example, Kindleberger, 'Dominance and Leadership'; Duncan Snidal, 'The Limits of Hegemonic Stability Theory,' *International Organization* 39 (Autumn 1985):579-614; and John Conybeare's description of the United States as a 'predatory hegemon' cited in Robert Gilpin, *The Political Economy of International Relations* (Princeton: Princeton University Press 1987), 345.

21 For example, Modelski (*Long Cycles*, 14) notes that 'Leadership cannot be viewed solely or primarily as a display of power or a manifestation of superiority.' But his description of what leadership entails ('it must be seen more essentially as the accomplishment of essential services that give impetus and example to the global polity') is incompletely worked out.

22 For an exploratory discussion, see Andrew Fenton Cooper, Richard A. Higgott, and Kim Richard Nossal, 'Bound to Follow? Leadership and Followership in the Gulf Conflict,' *Political Science Quarterly* 106 (Fall 1991):391-410.

23 Richard Stubbs, 'Reluctant Leader, Expectant Followers: Japan and Southeast Asia,' *International Journal* 46 (Summer 1991):649-67.

24 For one critique of structuralism that argues that it limits our understanding of leadership politics in Europe, see Stanley Hoffmann, 'The Case for Leadership,' *Foreign Policy* 81 (Winter 1990-1):20-38.

25 Robert O. Keohane and Joseph S. Nye, Jr., *Power and Interdependence*, 2nd edition (Boston: Scott Foresman 1989).

26 The work of Bernard Wood is indicative. In *The Middle Powers and the General Interest*, no. 1 in the series *Middle Powers in the International System* (Ottawa: North-South Institute 1990), table 1, p. 18. Wood uses a positional approach to identify a 'loose tier' of thirty-three states, which he asserts 'would likely be proposed as middle power candidates according to any criterion.'

27 In the nineteenth century, German theorists sought to analyze the role of the German states as *Mittelmachten*, located between the great powers of continental Europe. Interestingly, a century later, a study of West German foreign policy attributed middle power status to Germany on similar grounds. See Carsten

Holbraad, *Middle Powers in International Politics* (London: Macmillan 1984), 72.

28 For a discussion and critique of such an argument, see Kim Richard Nossal, *The Politics of Canadian Foreign Policy*, 2nd edition (Scarborough, ON: Prentice-Hall 1989), 50.

29 Holbraad, *Middle Powers in International Politics.*

30 For example, see the essays in J. King Gordon, ed., *Canada's Role as a Middle Power* (Toronto: Canadian Institute of International Affairs 1966). Also see the writings of John W. Holmes, particularly his *Canada: A Middle-Aged Power* (Toronto: McClelland and Stewart 1976). Two very useful reviews of the literature on middle powers in a Canadian context are to be found in: Michael K. Hawes, *Principal Power, Middle Power, or Satellite?* (North York, ON: York Research Programme in Strategic Studies 1984); and Maureen Appel Molot, 'Where Do We, Should We, or Can We Sit? A Review of Canadian Foreign Policy Literature,' *International Journal of Canadian Studies* 1-2 (Spring/Fall 1990):77-96.

31 Paul Keal, ed., *Ethics and Australian Foreign Policy* (Sydney: Allen and Unwin 1992), 16.

32 Cranford Pratt, ed., *Middle Power Internationalism: The North-South Dimension* (Kingston and Montreal: McGill-Queen's University Press 1990); Pratt, ed., *Internationalism Under Strain: The North-South Policies of Canada, the Netherlands, Norway, and Sweden* (Toronto: University of Toronto Press 1989).

33 Robert Rothstein, 'Regime Creation by a Coalition of the Weak: Lessons from the NIEO and the Integrated Program for Commodities,' *International Studies Quarterly* 28 (Summer 1984):307-28.

34 John W. Holmes, 'Is There a Future for Middlepowermanship?' and Paul Painchaud, 'Middlepowermanship as an Ideology,' both in Gordon, ed., *Canada's Role as a Middle Power*, 13-36.

35 Wood, *Middle Powers and the General Interest*, 20.

36 For Australia, see Gareth Evans, 'Australia's Place in the World,' *Australian Foreign Affairs Review* 59 (December 1988): 526-30; 'Australia's Foreign Policy: Responding to Change,' ibid., 61 (September 1990):586-94; 'Australia's Place in the World: The Dynamics of Foreign Policy Decision-Making,' in Desmond Ball, ed., *Australia and the World: Prologue and Prospects* (Canberra: Strategic and Defence Studies Centre, Australian National University 1990); Gareth Evans and Bruce Grant, *Australia's Foreign Relations in the World of the 1990s* (Melbourne: Melbourne University Press 1991), 322-6. For Canada: Joe Clark, 'Canada's New Internationalism,' in John Holmes and John Kirton, eds., *Canada and the New Internationalism* (Toronto: Canadian Institute of International Affairs 1988), 3-11.

37 For example, in December 1991, Barbara McDougall, Canada's secretary of state for external affairs, described Canadian policy in precisely these middle power terms but studiously avoided using the words 'middle power.' See Barbara McDougall, 'Introduction,' in John English and Norman Hillmer, eds., *Making a Difference? Canada's Foreign Policy in a Changing World Order* (Toronto: Lester 1992), ix-xvi.

38 *Department of Foreign Affairs and Trade - The Monthly Record* (hereafter *DFAT Monthly Record*) 61 (September 1990):592.

39 John W. Holmes, *The Shaping of Peace: Canada and the Search for World Order, 1943-1957*, vol. 1 (Toronto: University of Toronto Press 1979).

40 Bernard Wood, 'Towards North-South Power Coalitions,' in Pratt, ed., *Middle-Power Internationalism*, 69-107.

41 T.B. Millar, *Australia in Peace and War* (Canberra: Australian National University Press 1978); Nossal, *Politics of Canadian Foreign Policy*.

42 Robert O. Keohane, 'Big Influence of Small Allies,' *Foreign Policy* (Spring 1971):161-82.

43 Donald Puchala and R.A. Coate, *The State of the United Nations, 1988* (Hanover, NH: Academic Council on the United Nations System 1988).

44 W. Litzinger and T. Schaefer, 'Leadership Through Followership,' in William E. Rosenbach and Robert L. Taylor, eds., *Contemporary Issues in Leadership* (Boulder: Westview 1989); also Robert E. Kelly, 'In Praise of Followers,' *Harvard Business Review* 66 (November-December 1988):142-8.

45 The best formulation may be found in Barry Buzan, *People, States and Fear: An Agenda for International Security Studies in the Post Cold War Era* (London: Harvester Wheatsheaf 1991).

46 Robert Putnam, 'Diplomacy and Domestic Politics: The Logic of Two-Level Games,' *International Organization* 42 (Spring 1988):427-60.

47 A. Claire Cutler and Mark W. Zacher, 'Introduction,' in A. Claire Cutler and Mark W. Zacher, eds., *Canadian Foreign Policy and International Economic Regimes* (Vancouver: UBC Press 1992), 4.

48 For example, Glenn P. Jenkins, *Costs and Consequences of the New Protectionism: The Case of Canada's Clothing Sector* (Ottawa: North-South Institute 1980).

49 Robert Boardman, *Global Regimes and Nation-States: Environmental Issues in Australian Politics* (Ottawa: Carleton University Press 1990), 171-2.

50 *The African Famine and Canada's Response, A Report by the Honourable David MacDonald, Canadian Emergency Coordinator – African Famine, for the Period from November 1984 to March 1985* (Hull, PQ: Canadian International Development Agency 1985).

51 Cited in James Travers, 'Ethiopia: Is it a Fad or Step to Solution?' *Ottawa Citizen* (10 November 1984).

52 Burns, *Leadership*, 4.

53 Richard Rosecrance and Jennifer Taw, 'Japan and the Theory of International Leadership,' *World Politics* 42 (January 1990):290.

54 David Abshire, 'The Nature of American Global Economic Leadership in the 1990s,' in William Brock and Robert Hormats, eds., *The Global Economy: America's Role in the Decade Ahead* (New York: Norton for the American Assembly 1990), 175-8.

55 Kenneth Calder, 'Japanese Foreign Economic Policy Formation: Explaining the Reactive State,' *World Politics* 40 (July 1989):517-41.

56 Young, 'International Regime Formation,' 349-75; 'Political Leadership and Regime Reform,' 1-42.

57 Sylvia Ostry, 'Changing Multilateral Institutions: A Role for Canada,' in Cutler and Zacher, eds., *Canadian Foreign Policy and International Economic Regimes*, 337.

58 Robert O. Keohane, *Institutions and State Power: Essays in International Relations Theory* (Boulder: Westview 1990), 1-20.

59 Gareth Evans and Bruce Grant, *Australia's Foreign Relations in the World of the 1990s* (Melbourne: Melbourne University Press 1991), 323.

60 Indicative would be Annette Baker Fox, 'The Range of Choice for Middle Powers: Australia and Canada Compared,' *Australian Journal of Politics and History* 26 (1980):193-203.
61 Painchaud, 'Middlepowermanship as an Ideology,' argued that the belief systems of those who practised this kind of middle power role had all the features of a political ideology.
62 R.A. MacKay, 'The Canadian Doctrine of the Middle Powers,' in H.L. Dyck and H.P. Krosby, eds., *Empire and Nations: Essays in Honour of Frederic H. Soward* (Toronto: University of Toronto Press 1969), 133-43; reprinted in J.L. Granatstein, ed., *Towards a New World: Readings in the History of Canadian Foreign Policy* (Toronto: Copp Clark Pitman 1992), 65-75.
63 Examples would include Escott Reid, *On Duty: A Canadian at the Making of the United Nations, 1945-1946* (Kent, OH: Kent State University Press 1983); and Paul Hasluck, *Diplomatic Witness: Australian Foreign Affairs 1941-1947* (Melbourne: Melbourne University Press 1980).
64 For an exploration of some differences in the issue area of agriculture, see Andrew F. Cooper, 'Like-Minded Nations/Contrasting Diplomatic Styles: Australian and Canadian Approaches to Agricultural Trade,' *Canadian Journal of Political Science* 25 (June 1992):349-79.
65 On the concept of 'heroic' leadership, see Stanley Hoffmann, 'Heroic Leadership: The Case of Modern France,' in Lewis J. Edinger, ed., *Political Leadership in Industrialized Societies: Studies in Comparative Analysis* (New York: John Wiley 1967), 108-54; and J. Hayward, 'National Aptitudes for Planning in Britain, France and Italy,' *Government & Opposition* 9 (1974):397-410.
66 For example, Richard A. Higgott, 'International Constraints on Labor's Economic Policy,' in Brian Galligan and Gwyn Singleton, eds., *How Labor Governs: The Hawke Government and Business* (Melbourne: Longman Cheshire 1991); and 'The Politics of Australia's International Economic Relations: Adjustment and the Politics of Two-Level Games,' *Australian Journal of Political Science* 26 (March 1991):2-28; and Andrew Fenton Cooper, 'Australia: Domestic Political Management and International Trade Reform,' in Grace Skogstad and Andrew Fenton Cooper, eds., *Agricultural Trade: Domestic Pressures and International Trade* (Halifax, NS: Institute for Research on Public Policy 1990), 113-34.
67 On the peace initiative, see Richard and Sandra Gwyn, 'The Politics of Peace,' *Saturday Night* (May 1984), 19-32. On the North-South initiative, see Kim Richard Nossal, 'Personal Diplomacy and National Behaviour: Trudeau's North-South Initiatives,' *Dalhousie Review* 62 (Summer 1982), 278-91.
68 For example, Stephen Lewis, the former leader of the Ontario New Democratic Party, whom Brian Mulroney had appointed as Canada's permanent representative to the UN, was scathing in his attack on this approach: 'When the prime minister was engaged in an issue it was the centrepiece of Canadian public policy. But when Prime Minister Trudeau lost interest in or was not engaged in an issue, it was no longer the centrepiece.' Quoted in the *Toronto Star* (26 November 1987), A3.
69 For a discussion of Soviet fears of war at this time, see Michael McGwire, *Military Objectives in Soviet Foreign Policy* (Washington: Brookings Institution 1987), esp. ch. 13.

70 J.L. Granatstein and Robert Bothwell, *Pirouette: Pierre Trudeau and Canadian Foreign Policy* (Toronto: University of Toronto Press 1990), 375.

71 Richard A. Higgott, 'The Dilemmas of Interdependence: Australia and the International Division of Labor in the Asia Pacific Region,' in James Caporaso, ed., *The New International Division of Labor: International Political Economy Yearbook*, vol. 1 (Boulder: Lynne Reinner 1987), 147-86.

72 D. Porter, B. Allen and G. Thompson, *Development in Practice: Paved with Good Intentions* (London: Routledge 1991); and C. Gertzel and D. Goldsworthy, 'Australian Aid to Africa,' in P. Eldridge, D. Forbes and D. Porter, eds., *Australian Overseas Aid* (Canberra: Croom Helm 1986).

73 See, for example, Molot, 'Where Do We, Should We, or Can We Sit?'

74 John Kirton and Don Munton, 'The *Manhattan* Voyages and their Aftermath,' in Franklyn Griffiths, ed., *Politics of the Northwest Passage* (Montreal and Kingston: McGill-Queen's University Press 1987), 67-97.

75 Elizabeth Riddell-Dixon, *Canada and the International Seabed: Domestic Determinants and External Constraints* (Kingston/Montreal: McGill-Queen's University Press 1989).

76 Michael Tucker, *Canadian Foreign Policy: Contemporary Issues and Themes* (Toronto: McGraw-Hill Ryerson 1980), 33.

Chapter 2: State Reorganization

1 Robert Boardman, 'The Foreign Service and the Organization of the Foreign Policy Community: Views from Canada and Abroad,' in Canada, Royal Commission on the Economic Union and Development Prospects for Canada, *The Research Studies*, vol. 30: *Selected Problems in Formulating Foreign Economic Policy*, edited by Denis Stairs and Gilbert R. Winham (Toronto: University of Toronto Press 1985), 59-103; Zara Steiner, ed., *The Times Survey of Foreign Ministries of the World* (London: Time Books 1982).

2 Hugh Collins, 'Challenges and Options for the Department of Foreign Affairs in Its Fiftieth Year,' *Australian Foreign Affairs Record* 56 (November 1985):1077-8; Boardman, 'Foreign Service,' 79.

3 Stuart Harris, secretary of the Australian Department of Foreign Affairs between 1984 and 1988, notes that a senior Canadian official once said that in whatever country he visited, the preferred position on the amalgamation of the foreign and trade ministries was that they should be combined if separated and separated if combined. Harris, 'The Amalgamation of the Department of Foreign Affairs and Trade,' *Australian Foreign Affairs Record* 59 (March 1988): 71.

4 For example, foreign ministry reviews or reorganizations have been undertaken in Australia, Britain, Canada, Denmark, Germany, Ireland, Japan, Netherlands, New Zealand, Norway, Sweden, and the United States. See Zara Steiner, ed., *The Times Survey of Foreign Ministries of the World* (London: Time Books 1982).

5 Jacques Willequet, 'Belgium: The Ministry of Foreign Affairs,' in Steiner, ed., *Times Survey*, 75-93.

6 Klaus Kjølsen, 'The Royal Danish Ministry of Foreign Affairs,' in Steiner, ed., *Times Survey*, 172, 180; Kjølsen notes the symbolism in the current location of the foreign ministry: Asiatisk Plads was where eighteenth-century overseas trade and shipping companies had been located in the heyday of Danish commercial

power. See Geoffrey McDermott, *The New Diplomacy and Its Apparatus* (London: Plume 1973), 133: it is the foreign ministry's principal branch that deals with economic matters; 'political and legal affairs only come second.'

7 Jukka Nevakivi, 'The Finnish Foreign Service,' Steiner, ed., *Times Survey*, 185-201.

8 C.B. Wels, 'The Foreign Policy Institutions in the Dutch Republic and the Kingdom of the Netherlands, 1579 to 1980,' in Steiner, ed., *Times Survey*, 363-89.

9 Erik-Wilhelm Norman, 'The Royal Norwegian Ministry of Foreign Affairs,' in Steiner, ed., *Times Survey*, 391-408.

10 Wilhelm Carlgren, 'Sweden: The Ministry for Foreign Affairs,' in Steiner, ed., *Times Survey*, 455-69.

11 H. Gordon Skilling, *Canadian Representation Abroad: From Agency to Embassy* (Toronto: Ryerson 1945), 186.

12 As Gordon Osbaldeston, the under-secretary of state for external affairs (who oversaw the amalgamation), put it, 'The reorganization is not a case of External Affairs absorbing parts of the former Department of Industry, Trade and Commerce, or of the Trade Commissioner Service taking over control of External Affairs. Rather, there is a new department with a ... role in government which is essentially different from that of the old Department of External Affairs.' Osbaldeston, 'Reorganizing Canada's Department of External Affairs,' *International Journal* 37 (Summer 1982):455.

13 In the odd nomenclature adopted by the federal Canadian government in the 1980s, agencies of the state have two styles of appellation. On the one hand, they have formal statutory names in the style common to virtually every modern Weberian state – that is, 'Department of X,' or 'Ministry of State for Y.' However, this style is never used for official purposes. Instead, federal agencies also have what is known as an 'applied title,' which drops the identifier 'Department of' or 'Ministry of State for' and adds 'Canada' – as in Revenue Canada, Industry, Science, and Technology Canada, or Supply and Services Canada. External Affairs and International Trade Canada was given its 'applied title' effective 28 June 1989.

14 Canada, Office of the Prime Minister, *Release*, Ottawa, 12 January 1982, 1.

15 Ibid., 7.

16 For a good review, see Jock A. Finlayson with Stefano Bertasi, 'Evolution of Canadian Postwar International Trade Policy,' in A. Claire Cutler and Mark W. Zacher, eds., *Canadian Foreign Policy and International Economic Regimes* (Vancouver: UBC Press 1992), 19-46.

17 See O. Mary Hill, *Canada's Salesman to the World: The Department of Trade and Commerce, 1892-1939* (Montreal and Kingston: McGill-Queen's University Press 1977); John Hilliker, *Canada's Department of External Affairs*, vol. 1: *The Early Years, 1909-1946* (Montreal and Kingston: McGill-Queen's University Press 1990), 19; G.P. deT. Glazebrook, *A History of Canadian External Relations*, vol 1: *The Formative Years to 1914*, rev. edition (Toronto: McClelland and Stewart 1970), ch. 7. Canada's first trade commissioner had been despatched to Sydney in 1894. By 1909, there were Canadian trade commissioners in nineteen cities on five continents. See Canada, Royal Commission on Conditions of Foreign Service, Pamela A. McDougall, commissioner, *Report* (Ottawa: Supply and Services 1981), Table FST-2, 95-6.

18 James Eayrs, 'The Origins of Canada's Department of External Affairs,' *Canadian Journal of Economics and Political Science* 25 (May 1959):109-28.

19 The first came at the outset of the Great Depression, when the Conservative government of R.B. Bennett considered a series of proposals for amalgamation as a means of promoting Canadian exports. While the idea was embraced by External Affairs, the proposals were strongly resisted by bureaucrats in Trade and Commerce, and H.H. Stevens, the minister. The second occurred during the Second World War, when External Affairs proposed amalgamation as a means of solving its shortage of qualified officers for the conduct of Canada's burgeoning international relations. As Hugh Keenleyside, a DEA official, argued: 'trade and economic factors are fundamental to ninety per cent of all international relations and are thus worthy of, and in fact demand, consideration.' As in the early 1930s, opposition from both the Department of Trade and Commerce and its minister put an early end to these initiatives. Accounts of these proposals are to be found in Hilliker, *Canada's Department of External Affairs*, vol. 1, 153-4 and 260-1. See also J.L. Granatstein, 'Canada's Royal Commission on Conditions of Foreign Service,' *International Journal* 37 (Summer 1982):409. Between the wartime initiatives and 1968 no further initiatives were taken on reorganizing the foreign policy machinery, even though the Royal Commission on Government Organization (the Glassco Commission) highlighted the problems of poor coordination and the costly inefficiencies of having numerous departments represented abroad. R. Barry Farrell, *The Making of Canadian Foreign Policy* (Scarborough: Prentice-Hall 1969), 61.

20 J.L. Granatstein and Robert Bothwell, *Pirouette: Pierre Trudeau and Canadian Foreign Policy* (Toronto: University of Toronto Press 1990), 223.

21 His most frequently quoted scepticism about External Affairs was his assertion during a television interview on 1 January 1969: 'I think the whole concept of diplomacy today is a little bit outmoded ... I believe it all goes back to the early days of the telegraph when you needed a dispatch to know what was happening in Country A, whereas now most of the time you can read it in a good newspaper.' Quoted in Peter C. Dobell, 'The Management of a Foreign Policy for Canadians,' *International Journal* 26 (Winter 1970-1):202.

22 See Arthur Andrew, 'The Diplomat and the Manager,' *International Journal* 30 (Winter 1974-5):47; W.M. Dobell, 'Interdepartmental Management in External Affairs,' *Canadian Public Administration* 21 (Spring 1978):83-102.

23 James Eayrs, 'Canada: External Affairs,' in Steiner, ed., *Times Survey*, 105.

24 The purpose of this scheme was to allow posts abroad to operate more efficiently by giving the head of post authority over all officers at a post, regardless of their departmental affiliation. With this measure, the government finally implemented a recommendation about heads of post that had been made by the 1963 Royal Commission on Government Organization (the Glassco Commission). However, if a remembrance of Glassco survived the intervening seventeen years, it was not apparent in the official justifications offered for this move. See Jack Maybee, 'Foreign Service Consolidation,' *International Perspectives* (July/August 1980), 17-20.

25 Harold Nicholson popularized this term in the 1920s, though his focus then was on the 'new diplomacy' of the United States, particularly the changes in tradi-

tional nineteenth-century diplomatic practice introduced by such policymakers as Woodrow Wilson. In later manifestations, 'new' diplomacy came to refer to the ahistorical belief that contemporary international politics has rendered the practice of diplomacy obsolete. Such views were expressed in the early 1970s by such individuals as Zbigniew Brzezinski in the United States, Anthony Wedgwood Benn in Britain, and, as we have noted above, by Trudeau in Canada. See also McDermott, *The New Diplomacy*, 50-2; Steiner, 'Foreign Ministries Old and New,' 367.

26 Trudeau to McDougall, 28 August 1980, reprinted in Royal Commission on Conditions of Foreign Service, *Report*, viii.

27 A.E. Gotlieb, 'Canadian Diplomacy in the 1980s: Leadership and Service,' lecture to the Centre for International Studies and the Canadian Institute of International Affairs, Toronto, 15 February 1979:3, 4, and 15.

28 Royal Commission on Conditions of Foreign Service, *Report*, 80-1.

29 Granatstein and Bothwell, *Pirouette*, 228.

30 Because of his closeness to Trudeau, Pitfield was dismissed after Joe Clark became prime minister in June 1979. However, when the Liberals were returned to power in February 1980, Trudeau reappointed Pitfield as clerk.

31 Transcript of remarks to the Workshop on the Effects of the Reorganization of the Department of External Affairs, Canadian Institute of International Affairs and Institute for Research on Public Policy, Ottawa, 29 April 1982.

32 See Osbaldeston, 'Reorganizing Canada's Department of External Affairs,' 458-61.

33 Hawke press release of 14 July 1987, reprinted in *Australian Foreign Affairs Record* 58 (July 1987):399-402.

34 For example, Promotion Australia was transferred from the Department of Sport, Recreation and Tourism to Foreign Affairs in this reorganization. On 15 November 1987, this unit was renamed the Australian Overseas Information Service.

35 For a discussion of Austrade, see Ann Capling and Brian Galligan, *Beyond the Protective State: The Political Economy of Australia's Manufacturing Industry Policy* (Cambridge: Cambridge University Press 1992), 141-4.

36 For a more detailed discussion of these changes, see Patrick Weller, 'The Cabinet,' and Kenneth Wiltshire, 'The Bureaucracy,' both in Christine Jennett and Randal G. Stewart, eds., *Hawke and Australian Public Policy: Consensus and Restructuring* (Melbourne: Macmillan of Australia 1990), 16-41.

37 See Michael Stuchbury, 'Macroeconomic Policy,' in Jennett and Stewart, eds., *Hawke and Australian Public Policy*, 54-78; Richard Higgott, 'Australia: Economic Crises and the Politics of Regional Economic Adjustment,' in Richard Robison, Kevin Hewison, and Richard Higgott, eds., *Southeast Asia in the 1980s: The Politics of Economic Crisis* (Sydney: Allen and Unwin 1987), 177-217; Stuart Harris, 'Australia in the Global Economy in the 1980s,' in P.J. Boyce and J.R. Angel, eds., *Diplomacy in the Marketplace: Australia in World Affairs, 1981-90* (Melbourne: Longman Cheshire 1992), 30-50.

38 Some have argued that such innovations as the 1983 'Accord' reached between the Australian Labor Party and the peak labour organization, the Australian Council of Trade Unions, on wage demands and the tripartite Economic Summit convened to ratify the Accord were examples of corporatism. Paul Boreham,

'Corporatism,' in Jennett and Stewart, *Hawke and Australian Public Policy*, 42-53; for a more sceptical view, however, see Margaret Gardner, 'Wage Policy,' in ibid., 82-4.

39 Gareth Evans, 'Australia Offshore – Diplomats and Traders,' *Australian Foreign Affairs Record* 59 (November 1988):457.

40 See 'Machinery of Government Changes and the Department of Foreign Affairs and Trade,' *Australian Foreign Affairs Record* 59 (June 1988): 231; organization charts: 232-5.

41 To France and the United States in 1918, China in 1921, Singapore in 1922, and Canada in 1929; a Trade Commissioners Act was adopted in 1933: T.B. Millar, 'Managing the Australian Foreign Affairs Department,' *International Journal* 37 (Summer 1982):442.

42 A Department of External Affairs had been created when the Commonwealth was founded in 1901, but it had what Alan Watt, a former secretary of the department, termed an 'arrested childhood': it was soon absorbed by the Prime Minister's Department and was eventually abolished in 1916. It was not 'founded' again until November 1935. Watt, 'Australia: The Department of Foreign Affairs,' in Steiner, ed., *Times Survey*, 34-45.

43 Evans, 'Australia Offshore – Diplomats and Traders,' 457. Nancy Viviani also uses 'warfare' to describe the relations between the 'political' and 'economic' sides: 'Foreign Economic Policy,' in Jennett and Stewart, eds., *Hawke and Australian Public Policy*, 403.

44 For example, the impact of McEwen on Australian policy following the 1967 devaluation of the pound: H.W. Arndt, 'Foreign Payments,' in Gordon Greenwood and Norman Harper, eds., *Australia in World Affairs* (Melbourne/Vancouver: Australian Institute of International Affairs 1974), 140.

45 The dispute between Alan Renouf, the secretary of the Department of Foreign Affairs, and R.F.X. Connor, the minister for minerals and energy, and Lenox Hewitt, the secretary of the department, led to 'a virtual standstill' in communications between the two departments: Henry S. Albinski, *Australian External Policy Under Labor* (Vancouver: University of British Columbia Press 1977), 295-6.

46 The problem was particularly acute in Britain: Australia House in London 'came to constitute a mini Canberra, with a range of home departments represented by their own people, dealing directly with their opposite numbers in the relevant British ministry and reporting to the departmental home base in Australia.' Millar, 'Managing the Australian Foreign Affairs Department,' 445.

47 For a critique of the report, see Hugh Collins, 'The "Coombs Report": Bureaucracy, Diplomacy and Australian Foreign Policy,' *Australian Outlook* 30 (December 1976):387-413.

48 Watt, 'Australia,' 43-4.

49 See Michael Pusey, *Economic Rationalism in Canberra: A Nation-Building State Changes Its Mind* (Melbourne: Melbourne University Press 1991); for a critique, however, see the views of Des Moore, a former deputy secretary of the treasury: 'Economic Rationalism: Myth or Reality?' *IPA Review* 45 (1992):35-7.

50 Alan Rix, *Coming to Terms: The Politics of Australia's Trade with Japan, 1945-1957* (Sydney: Allen and Unwin 1986).

51 For example, the Garnaut Report's neoclassical economic blueprint for Australia

called for the abolition of all tariffs by 2000. Ross Garnaut, *Australia and the Northeast Asian Ascendency* (Canberra: Australian Government Publishing Service 1989). See, however, Trevor Matthews and John Ravenhill, 'The Economic Challenge: Is Unilateral Free Trade the Answer?' in J.L. Richardson, ed., *Northeast Asian Challenge: Debating the Garnaut Report*, Canberra Studies in World Affairs 27 (Canberra: Australian National University 1991), 68-94.

52 For a detailed account of this reversal, see Capling and Galligan, *Beyond the Protective State*.

53 Until then, all secretaries of the department had been senior career officers from Foreign Affairs, all with overseas experience: Watt, 'Australia,' 38.

54 Viviani, 'Foreign Economic Policy,' 403. Many of these outside experts were economists at the Australian National University.

55 Stuart Harris, 'The Separation of Economics and Politics: A Luxury We Can No Longer Afford,' in Coral Bell, ed., *Academic Studies and International Politics*, Canberra Studies in World Affairs 6 (Canberra 1982).

56 A refined and extended version of this argument was given as the Roy Milne Memorial Lecture delivered in Darwin in August 1985: Stuart Harris, 'The Linking of Politics and Economics in Foreign Policy,' *Australian Outlook: The Australian Journal of International Affairs* 40 (April 1986):5-10.

57 *Australian Foreign Affairs Record* 56 (April 1985):375-6.

58 Department of Foreign Affairs, *Review of Australia's Overseas Representation*, by Stuart Harris (Canberra: Department of Foreign Affairs 1986), xxii.

59 Harris's addresses are reproduced in *Australian Foreign Affairs Record*, vol. 59: 'Australia's Foreign Service in the 1990s' (January 1988), 4-8; 'The Amalgamation of the Department of Foreign Affairs and Trade' (March 1988), 71-4; 'Australian Trade Policy' (May 1988), 195-6. Also Department of Foreign Affairs and Trade, *The 1986 Review of Australia's Overseas Representation Revisited*, by Dr S. Harris (Canberra: Department of Foreign Affairs and Trade 1988), esp. 6-7.

60 Bill Hayden, 'Transforming Australia's Trade,' *Australian Foreign Affairs Record* 59 (March 1988):90-4; Gareth Evans, 'Australia Offshore Diplomats and Traders,' *Australian Foreign Affairs Record* 59 (November 1988):457-9; Senator Gareth Evans, 'Australian Foreign Policy: Priorities in a Changing World,' *Australian Outlook: The Australian Journal of International Affairs* 43 (August 1989):1-15; Gareth Evans and Bruce Grant, *Australia's Foreign Relations in the World of the 1990s* (Melbourne: Melbourne University Press 1991), 40.

61 For a fuller examination of this argument, see Ernie Keenes, 'Rearranging the Deck Chairs: A Political Economy Approach to Foreign Policy Management in Canada,' *Canadian Public Administration* 35 (Autumn 1992):381-401.

62 Stuart Harris, 'Australian Trade Policy,' *Australian Foreign Affairs Record* 59 (May 1988):196.

63 Indeed, a number of Liberal/National members of Parliament criticized DFAT for its preoccupation with multilateral and regional foreign economic diplomacy, suggesting that they were not wedded to the permanency of the merger.

Chapter 3: The Cairns Group

1 Henry Nau, ed., *Domestic Trade Politics and the Uruguay Round* (New York: Columbia University Press 1989); and Gilbert R. Winham, 'The Pre-Negotiation

Phase of the Uruguay Round,' *International Journal* 44 (Spring 1989):280-303.

2 William J. Drake and Kalypso Nicolaïdis, 'Ideas, Interests, and Institutionalization: "Trade in Services" and the Uruguay Round,' *International Organization* 46 (Winter 1992):37-100.

3 Krasner has persuasively argued that a change in the configuration of power was in fact under way in the Tokyo Round: Stephen D. Krasner, 'The Tokyo Round: Particularistic Interests and Prospects for Stability in the Global Trading System,' *International Studies Quarterly* 23 (December 1979):491-531.

4 Winham, 'Pre-Negotiation Phase,' 290; also see Gilbert R. Winham, *The Evolution of International Trade Agreements* (Toronto: University of Toronto Press 1992).

5 Ibid., 286-7.

6 As we noted in the introductory chapter, the nature of this change is much contested: see Robert Keohane, 'The World Political Economy: The Crisis of Embedded Liberalism,' in John Goldthorpe, ed., *Order and Conflict in Contemporary Capitalism* (Oxford: Clarendon 1984), 15-38; Robert Gilpin, *The Political Economy of International Relations* (Princeton, NJ: Princeton University Press 1987); Stephen Gill and David Law, *Global Political Economy* (Baltimore, MD: Johns Hopkins University Press 1988); Bruce Russett, 'The Mysterious Case of Vanishing Hegemony,' *International Organization* 39 (Spring 1985):207-31; Susan Strange, 'The Persistent Myth of Lost Hegemony,' *International Organization* 41 (Autumn 1987):551-74; and Walter Russell-Mead, 'The United States and the World Economy,' *World Policy* 6 (Winter 1988):1-47.

7 John Odell, *U.S. International Monetary Policy* (Princeton, NJ: Princeton University Press 1982); and Fred Block, *The Origins of International Economic Disorder* (Berkeley: University of California Press 1977).

8 Michael C. Webb and Stephen D. Krasner, 'Hegemonic Stability Theory: An Empirical Assessment,' *Review of International Studies* 15 (Spring 1989):183-98.

9 Gilbert R. Winham, *International Trade and the Tokyo Round Negotiation* (Princeton, NJ: Princeton University Press 1986); also Jock A. Finlayson and Mark W. Zacher, 'The GATT and the Regulation of Trade Barriers: Regime Dynamics and Functions,' in Stephen D. Krasner, ed., *International Regimes* (Ithaca: Cornell University Press 1983), 273-314.

10 For a discussion about the early period, see Gerald Maier, 'The Politics of Productivity: Foundations of American International Economic Policy after World War II,' *International Organization* 31 (Summer 1977):607-34.

11 Gilpin, *Political Economy of International Relations*.

12 Paul Krugman, ed., *Strategic Trade Policy and the New International Economics* (Cambridge, MA: MIT Press 1986); Jagdish Bhagwati, *Protectionism* (Cambridge, MA: MIT Press 1988); and R. Ponfret, *Unequal Trade: The Economics of Discriminatory International Trade Policies* (Oxford: Basil Blackwell 1988).

13 Raymond Hopkins and Donald J. Puchala, eds., *The Global Political Economy of Food*, special issue of *International Organization* 32 (Spring 1978).

14 On American agricultural policy in this period, see Ivan Roberts, et al., *U.S. Grain Policies and the World Market* (Canberra: Australian Bureau of Agricultural and Resource Economics 1989), 17-27.

15 D.G. Johnson, 'Food Reserves and International Trade Policy,' in J.S. Hillman and A. Schmitz, eds., *International Trade and Agriculture: Theory and Policy* (Boul-

der: Lynne Reinner 1979), 247; also Andrew F. Cooper, 'The Protein Link: Complexity in the U.S.-EC Agricultural Trade Relationship,' *Journal of European Integration* 11 (Winter 1987):29-45.

16 Fred H. Sanderson, *Japan's Food Prospects and Policies* (Washington: Brookings Institution 1978).

17 *Economist*, 28 December 1974, 44.

18 D.G. Johnson, Z.K. Hemmi, and P. Lardinois, *Agricultural Policy and Trade: Adjusting Domestic Programs in an International Framework – A Report to the Trilateral Commission* (New York: New York University Press 1985).

19 Paul Lewis, 'Europe's Farm Policies Clash with American Export Goals,' *New York Times* (22 February 1983), 1, 5.

20 For example, Elaine Frost, *For Richer, For Poorer: The New U.S.-Japan Relationship* (New York: Council on Foreign Relations 1987); Benjamin J. Cohen, 'An Explosion in the Kitchen? Economic Relations with other Advanced Countries,' in Kenneth Oye, Robert J. Leiber, and Donald Rothchild, eds., *Eagle Defiant: United States Foreign Policy in the 1980s* (Boston: Little, Brown 1983), 105-30; and Stephen D. Krasner, *Asymmetries in Japanese-American Trade: The Case for Specific Reciprocity* (Berkeley: University of California, Institute of International Studies 1987).

21 Clyde Sanger, *Ordering the Oceans: The Making of the Law of the Sea* (Toronto: University of Toronto Press 1987), 52-3, 55.

22 Percentages for other states in the Cairns Group: Australia (39); Brazil (41); Chile (25); Colombia (67); Hungary (23); Indonesia (21); Malaysia (38); New Zealand (68); Philippines (26); Thailand (54); Uruguay (58). Comparable data for Fiji unavailable. All percentages are from 1986, the year the Cairns Group was founded: International Bank for Reconstruction and Development, *World Development Report 1988* (Oxford: Oxford University Press 1988), 222-3.

23 In 1986, Cairns Group members provided 28 per cent of the global market in oilseeds; 30 per cent in cocoa; 31 per cent in barley; 31 per cent in frozen meat; 38 per cent in rice; 39 per cent in animal feedstuffs; 41 per cent in wheat; 46 per cent in cereals; 56 per cent in coffee; 64 per cent in wool; and 69 per cent in rubber. United Nations, *UN International Trade Statistics*, vols. 1 and 2 (New York: United Nations 1988).

24 On the division between food-exporting and food-importing LDCs, see Andrew F. Cooper, 'Exporters Versus Importers: LDCs, Agricultural Trade and the Uruguay Round,' *Intereconomics* 25 (Winter 1990):13-17.

25 Australia, Department of Trade, *Annual Report, 1986-87* (Canberra: Australian Government Publishing Service 1987), 18.

26 John W. Holmes, *The Shaping of Peace: Canada and the Search for World Order, 1943-1957*, vol. 1 (Toronto: University of Toronto Press 1979); Escott Reid, *On Duty: A Canadian at the Making of the United Nations, 1945-1946* (Kent, OH: Kent State University Press 1983).

27 Fox, 'Range of Choice for Middle Powers,' 194.

28 Canada, Parliament, House of Commons, *Debates*, 21 July 1969, 11398.

29 Tom Connors, *The Australian Wheat Industry: Its Economics and Politics* (Armidale, NSW: Gill 1972), 120-1.

30 These differences in style have been explored in Andrew F. Cooper, 'Like-Minded

Nations/Contrasting Diplomatic Styles: Australian and Canadian Approaches to Agricultural Trade,' *Canadian Journal of Political Science* 25 (June 1992):349-79.

31 Alan Renouf, *The Frightened Country* (Melbourne: Macmillan 1979).

32 'Canada Reassured on Crop Disposal,' *New York Times* (17 March 1954), 21.

33 Grace Skogstad, *The Politics of Agricultural Policy-Making in Canada* (Toronto: University of Toronto Press 1987); Theodore H. Cohn, 'Canada and the On-Going Impasse Over Agricultural Protectionism,' in A. Claire Cutler and Mark W. Zacher, eds., *Canadian Foreign Policy and International Economic Regimes* (Vancouver: UBC Press 1992), 62-88.

34 Richard A. Higgott, 'Australia and the New International Division of Labor in the Asia Pacific Region,' in J. Caporaso, ed., *A Changing International Division of Labor* (Boulder: Lynne Reiner 1987), 147-85; Stuart Harris, 'Australia in the Global Economy in the 1980s,' in P.J. Boyce and J.R. Angel, eds., *Diplomacy in the Marketplace: Australia in World Affairs, 1981-90* (Melbourne: Longman Cheshire 1992), 30-50.

35 David Dewitt and John Kirton, *Canada as a Principal Power* (Toronto: John Wiley 1983); Richard A. Higgott, *The Evolving World Economy: Some Alternative Security Questions for Australia* (Canberra: Strategic and Defence Studies Centre, ANU 1989); also Richard A. Higgott, 'The Ascendancy of the Economic Dimension in Australian-American Relations,' in John Ravenhill, ed., *No Longer an American Lake: U.S. Policy in the Pacific in the 1980s* (Berkeley: University of California, Institute of International Studies 1989), 132-68.

36 Peter Field, 'Without the GATT Round: What Else?' in *Recent Trends in World Trade: Implications for Australia* (Sydney: Australian Institute of International Affairs 1987), 1-6.

37 Anthony Hoy, 'Australia Must Attack in Farm War,' *The Australian* (28 May 1986), 9.

38 *Globe and Mail* (28 December 1981); *Australian* (6 April 1983).

39 Paul Hasluck, *Diplomatic Witness: Australian Foreign Affairs, 1941-1947* (Melbourne: Melbourne University Press 1980); Reid, *On Duty*.

40 Australia, Parliament, *Commonwealth Parliament Debates* (hereafter *CPD*), House of Representatives, 10 May 1965, 1635.

41 See, for example, the following studies by the Bureau of Agricultural Economics (Canberra: Australian Government Publishing Service): *Japanese Agricultural Policies: Their Origins, Nature and Effects on Production and Trade* (1981); *Agricultural Policies in the European Community: Their Origins, Nature and Effects on Production and Trade* (1985); *Japanese Beef Policies: Implications for Trade Prices and Market Shares* (1988). Also A. Stoekel, *Intersectoral Effects of the CAP: Growth, Trade and Unemployment* (Canberra: Australian Government Publishing Service 1985); G. Miller, *The Political Economy of International Agricultural Policy Reform* (Canberra: Department of Primary Industry 1986); Centre for International Economics, *The Game Plan: Successful Strategies for Australian Trade* (Canberra: Centre for International Economics 1987).

42 Organization for Economic Cooperation and Development, *National Policies and Agricultural Trade* (Paris: OECD 1987).

43 Amanda Buckley, 'Aust Hopes to Help Found Group to Counter Protectionist Traders,' *Australian Financial Review* (25 August 1986), 10.

44 *Weekend Australian* (16-17 August 1986), 1; Barry Critchley, 'Fair Traders Taking Aim at Agricultural Subsidies' (23 August 1986), 7.

45 Cairns Group, 'Comprehensive Proposal for the Reform of Agriculture,' Chiang Mai, Thailand, 21-23 November 1989.

46 R.A. Byers, Stephen F. Larrabee, and A. Lynch, eds., *Confidence-Building Measures and International Security* (New York: East-West Security Studies Center 1987); cf., however, J. Alford, 'The Usefulness and Limitations of CBMs,' and H.G. Brauch, 'Confidence-Building and Disarmament-Supporting Measures,' both in William Epstein and B. Feld, eds., *New Directions in Disarmament* (New York: Praeger 1981), 133-60.

47 Australia, Department of Foreign Affairs and Trade, *Measuring the Impact of Trade Protection* and *Using the Effective Rate of Assistance in Trade Negotiations* (Canberra: DFAT 1989).

48 *The Age* (26 August 1986); also P. Gallagher, 'Setting the Agenda for Trade Negotiations: Australia and the Cairns Group,' *Australian Outlook* 44 (April 1988):3-8.

49 'Declaration of the Ministerial Meeting of Fair Traders in Agriculture,' Cairns, Qld, 26 August 1986.

50 *CPD*, House of Representatives, 10 October 1986; also Department of Trade, *Transforming Australia's Trade: Annual Report, 1986-87* (Canberra: Australian Government Publishing Service 1987), 17-20.

51 For a discussion of how the Hawke government reversed Australia's historical attachment to protectionism in key manufacturing industries, see Ann Capling and Brian Galligan, *Beyond the Protective State: The Political Economy of Australia's Manufacturing Industry Policy* (Cambridge: Cambridge University Press 1992).

52 Jeffrey J. Schott, ed., *Free Trade Areas and U.S. Trade Policy* (Washington: Institute for International Economics 1989).

53 Cairns Group, 'Declaration of the Ministerial Meeting,' 26 August 1986.

54 Dale E. Hathaway, *Agriculture and the GATT: Rewriting the Rules* (Washington: Institute for International Economics 1988).

55 *United States Journal of Commerce*, 27 May 1987, 10A; also 'Cairns Group Brings Sanity to GATT,' *Agra Europe*, (23 October 1987), 1. For some, the argument that it was the whip of the Cairns Group that secured the agenda would almost certainly be seen as inverted. For example, Winham's discussion of the Punte del Este meeting makes no mention of the Cairns Group: Winham, 'Pre-Negotiation Phase.'

56 Cf. Cairns Group, 'Proposal to the Uruguay Round Negotiating Group on Agriculture,' GATT, UR-87-0322, 10 December 1987; United States, 'Proposal for Negotiations on Agriculture,' GATT, UR-87-0186, 7 July 1987.

57 Personal communication from Peter Field, Australia's chief negotiator at the Uruguay Round, 22 September 1989.

58 *Australian Financial Review* (4 January 1988), 10.

59 Cranford Pratt, *Internationalism Under Strain: The North-South Policies of Canada, the Netherlands, Norway and Sweden* (Toronto: University of Toronto Press 1989), 45-9.

60 Canada, Parliament, House of Commons, *Debates*, 28 April 1987, 5357.

61 Peter Benesh, 'Canada Breaks Free Trade Solidarity with Subsidies,' *The Age* (18

December 1987), 9.

62 On this issue, see, in particular, Cohn, 'Canada and Agricultural Protectionism,' 71-8.

63 Richard H. Snape, 'Should Australia Seek a Trade Agreement with the United States?' Australian Economic Planning Advisory Council/Department of Trade discussion paper 86/01, 1986.

64 The proposal explicitly stated that LDCs 'should be exempted from contributing to the first steps to long-term reform.' Cairns Group, 'Time for Action: A Proposal for a Framework Approach for Agriculture,' GATT, MTN.GNG/NG5/W/69, 13 July 1988, 5; also *Australian Financial Review* (22 May 1988), 6.

65 For example, Bernard Heokan, 'Determining the Need for Issue Linkages in Multilateral Trade Negotiations,' *International Organization* 43 (Autumn 1989):693-714.

66 Michael Aho, 'Foreword,' in Robert L. Paarlberg, *Fixing Farm Trade: Options for the United States* (Cambridge, MA: Ballinger 1988), viii.

67 Canada, 'Proposal by Canada Regarding the Multilateral Trade Negotiations in Agriculture,' GATT, MTN.GNG/NG5/W/19, 20 October 1987, 1.

68 For example, Sarah Sargent, 'Cairns Group May Lose Canada,' *Australian Financial Review* (7 July 1988), 5.

69 Peter Dockrill, 'Aussies Pressed to Cut Subsidies,' *Calgary Herald* (8 July 1988); *Winnipeg Free Press* (23 July 1988), 41.

70 Australia, 'Illustrative Elements of Commitments to Reduce Support as Part of First Steps to Long-Term Reform,' GATT, MTN.GNG/NG5/W/70/REV.1, 13 July 1988.

71 Trade Negotiations Committee, 'Meeting at the Level of High Officials,' GATT, UR-89-0029, MTN-TNC/9, 11 April 1989, 3-7.

72 Field, personal correspondence, 22 September 1989.

73 United States, 'Submission of the United States on Comprehensive Long-Term Agricultural Reform,' GATT, MTN.GNG/NG5/W/118, 28 October 1989.

74 *Australian Financial Review* (23 October 1989), 12.

75 'Preface,' in Nau, ed., *Domestic Trade Politics*, xiii.

76 Gallagher, 'Setting the Agenda,' 5.

77 Capling and Galligan, *Beyond the Protective State*; also Kym Anderson and Ross Garnaut, *Australian Protectionism: Extent, Causes, and Effect* (Sydney: Allen and Unwin 1986).

Chapter 4: Regional Economic Cooperation

1 Robert O. Keohane, *International Institutions and State Power* (Boulder: Westview 1989), 1-20; Beverly Crawford, ed., *The New Europe Asserts Itself: A Changing Role in International Relations*, Research Series, No. 77 (Berkeley: University of California, International and Area Studies 1990); see also the special issues on multilateralism in *International Journal* 44 (Autumn 1990) and *International Organization* 46 (Summer 1992).

2 See J. Bhagwati, *Protectionism* (Cambridge, MA: MIT Press 1988) and R. Pomfret, *Unequal Trade: The Economics of Discriminatory International Trade Policies* (Oxford: Basil Blackwell 1988).

3 Our focus in this chapter is on the states of the Pacific participating in the APEC

meeting in Canberra in 1989: Australia, Brunei Darussalem, Canada, Indonesia, Japan, the Republic of Korea, Malaysia, New Zealand, the Philippines, Singapore, Thailand, and the United States. This limited membership excluded numerous other states – from the micro island states of the South Pacific to the former Soviet Union, the People's Republic of China, the socialist states of East Asia, and Taiwan. In addition, there are states of the Latin American littoral that lay claim to regional inclusion. Despite its initial opposition to the APEC gathering, even the European Community staked a claim to representation based on its trade and investment links with the region.

4 Gerald Segal, *Rethinking the Pacific* (Oxford: Clarendon 1990).
5 L. Krause, 'The Pacific Economy in an Interdependent World: A New Institution for the Pacific Basin,' in J. Crawford and G. Seow, eds., *Pacific Economic Cooperation: Suggestions for Action* (Kuala Lumpur: Heinemann Asia 1981) and S.J. Han, 'Political Conditions of Pacific Regional Cooperation: Theoretical and Practical Considerations,' in H. Soesastro and S.J. Han, eds., *Pacific Economic Cooperation: The Next Phase* (Jakarta: Centre for Strategic and International Studies 1983); Paul M. Evans, 'A North American Perspective on the Pacific in the 1990s: On the Pacific or of the Pacific?' *Australian-Canadian Studies* 10 (1992):61-80, esp. 62-4.
6 James Kurth, 'The Pacific Basin Versus the Atlantic Alliance: Two Paradigms of International Relations,' *Annals of the Academy of Political and Social Science* 505 (September 1989):34-45.
7 Peter Drysdale, *International Economic Pluralism: Economic Policy in East Asia and the Pacific* (Sydney: Allen and Unwin 1988), 204.
8 Peter Drysdale and Ross Garnaut, 'A Pacific Free Trade Area?' Jeffrey J. Schott, ed., *Free Trade Areas and U.S. Trade Policy* (Washington: Institute for International Economics 1989), 219-31.
9 For the gloomier proponents of this position, see: Clyde Prestowitz, Jr., *Trading Places: How We Allowed Japan to Take the Lead* (New York: Basic Books 1988); Karl von Wolferen, *The Enigma of Japanese Power* (New York: Alfred A. Knopf 1989); Shintaro Ishihara and Akio Morita, *The Japan That Can Say No* (unauthorized version). A discussion that puts this polemical literature into a more measured perspective is found in Michael K. Hawes, 'Japan and the International System: Challenge from the Pacific,' *International Journal* 46 (Winter 1990-1):164-82.
10 For example, J.F. Helliwell, 'From Now Until Then: Globalization and Economic Cooperation,' *Canadian Public Policy* 15 (1989):70-8.
11 P.R. Krugman, ed., *Strategic Trade Policy and the New International Economics* (Cambridge, MA: MIT Press 1986); J.D. Richardson, 'The Political Economy of Strategic Trade Policy,' *International Organization* 44 (Winter 1989): 107-35.
12 For the debate over the role of the state in the development process in the Asia-Pacific region, see Robert Wade, *Governing the Market: Economic Theory and the Role of Government in East Asian Industrialization* (Princeton: Princeton University Press 1990); Stephen Haggard, *Pathways from the Periphery: The Politics of Growth in the Newly Industrializing Countries* (Ithaca: Cornell University Press 1990); Frederic C. Deyo, ed., *The Political Economy of the New Asian Industrialism* (Ithaca: Cornell University Press 1987).
13 Stephen D. Krasner, *Asymmetries in Japanese-American Trade: The Case for Specific Reciprocity*, Papers in International Affairs 32 (Berkeley: Institute of International

Studies, University of California 1988).

14 See, for example, David A. Lake, *Power, Protection and Free Trade* (Ithaca: Cornell University Press 1988).

15 John Conybeare, *Trade Wars: The Theory and Practice of International Commercial Policy* (New York: Columbia University Press 1985). On the history of American protectionism, see I.M. Destler, *American Trade Politics* (Washington: Institute for International Economics 1986); P.S. Nivola, 'The New Protectionism: U.S. Trade Policy in Historical Perspective,' *Political Science Quarterly* 100 (Autumn 1986):577-600.

16 Richard A. Higgott, 'From High Politics To Low Politics: The Ascendancy of the Economic Dimension in Australian-American Relations,' in John Ravenhill, ed., *No Longer an American Lake: Alliance Problems in the Pacific* (Berkeley: Institute of International Studies, University of California 1989), 132-68.

17 K. Kojima, *Japan and a Pacific Free Trade Area* (London: Macmillan 1971).

18 Drysdale, *International Economic Pluralism*, 207-09.

19 Ibid., 212-13. But also see Peter Drysdale and H. Patrick, *An Asia-Pacific Regional Economic Organization: An Exploratory Concept Paper* (Washington: United States Congress, Congressional Research Service 1979).

20 Stuart Harris, 'Regional Economic Co-operation: Trading Blocs and Australian Interests,' *Australian Outlook* 43 (August 1989):16-25.

21 Harris, 'Regional Economic Co-operation,' 18.

22 Stephen Gill, *American Hegemony and the Trilateral Commission* (London: Cambridge University Press 1990).

23 Peter Drysdale, 'Growing Pains: New Group Could Calm U.S.-Asian Friction,' *Far Eastern Economic Review* (16 November 1989), 19.

24 Robert J. Hawke, *Regional Co-operation: Challenges for Korea and Australia* (Seoul: Korean Business Association 1989), 4.

25 APEC ministerial meeting, 'Joint Statement,' Canberra, 7 November 1989; Gareth Evans, 'Summary Statement by the Chairman,' Canberra, 7 November 1989. Also Andrew Elek, 'The Evolution of Asia-Pacific Economic Co-operation,' in Australia, Department of Foreign Affairs and Trade, *Backgrounder* 17 (1990): 4-8.

26 See Jennelle Bonnor, 'The Politics of Asia-Pacific Economic Co-operation,' MA thesis, Australian National University, Canberra, 1990, 59-66.

27 *Far Eastern Economic Review,* (16 November 1989), 10.

28 Andrew Elek, 'Pacific Economic Co-operation: Policy Choices for the 1990s,' *Asian Pacific Economic Literature* (May 1992), 1-16.

29 Keohane, *International Institutions*, 1-20.

30 Ibid., 12.

31 Ibid., 119.

32 Ibid., 118.

33 Friedrich Kratochwil and John Ruggie, 'International Organization: A State of the Art or an Art of the State?' *International Organization* 40 (Summer 1986):753-76.

34 Lawrence T. Woods, 'Diplomacy and Non-Governmental International Organization: A Study of the Pacific Economic Co-operation Movement,' PhD thesis, Australian National University, Canberra, 1988.

35 Gareth Evans and Bruce Grant, *Australia's Foreign Relations in the World of the 1990s* (Melbourne: Melbourne University Press 1991), 125-6.

36 Richard A. Higgott, 'The Dilemmas of Interdependence: Australia and the International Division of Labor in the Asia-Pacific Region,' in James Caporaso, ed., *A Changing International Division of Labor: International Political Economy Yearbook*, vol. 2 (Boulder: Lynne Reinner 1987), 147-85.

37 For example, M.K. George, 'Hawke Bids for Stardom,' *South* (November 1989):12-16.

38 For example, a ministerial meeting had been on PECC's own agenda for some time before Hawke raised the idea in Korea in 1989.

39 Robert D. Putnam, 'Diplomacy and Domestic Politics: The Logic of Two-Level Games,' *International Organization* 42 (Spring 1988):427-60.

40 Stuart Harris, 'Economic Change in the International System: Implications for Australia's Prospects,' in Coral Bell, ed., *Agenda for the Nineties: Australian Choices in Foreign and Defence Policy* (Melbourne: Longman Cheshire 1990).

41 H. Hughes, 'Too Little, Too Late: Australia's Future in the Pacific Economy,' *Australian Economic Papers* 27 (1988):187-96.

42 However, it should be noted that at least one analyst has argued that despite the APEC initiative, domestic attitudes in Australia had yet to 'catch up' with the profound changes in the region: see Nancy Viviani, 'The 1990s in the Region – Political/Strategic,' in Stuart Harris and James Cotton, eds., *The End of the Cold War in Northeast Asia* (Melbourne: Longman Cheshire/Boulder: Lynne Reinner 1991), 257.

43 These signals include the publication of a major report on Australia's regional relations: see Ross Garnaut, *Australia and the Northeast Asian Ascendancy* (Canberra: Australian Government Publishing Service 1989).

44 R. Snape, 'Should Australia Seek a Free Trade Agreement with the United States?' *Discussion Paper* 86/01 (Canberra: Economic Planning Advisory Council and Department of Trade 1986).

45 Owen Harries, *Australia's Relations with the Third World* (Canberra: Australian Government Publishing Service 1979), 131-2.

46 James Kurth, 'The United States and the North Pacific,' in Andrew Mack and Paul Keal, eds., *Security and Arms Control in the North Pacific* (Sydney: Allen and Unwin 1988), 27.

47 J. Wanandi, 'The Role of PECC in the 1990s and Pacific Institutions,' *Background Paper*, APEC Ministerial Meeting, Canberra, 5-7 November 1989.

48 James A. Baker 3d, 'Speech to the Asia Society,' New York, 26 June 1989, 2.

49 Richard Stubbs, 'Reluctant Leader, Expectant Followers: Japan and Southeast Asia,' *International Journal* 46 (Autumn 1991):649-67.

50 *Japan Economic Journal* (8 April 1989), 1, 4.

51 T. Nakayama, 'Opening Statement by the Minister for Foreign Affairs,' APEC Ministerial Meeting, Canberra, 5 November 1989.

52 K. Hagegawa and K. Koike, 'Nations Test Waters for Pacific Rim Bloc,' *Japan Economic Journal* (10 June 1989), 9.

53 *Far Eastern Economic Review* (20 July 1989), 10-11.

54 S. Isaka, 'ASEAN Asserts Its Regional Influence at Meeting of New Economic Organization,' *Japan Economic Journal* (18 November 1989), 5.

55 See David Crone, 'The Politics of Emerging Pacific Cooperation,' *Pacific Affairs* 65 (1992):68-83.

56 Christopher Thomas, 'Reflections on the Canada-U.S. Free Trade Agreement in the Context of the Multilateral Trading System,' in A. Claire Cutler and Mark W. Zacher, eds., *Canadian Foreign Policy and International Economic Regimes* (Vancouver: UBC Press 1992), 47-61.

57 Lawrence T. Woods, 'The Business of Canada's Pacific Relations,' *Canadian Journal of Administrative Sciences* 4 (1987):418. Canada, for example, has been an active member of PECC: for an indication of the nature of Canadian economic interest in the Pacific, see Murray G. Smith, ed., *Canada, the Pacific and Global Trade: Proceedings of a Conference* (Halifax: Institute for Research on Public Policy 1989); H. Edward English, *Tomorrow the Pacific* (Toronto: C.D. Howe Institute 1991); Evans, 'A North American Perspective,' 61-80.

58 For example, Jean McCloskey, the assistant under-secretary of state in the Asia and Pacific branch of the Department of External Affairs argued that subregional arrangements such as ASEAN and the Australia New Zealand Closer Economic Relations and Trade Agreement – the CER – could not be extended to the rest of the Pacific for political as well as for economic reasons. McCloskey, 'New Realities in the Pacific: The Political Perspective,' *Behind the Headlines* (Winter 1988-9):10-11.

59 Edith Terry, 'Crosbie Warns Against Trade Bloc Excluding North America,' *Globe and Mail* (27 February 1989), B13; 'Canada Says it Wants Role in Asia Trade Talks,' *Globe and Mail* (9 March 1989), B12.

60 Quoted in Patricia Roy, 'Has Canada Made a Difference? North Pacific Connections: Canada, China, and Japan,' in John English and Norman Hillmer, eds., *Making a Difference? Canada's Foreign Policy in a Changing World Order* (Toronto: Lester Publishing 1992), 150.

61 Canada, External Affairs and International Trade Canada, *Canadian Foreign Policy Series*, 89/14, speech by Clark to the Corporate Higher Education Forum, Edmonton, AB, 16 May 1989, 2.

62 John Crosbie, 'Statement to OECD Ministerial Meeting: Canadian Minister of International Trade,' *Canadian Foreign Policy Series*, 89/20, 31 May 1989.

63 External Affairs and International Trade, *Canadian Foreign Policy Series*, 89/20, 31 May 1989, 4.

64 Douglas A. Ross, 'Canadian Foreign Policy and the Pacific Rim: From National Security Anxiety to Creative Economic Co-operation,' in F. Quei Quo, ed., *Politics of the Pacific Rim: Perspectives on the 1980s* (Burnaby, BC: Simon Fraser University Publications 1982), 28.

65 Stephen J. Randall, 'Canada, the United States and Mexico: The Development of Trilateralism,' *Frontera Norte* 3 (julio-diciembre 1991):121-36.

66 Anne Kreuger, 'The Effects of Regional Trade Blocs on World Trade,' in John Higley, Robert Cushing, and Michael Sutton, eds., *NAFTA, the Pacific, and Australia/New Zealand* (Austin, TX: University of Texas Press 1993). On Australian reactions to NAFTA, see Richard Snape, Jan Adams, and David Morgan, *Regional Trade Agreements: Implications and Options for Australia*, 2 vols. (Melbourne: Monash University 1992).

67 J.L. Granatstein and Robert Bothwell, *Pirouette: Pierre Trudeau and Canadian*

Foreign Policy (Toronto: University of Toronto Press 1990), 269; for a discussion of economic linkages between the two countries, see Maxwell A. Cameron, Lorraine Eden, and Maureen Appel Molot, 'North American Free Trade: Co-operation and Conflict in Canada-Mexico Relations,' in Fen Osler Hampson and Christopher J. Maule, eds., *Canada Among Nations, 1992-93: A New World Order* (Ottawa: Carleton University Press 1992), 175-9.

68 Robert Lindsey, 'Reagan, Entering Presidency Race, Calls for North American "Accord,"' *New York Times* (14 November 1979); Alan Richman, '2 Nations are Cool to Reagan Plan,' *New York Times* (15 November 1979).

69 Michael Hart, *A North American Free Trade Agreement: The Strategic Implications for Canada* (Ottawa: Centre for Trade Policy 1990).

70 Richard Lipsey, 'Canada at the U.S.-Mexico Trade Dance: Wallflower or Partner?' *C.D. Howe Institute Commentary* 20 (Toronto: C.D. Howe Institute 1990); Ronald J. Wonnacott, 'U.S. Hub-and-Spoke Bilaterals and the Multilateral Trading System,' *C.D. Howe Institute Commentary* 23 (Toronto: C.D. Howe Institute October 1990).

71 Lorraine Eden and Maureen Appel Molot, 'The View from the Spokes: Canada and Mexico Face the U.S.,' in Stephen J. Randall, H. Konrad, and S. Silverman, eds., *The Challenge of North American Integration* (Calgary: University of Calgary Press 1993).

72 Quoted in Maxwell Cameron, 'Canada and Latin America,' in Fen Osler Hampson and Christopher J. Maule, eds., *After the Cold War: Canada Among Nations, 1990-91* (Ottawa: Carleton University Press), 113.

73 Sylvia Ostry, 'The NAFTA: Its International Economic Background,' in Stephen J. Randall et al., eds., *North America Without Borders? Integrating Canada, the United States and Mexico* (Calgary: University of Calgary Press 1992), 28.

74 'Trying to Avoid a Mexican Standoff,' *Globe and Mail* (20 July 1992).

75 A particularly narrow interpretation of rules of origin applied to Hondas manufactured in Alliston, Ontario, led, in the fall of 1991 (at the U.S. border), to Canadian allegations of unfair harassment concerning these products.

76 Clyde Graham, 'Canada Resists U.S. Move to Re-Open Free-Trade Pact to admit Latin America,' *Ottawa Citizen* (8 May 1992).

77 Michael Hart, 'Canada Discovers Its Vocation as a Nation of the Americas,' in Hampson and Maule, eds., *Canada Among Nations, 1990-91*, 83-107.

78 Gilbert R. Winham, 'Canada, GATT, and the World Trading System,' in Hampson and Maule, eds., *Canada Among Nations, 1992-93*, 126.

79 Stephen Mills, 'APEC Warns U.S. Not to Turn NAFTA into Trade Fortress,' *Australian Financial Review* (11 September 1992).

80 See, for example, Robert Gilpin, *The Political Economy of International Relations* (Princeton: Princeton University Press 1987), 336-9.

81 Peter Drysdale, 'Change and Response in Japan's International Economic Policy,' *Workshop on Change in Northeast Asia: Implications for the 1990s* (Canberra: Northeast Asia Research Programme, Australian National University 1990), 26.

82 Ibid., 29.

83 Ken Calder, 'Japanese Foreign Economic Policy Formation: Explaining the Reactive State,' *World Politics* 40 (July 1989):517-41.

84 Samuel P. Huntington, 'The U.S. – Decline or Renewal?' *Foreign Affairs* 67 (Spring

1989):76-96.
85 Nye, *Bound to Lead*, 182-8; Raymond Vernon and Debora Spar, *Beyond Globalism: Remaking American Foreign Economic Policy* (New York: Free Press 1989), 4.
86 David Abshire, 'The Nature of American Global Economic Leadership in the 1990s,' in William Brock and Richard Hormats, *The Global Economy: America's Role in the Decade Ahead* (New York: W.W. Norton for the American Assembly 1990), 175.
87 Ibid., 178.
88 Young, 'Political Leadership,' 10.
89 Chalmers Johnson, 'History Restarted: Japanese-American Relations at the End of the Century,' in Richard A. Higgott, Richard Leaver, and John Ravenhill, *Pacific Economic Relations in the 1990s: Co-operation or Conflict?* (Sydney: Allen and Unwin 1992).
90 Richard Leaver, 'The Future of Northeast Asian Regional Growth: The Regionalist Alternative,' in J.L. Richardson, ed., *Northeast Asian Challenge: Debating the Garnaut Report*, Canberra Studies in World Affairs, No. 27 (Canberra: Australian National University 1991), 66.

Chapter 5: The Gulf Conflict

1 For example, standing instructions to Canadian delegations to the United Nations in 1946 noted that: 'Experience has demonstrated that, in general, the interests of the middle powers coincide more with the general interest than do the interests of the small powers or of the great powers.' Cited in Bernard Wood, *The Middle Powers and the General Interest*, no. 1 in the series *Middle Powers in the International System* (Ottawa: North-South Institute 1988), iii.
2 This argument is put most elegantly by John W. Holmes, 'Most Safely in the Middle,' *International Journal* 39 (Spring 1984):366-88; reprinted in J.L. Granatstein, *Towards a New World Order? Readings in the History of Canadian Foreign Policy* (Toronto: Copp Clark Pitman 1992), 90-105.
3 Carsten Holbraad, *Middle Powers in International Politics* (London: Macmillan 1984); Annette Baker Fox, *The Politics of Attraction: Four Middle Powers and the United States* (Columbia University Press 1977), ch. 5.
4 For discussions of these different issues, see Clyde Sanger, *Ordering the Oceans: The Making of the Law of the Sea* (Toronto: University of Toronto Press 1987), 23-39; Elizabeth Riddell-Dixon, *Canada and the International Seabed: Domestic Interests and External Constraints* (Kingston and Montreal: McGill-Queen's University Press 1989), 50-1; Asbjørn Løvbræk, 'International Reform and the Like-Minded Countries in the North-South Dialogue, 1975-1985,' in Cranford Pratt, ed., *Middle Power Internationalism: The North-South Dimension* (Kingston and Montreal: McGill-Queen's University Press 1990), 25-68; Margaret Doxey, 'Evolution and Adaptation in the Modern Commonwealth,' *International Journal* 45 (Autumn 1990):889-912; Louis A. Delvoie, 'The Commonwealth in Canadian Foreign Policy,' *The Round Table* 310 (1989):137-43.
5 Margaret Doxey, 'Constructive Internationalism: A Continuing Theme in Canadian Foreign Policy,' *The Round Table* 311 (1989):288-304.
6 Accounts of the five and a half months between the invasion and the use of force against Iraq by the coalition may be found in: Jean Edward Smith, *George Bush's*

War (New York: Henry Holt 1992); Bob Woodward, *The Commanders* (New York: Simon and Schuster 1991), pt. 2, 197ff; Tom Mathews, 'The Road to War,' *Newsweek* (28 January 1991), 54-65.

7 Quoted in Woodward, *The Commanders*, 260. For Thatcher's role, see Mathews, 'Road to War,' 58; Craig R. Whitney, 'The Empire Strikes Back,' *New York Times Magazine* (10 March 1991), 34.

8 For a discussion of American coalition-building diplomacy, see Andrew Fenton Cooper, Richard A. Higgott, and Kim Richard Nossal, 'Bound to Follow? Leadership and Followership in the Gulf Conflict,' *Political Science Quarterly* 106 (Fall 1991):391-410.

9 Woodward, *The Commanders*, 231-73, and Mathews, 'Road to War,' 58-9, describe the intricate process by which the United States and Saudi Arabia came to an agreement on the temporary basing of foreign troops on Saudi territory.

10 *New York Times* (9 August 1990), A15.

11 *The Australian* (3 August 1990); *Globe and Mail* (3 August 1990).

12 *Globe and Mail* (4 August 1990).

13 *The Age* (7 August 1990).

14 Explicit promises of support for whatever UN sanctions were imposed in the *Weekend Australian* (4-5 August 1990); *The Age* (6 August 1990); and the *Globe and Mail* (4 August 1990). Chapter VII of the UN Charter (arts. 39-51) outlines what steps may be taken by the UN 'with respect to threats to the peace, breaches of the peace, and acts of aggression.'

15 *Weekend Australian* (4-5 August 1990); *Globe and Mail* (8 August 1990).

16 Press release, cited in the *Globe and Mail* (6 August 1990).

17 *The Age* (6 August 1990).

18 See the account by Greg Sheridan in the *The Australian* (10 August 1990).

19 Quoted in *Australian Financial Review* (6 August 1990).

20 *DFAT Monthly Record* 61 (August 1990):564-5.

21 *The Age* (7 August 1990).

22 *Australian Financial Review* (8 August 1990); *Globe and Mail* (8 August 1990).

23 The language in paragraph 3(c) of Resolution 661 was somewhat ambiguous on the issue of food, asserting that all states should halt the sale or supply of all goods, 'but not including supplies intended strictly for medical purposes and, in humanitarian circumstances, foodstuffs.'

24 For the comments of officials of the Canadian Wheat Board, see the *Globe and Mail* (8 August 1990). The Australian Wheat Board had sent an official from its Melbourne headquarters to argue against including food in the Australian sanctions: *The Age* (7 August 1990); *Australian Financial Review* (8 August 1990).

25 *The Age* (9 August 1990).

26 Quoted in the *Sydney Morning Herald* (1 September 1990).

27 Michelle Grattan, *The Age* (11 August 1990); Laurie Oakes, the *Bulletin* (21 August 1990); and Paul Grigson, the *Sydney Morning Herald* (1 September 1990).

28 Mark Baker, 'The Imperious Hawke Style,' *The Age* (7 September 1990).

29 *The Age* (10 August 1990).

30 Indeed, according to Grigson's account of this meeting, Keating was exceedingly 'gung ho' about a naval commitment against Saddam Hussein, whom he apparently described as a 'turd.'

31 *Bulletin* (21 August 1990).
32 Clause 15 of the ALP's international relations policy asserts that the ALP will 'not commit Australian forces for combat overseas unless there is a clear and imminent threat to Australian security and lives.'
33 For accounts, see the *Sydney Morning Herald* (21 August 1990); *The Australian*, the *Australian Financial Review* (22 August 1990); and the *Canberra Times* (23 August 1990).
34 *Bulletin*, 21 August 1990.
35 *Globe and Mail* (9 August 1990) and (28 August 1990).
36 *Sydney Morning Herald* (1 September 1990); *Globe and Mail* (9 August 1990) and (28 August 1990).
37 And, according to Grigson's account, to urge him to make a similar commitment. In his own reference to this phone call – on ABC's *7:30 Report* on 10 August – Hawke indicated only that Mulroney told him that a Canadian decision was expected soon. *Canberra Times* (11 August 1990).
38 See, for example, Clark's comments on 3 August ruling out the use of force by Canada in the *Globe and Mail* (4 August 1990).
39 At separate news conferences on 8 August, both Mulroney and Clark asserted that no forces had been requested or volunteered: *Globe and Mail* (9 August 1990).
40 *Globe and Mail* (24 August 1990); Charlotte Gray, 'War Games,' *Saturday Night* (March 1991), 10; Geoffrey Stevens, 'How We Entered War: Decision Was All Up To Prime Minister,' *Toronto Star* (20 January 1991).
41 *Globe and Mail* (11 August 1990); *Economist* (22 September 1990), 45-6.
42 *Toronto Star* and *Globe and Mail* (11 August 1990).
43 Martin Rudner, 'Canada, the Gulf Crisis and Collective Security,' in Fen Osler Hampson and Christopher J. Maule, eds., *Canada Among Nations 1990-91: After the Cold War* (Ottawa: Carleton University Press 1991), 268.
44 Order-in-Council PC1990-1995, 15 September 1990.
45 *Globe and Mail* (13 September 1990); Canada, Parliament, House of Commons, *Debates*, 24 September 1990, 13218.
46 The original Pentagon plan agreed to by Bush called for 200,000 to 250,000 troops to be deployed over 17 weeks. However, the exact number was purposely fudged: John Sununu, Bush's chief of staff, put out the figure of 50,000 to the media. An official at the Pentagon later leaked the real figure to the Associated Press. Woodward, *The Commanders*, 249, 279. Despite the AP story, however, the original figure of 50,000 stuck in public perceptions, making the arrival of some 100,000 troops by September seem to be a doubling of the original commitment.
47 By contrast, having a naval task force lingering for months on the high seas in the Gulf, enforcing a blockade and waiting for sanctions to 'work,' involved few of the political costs and a fraction of the financial costs.
48 This decision was taken without the prior knowledge of the Saudi government. Only after the decision was made was Baker sent to speak to key allies in Europe and the Middle East. See Woodward, *The Commanders*, 321. Woodward also notes (312-13, 322) that the decision was taken without the participation of Colin Powell, chairman of the Joint Chiefs of Staff. Sam Nunn, chairman of the Senate Armed Services Committee, was also reported to be unhappy about being informed rather than consulted: Thomas L. Friedman and Patrick E. Tyler, 'The

Path to War: Bush's Crucial Decisions,' *New York Times* (3 March 1991), 1, 12.

49 Resolution 678 had indicated a deadline for withdrawal – 'on or before 15 January' – but was silent as to in which time zone the resolution became effective. The determination that the resolution meant midnight Eastern Standard Time (rather than midnight Kuwait time, eight hours earlier) was made by American, not UN, officials. See *Globe and Mail* (12 January 1991).

50 For prime ministerial statements, see, in Australia: Australia, Parliament, *Commonwealth Parliamentary Debates* (hereafter *CPD*), Representatives, 4 December 1990, 4319-25; 21 January 1991, 3-9; 22 January 1991, 266-8. In Canada: House of Commons, *Debates*: 29 November 1990, 15958-61; 15 January 1991, 16984-91.

51 For a comparison of the Gulf debate in both countries, see Kim Richard Nossal, 'Quantum Leaping: The Gulf Debate in Australia and Canada,' in Michael McKinley, ed., *Allied Perspectives on the Gulf Conflict* (Sydney: Allen and Unwin 1993, forthcoming); also Gregory Wirick, 'Canada, Peacekeeping and the United Nations,' in Fen Osler Hampson and Christopher J. Maule, eds., *Canada Among Nations, 1992-93: A New World Order?* (Ottawa: Carleton University Press 1992), 96-100.

52 Because under Australian parliamentary rules a formal division requires the call of two members, motions on the Gulf never came to a vote in the House; Mack had to invoke a special provision in the standing orders to have his opposition registered in *Hansard*.

53 J.L. Granatstein, 'Peacekeeping: Did Canada Make a Difference? And What Difference Did Peacekeeping Make to Canada?,' in John English and Norman Hillmer, eds., *Making a Difference? Canada's Foreign Policy in a Changing World Order* (Toronto: Lester Publishing 1992), 233.

54 House of Commons, *Debates*, 16 January 1991, 17131-5.

55 House of Commons, *Debates*, 16 January 1991, 17165-6.

56 House of Commons, *Debates*, 16 January 1991, 17166-7.

57 See poll results reported in the *Weekend Australian* (1-2 September 1990); *The Age* (10 September 1990); the *Globe and Mail* (30 October 1990); the *PAI Report* (November 1990), 31; the *Sydney Morning Herald* (8 December 1990); and the Angus Reid-Southam News poll, 17-22 December 1990. It should be noted that by December, fully 80 per cent of Australians supported Canberra's Gulf policies.

58 *The Australian* (12 September 1990); *Australian Financial Review* (14 September 1990).

59 *DFAT Monthly Record* (September 1990), 665.

60 *CPD*, Representatives, 4 December 1990, 4322.

61 *Pacific Research* 4 (February 1991):29-30.

62 *Globe and Mail* (15 September 1990).

63 *Globe and Mail* (12 January 1991).

64 *Globe and Mail* (21 February 1991).

65 See, for example, Reg Whitaker, 'Prisoners of the American Dream: Canada, the Gulf, and the New World Order,' *Studies in Political Economy* 35 (Summer 1991):13-27; Richard Leaver, 'The Costs of Australia "Being Seen to Be There,"' *Pacific Research* 3 (November 1990):7.

66 For one explanation of Canadian involvement that seems overly monocausal,

see John Kirton, 'Liberating Kuwait: Canada and the Persian Gulf War, 1990-91,' in Don Munton and John Kirton, eds., *Canadian Foreign Policy: Selected Cases* (Scarborough: Prentice-Hall 1992), esp. 383.

67 Many critics in Australia and Canada argued that because their governments had not condemned all cases of invasion (Indonesia for invading East Timor or the United States for invading Grenada and Panama), their expressions of concern for Kuwait's territorial integrity had to be disingenuous. However, while their public reactions to invasions will always be tempered by political considerations and the nuances of context, secondary states will nonetheless always experience private concern at violations of territorial integrity.

68 Indeed, T.B. Millar suggests that the roots of this fear go much deeper: he notes that a fear of invasion by neighbours – 'pervasive in Britain since 1066' – was brought to Australia by European settlers. See *Australia in Peace and War*, 2nd edition (Canberra: Australian National University Press 1991), 376. For how this fear was reflected in defence policy in the 1980s, see Graeme Cheeseman, 'Defence Policy and Organisation: The Search for Self-Reliance,' in P.J. Boyce and J.R. Angel, eds., *Diplomacy in the Marketplace: Australia in World Affairs, 1981-90* (Melbourne: Longman Cheshire 1992), 63-81.

69 As Eric Fitzgibbon (ALP: Hunter, NSW), for example, put it, 'I am glad that my Returned Services League mates and all those who sacrificed their lives for their country did not merely sit around Australia's coastline singing "Give peace a chance" in 1942.' *CPD*, Representatives, 21 January 1991, 89.

70 See J. Mohan Malik, *The Gulf War: Australia's Role and Asian-Pacific Responses*, Canberra Papers on Strategy and Defence 90 (Canberra: Strategic and Defence Studies Centre, Australian National University 1992).

71 See the accounts in Denis Stairs, *The Diplomacy of Constraint: Canada, the Korean War, and the United States* (Toronto: University of Toronto Press 1974); Douglas A. Ross, *In the Interests of Peace: Canada and Vietnam, 1954-73* (Toronto: University of Toronto Press 1984).

72 Gray, 'War Games,' 13; *Globe and Mail* (14 August 1990).

73 For example, Stephen Lewis, a former permanent representative at the UN, has suggested that 'to an extraordinary degree, Canadian foreign policy is driven by the prime minister's friendships.' Cited in Gray, 'War Games,' 13. Gray herself noted that Mulroney was eager to please 'his pal in the White House.' In Australia, such critics as former ALP minister Tom Uren criticized Hawke for taking telephone calls from his 'mate George': *Sunday Herald* (12 August 1990); Robert Springborg likened Hawke's friendship with Bush to Sir Robert Menzies's friendship with Anthony Eden, and suggested that Hawke went further in his response to Bush's Gulf policy than Menzies went in response to Eden's Suez policy in 1956: the *Herald* (13 August 1990). Even *The Age*, which supported the deployment, editorialized that Hawke seemed 'just too anxious to please in responding to his friends' Bush and Baker: *The Age* (19 August 1990). Also see the comments of Janet Powell, leader of the Australian Democrats in the Senate: *CPD*, Senate, 21 January 1991, 18.

74 As Leaver put it, Hawke chose 'good American citizenship' over 'good international citizenship': '"Being Seen to Be There,"' 7. In Canada, a number of critics chastised Mulroney for his 'ready, aye, ready' response to Bush: House of

Commons, *Debates*, 24 September 1990, 14301, 14375; also Gray, 'War Games,'
11. The negative connotation of the phrase comes from a speech made by the
leader of the opposition Conservatives, Arthur Meighen, during the Chanak
crisis of 1922. He argued that Canada should have responded 'Ready, aye, ready'
to a British request to send troops to Gallipoli. Since then, like 'All the way with
LBJ' in Australia, 'Ready, aye, ready' has become Canadian code to describe
unwarranted subservience to the 'imperial' powers – Britain, and after 1945, the
United States.

75 For example, another erstwhile colleague of Hawke's, former deputy prime
minister Jim Cairns, sneered publicly at prime ministers with 'a need to please
big men and big nations': *The Australian* (20 August 1990). The *Canberra Times*
(18 September 1990) likened Hawke to a small boy in a schoolyard 'hanging
around the larger kids for kudos.' A comparable analysis of Brian Mulroney was
advanced by Geoffrey Stevens, a senior columnist with the *Toronto Star* (26
August 1990).

76 Samples of the argument that Australian and Canadian policy was the result of
a prime minister who was a toady, a lap dog, or simply servile would include,
for Australia: Manning Clark in *Sunday Age* (19 August 1990); 2GB radio personality Mike Carlton, cited in *Sunday Age* (19 August 1990); Brian Toohey's column,
Sunday Herald (26 August 1990); Arab-Australians cited in the *Bulletin* (28 August
1990); and the editorial in the *Advertiser* (13 September 1990). In Canada, K.B.
Sayeed of Queen's University, cited in the *Globe and Mail* (18 August 1990);
Gerald Caplan, an NDP columnist, the *Toronto Star* (13 January 1991); and
Geoffrey Stevens, the *Toronto Star* (31 March 1991). For MPs' comments, House
of Commons, *Debates*: Svend J. Robinson (NDP: Burnaby-Kingsway), 17 October
1990, 13211; Jesse Flis (Lib: Parkdale-High Park), 17 October 1990, 14311; Joseph
Volpe (Lib: Eglinton-Lawrence), 18 October 1990, 14397.

77 *Sunday Age* (19 August 1990). Mulroney was less colourful but no less dismissive.
Calling the charge that Canada was merely toadying to the United States 'the
most tired and threadbare accusation of all,' Mulroney reminded the House that
Pearson had written in his memoirs that: 'A sure way to get applause and support
at home is to exploit [Canadians'] anxieties and exaggerate [their] suspicions
over United States power and policies.' House of Commons, *Debates*, 15 January
1991, 16989.

78 *Toronto Star* and *Globe and Mail* (11 August 1990).

79 Australia, Department of Foreign Affairs and Trade, *Backgrounder* 1:25 (21 September 1990), 7.

80 *Globe and Mail* (13 November 1990).

81 *CPD*, Representatives, 4 December 1990, 4323.

82 *The Age* (3 December 1990); *Sydney Morning Herald* (7 December 1990).

83 Australia, Department of Foreign Affairs and Trade, *Backgrounder* 1:25 (21 September 1990), 4.

84 *Globe and Mail* (27 October 1990).

Chapter 6: The Widening Global Agenda

1 Fred Halliday, 'International Relations: Is There a New Agenda?' *Millennium* 20
(Spring 1991):57-72; and Barry Buzan, *People States and Fear: An Agenda for*

International Security Studies in the Post Cold War Era, 2nd edition (London: Harvester Wheatsheaf 1991).

2 For a discussion of 'niche diplomacy,' see Gareth Evans and Bruce Grant, *Australia's Foreign Relations in the World of the 1990s* (Melbourne: Melbourne University Press 1991), 323; also see above, chapter 1.

3 The members of the Australia Group include: Australia, Austria, Belgium, Canada, Denmark, Finland, France, Germany, Greece, Ireland, Italy, Japan, Luxembourg, Netherlands, New Zealand, Norway, Portugal, Spain, Sweden, Switzerland, the United Kingdom, and the United States.

4 Australia, Department of Foreign Affairs and Trade, *Final Record: Government Industry Conference Against Chemical Weapons*, Canberra, September 1989.

5 Notably Brazil, Egypt, Germany, India, Japan, the Netherlands, Norway, Sweden, the Soviet Union, and the United States: Evans and Grant, *Australia's Foreign Relations*, 323.

6 Bronwyn Young, 'Hopes High for Chemical Weapons Ban,' *Australian Financial Review* (19 September 1989), 13.

7 Martine Letts, 'The Year of the CWC?' *Pacific Research* 5 (August 1992):6-9.

8 Richard Butler, 'Australia and Disarmament,' in Desmond Ball, ed., *Australia and the World: Prologue and Prospect* (Canberra: Australian National University, Strategic and Defence Studies Centre 1990).

9 *Pacific Research* (May 1991):23.

10 Mary Louise O'Callaghan, 'Hawke Faces S. Pacific Row over Weapons,' *The Age* (28 July 1990), 9. It should be noted that the JACADS operation shut down temporarily in February 1991 because of mechanical problems. *Pacific Research* (May 1991):25.

11 *Globe and Mail* (14 February 1990), A3.

12 Iain Hunter, 'Open Skies: Canada Takes a Leading Role in Reviving an Old Concept,' *Ottawa Citizen* (20 January 1990); *Le Devoir* (29 January 1990).

13 Alan Ferguson, '34 States Back Canada's Arms Control Plan,' *Toronto Star* (21 June 1991).

14 John Hay, *Ottawa Citizen* (13 February 1991), cited in Gregory Wirick, 'Canada, Peacekeeping and the United Nations,' in Fen Osler Hampson and Christopher J. Maule, eds., *Canada Among Nations, 1992-93: A New World Order?* (Ottawa: Carleton University Press 1992), 98-9.

15 John Cruickshank, 'Not Just Two Dudes on 'Ludes,' *Globe and Mail* (5 April 1991).

16 For a discussion of this tradition see Richard Higgott and Jim George, 'Tradition and Change in Australia's International Relations,' *International Political Science Review* 11 (1990):423-38.

17 The most forceful statement of this position is to be found in Ross Garnaut, *Australia and the Northeast Asian Ascendency* (Canberra: Australian Government Publishing Service 1989).

18 Speech by Bob Hawke, Washington Press Club, Washington, 15 June 1983.

19 Gareth Evans, cited in Mark Metherell, 'Flight Path to Cambodian Peace,' *The Age* (18 January 1990), 13.

20 Australia, Department of Foreign Affairs and Trade, *Cambodia: An Australian Peace Proposal* (Canberra: Australian Government Publishing Service 1990). Also Bronwyn Young 'Australia Prepares Major Paper for Cambodia Talks,' *Australian*

Financial Review (13 February 1990).

21 Metherell, 'Flight Path to Cambodian Peace,' *The Age* (18 January 1990), 13.

22 Lindsay Murdoch, 'ASEAN to Support Cambodia's New Council,' *Sydney Morning Herald* (20 July 1991).

23 Bill Hayden, 'Security and Arms Control in the North Pacific,' in Andrew Mack and Paul Keal, eds., *Security and Arms Control in the North Pacific* (Sydney: Allen and Unwin 1988).

24 Innovative work on these questions in Australia was first undertaken by the Peace Research Centre at the Australian National University. See in particular the working papers by Trevor Findlay: *North Pacific Confidence-Building: The Helsinki/Stockholm Model* (1988) and *Asia-Pacific CSBMs: A Prospectus* (1990). Findlay's ideas caught the attention of the policymaking community in Canberra more quickly than did the work of the mainstream security studies community, such as Desmond Ball's study, *Building Blocks for Regional Security: An Australian Perspective on Confidence and Security Building Measures in the Asia-Pacific Region*, Canberra Papers on Strategy and Defence No. 83 (Canberra: Strategic and Defence Studies Centre, ANU 1991).

25 Gareth Evans, *The Asia-Pacific and the Global Challenge* (Tokyo: Trilateral Commission 1991), 6.

26 Stuart Harris, *Security Issues in Northeast Asia: Strategic Studies in a Changing World* (Canberra: Strategic and Defence Studies Centre Conference 1991, mimeo), 19.

27 The preferred analogy of James Baker, the United States secretary of state, was of a fan, with the base being the United States and the bilateral spokes being the individual Asian states. James Baker, 'America in Asia: Emerging Architecture for a Pacific Community,' *Foreign Affairs* 70 (Winter 1991-2):4-6.

28 And, as Andrew Mack noted, the United States Navy persistently resisted naval arms control on the grounds that such agreements could create 'dangerous precedents' that might impede United States naval operations and, hence, affect deterrence. Andrew Mack, *Naval Arms Control and Confidence-Building for Northeast Asian Waters*, North Pacific Cooperative Security Dialogue Working Paper 13 (August 1992), 15, fn. 40.

29 For a critique of this maxim in the context of Asia-Pacific, see Andrew Mack, *After the Cold War and the Gulf War: Prospects for Security in the Asia-Pacific*, Department of International Relations, Australian National University Working Paper, (1992).

30 *Australian* (24 April 1991), 1-2.

31 Indeed, one analyst has suggested that Russia may emerge with 'a completely new role to play' by the year 2000: Vladimir I. Ivanov, *Emerging Asian-Pacific Multilateralism: Its Impact on Regional Development and Stability Beyond the Cold War*, North Pacific Cooperative Security Dialogue Working Paper No. 6 (February 1992).

32 For example, Gareth Evans, *Australia's Regional Security: A Ministerial Statement* (Canberra: Department of Foreign Affairs and Trade 1989); and Garnaut, *Northeast Asian Ascendency*, 159.

33 Canada, Secretary of State for External Affairs, *Statement 90/40*, 17 July 1990; *Globe and Mail* (24 July 1990).

34 Brian L. Job, *Canadian Interests and Perspectives Regarding the Emerging Pacific*

Security Order, North Pacific Co-operative Security Dialogue Working Paper No. 2 (1991), 13.

35 Job, *Canadian Interests*, 12, esp. fn. 3.

36 Hiroshi Kitamura, 'Asia-Pacific Cooperation in the 1990s: Opportunities and Challenges,' speech to the Conference on the United States, Japan and Canada: The Political Economy of System Change, Queen's University, Kingston, 10 October 1990.

37 David Lague, 'U.S. Reverses Stance on Regional Security,' *Australian Financial Review* (23 July 1991), 3.

38 For a more detailed discussion of Canada's diplomacy in this period, see Margaret Doxey, 'Constructive Internationalism: A Continuing Theme in Canadian Foreign Policy,' *The Round Table* 31 (July 1989):288-304.

39 For example, Robert O. Matthews and Cranford Pratt, eds., *Human Rights in Canadian Foreign Policy* (Montreal and Kingston: McGill-Queen's University Press 1988).

40 On Diefenbaker, see Frank R. Hayes, 'South Africa's Departure from the Commonwealth, 1960-61' *International History Review* 2 (July 1980):453-84. On Trudeau, see Clarence G. Redekop, 'Trudeau at Singapore: The Commonwealth and Arms Sales to South Africa,' in Kim Richard Nossal, ed., *An Acceptance of Paradox: Essays on Canadian Diplomacy in Honour of John W. Holmes* (Toronto: Canadian Institute of International Affairs 1982), 174-95; and J.L. Granatstein and Robert Bothwell, *Pirouette: Pierre Trudeau and Canadian Foreign Policy* (Toronto: University of Toronto Press 1990), 280-2. On Clark at Lusaka, see Margaret Doxey, 'Canada and the Evolution of the Modern Commonwealth,' *Behind the Headlines* 40 (November 1982):1-20, esp. n. 17.

41 Clarence G. Redekop, 'The Mulroney Government and South Africa: Constructive Disengagement,' *Behind the Headlines* 44 (December 1986):1-16; Linda Freeman, 'What's Right with Mulroney? Canada and Sanctions, 1986,' *Southern Africa Report* (October 1986), 3.

42 Cited in Chris Brown, 'Canada and Southern Africa: Autonomy, Image and Capacity in Foreign Policy,' in Maureen Appel Molot and Fen Osler Hampson, eds., *Canada Among Nations – 1989* (Ottawa: Carleton University Press 1990), 207.

43 D. Braid, 'Mulroney Inheriting Commonwealth Leadership,' *Montreal Gazette* (7 August 1986), B3.

44 Kim Richard Nossal, 'Canadian Sanctions Against South Africa: Explaining the Mulroney Initiatives, 1985-86,' *Journal of Canadian Studies* 25 (Winter 1990-1):17-33.

45 For example, the other G-7 states refused a Canadian suggestion to incorporate a statement on South Africa into the final communique of the Venice Summit in June 1987.

46 Bernard Wood, 'Canada and Southern Africa: A Return to Middle Power Activism,' *The Round Table* 315 (1990):280-90.

47 For example, one source of friction, highlighted by Canadian anti-apartheid groups, was the question of whether a Canadian bank had broken the Commonwealth ban on new loans to South Africa. David R. Black, 'Middle Power Diplomacy and the Pursuit of Change in South Africa: Canada, Australia and the

Commonwealth Committee of Foreign Ministers on Southern Africa,' paper presented to the International Studies Association, Vancouver BC, 22 March 1991.

48 Canada, Department of External Affairs, 'Canadian Government Support for the Promotion of Dialogue, Countering South African Propaganda and Censorship, and Canadian Embassy Special Initiatives,' Ottawa, 10 January 1990.

49 Black, 'Middle Power Diplomacy,' 6.

50 Gerald J. Schmitz, 'Human Rights, Democratization, and International Conflict,' in Hampson and Maule, eds., *Canada Among Nations, 1992-93*, 244-5.

51 Keith Ovenden and Tony Cole, *Apartheid and International Finance: A Programme for Change* (Ringwood, Victoria: Penguin Books 1989). For a discussion of the earlier era, see Richard Higgott, 'Australia and Africa, 1970-80: A Decade of Change and Growth,' *Africa Contemporary Record, 1981-2*, 219-35.

52 Commonwealth Secretariat, Commonwealth Committee of Foreign Ministers on Southern Africa, 'First Meeting: Lusaka,' Commonwealth News Release, 1-2 February, 1988, 1.

53 Robert O. Matthews and Cranford Pratt, 'Introduction: Concepts and Instruments,' in Matthews and Pratt, eds., *Human Rights in Canadian Foreign Policy*, esp. 6-20; also Kim Richard Nossal, *The Politics of Canadian Foreign Policy*, 2nd edition (Scarborough, ON: Prentice-Hall 1989), 106.

54 Michael Valpy, 'Canadian Credited at Women's Conference,' *Globe and Mail* (16 July 1985). Also Danié le Blair, 'Le Canada se dit satisfait du fragile consensus de Nairobi,' *Le Devoir* (29 July 1985).

55 Tom Axworthy, 'Canada Can be Proud of Its Role in Nairobi,' *Toronto Star* (16 July 1985). Axworthy was a senior aide to Pierre Trudeau; he is the brother of Lloyd Axworthy, a prominent Liberal front-bencher and former cabinet minister in the Trudeau government.

56 Stephen Lewis, 'Speech to Symposium – An Equal Society: Into the Year 2000,' *Toronto Star* (4 November 1986), G4.

57 Lynda Hurst 'Our Woman in Nairobi Has Plenty of Savvy,' *Toronto Star* (23 July 1985), B1. This laudatory assessment was shared by other commentators: for example, Tom Axworthy (*Toronto Star*, 16 July 1985), stated that 'Officials from External Affairs along with O'Neil worked actively to gain acceptance of the compromise wording that prevented an American withdrawal.'

58 Canada, Department of External Affairs, *Annual Report, 1988* (Ottawa: Supply and Services 1989), 28; *Annual Report, 1989*, 30.

59 D. Landsberg, 'Canada Works Stubbornly for International Women's Rights,' *Globe and Mail* (26 April 1986), A2.

60 Paul Lewis, 'World's Leaders Gather for Summit Meeting on Children,' *New York Times* (30 September 1990).

61 'A Better Start for the World's Children,' *Globe and Mail* (29 September 1990).

62 Stuart Harris, 'The Environmental Challenge: The New International Agenda,' *Working Paper 1990/3*, Canberra: Department of International Relations, Australian National University, May 1990, 1; also Jennifer Tuchman Mathews, 'Redefining Security,' *Foreign Affairs* 68 (1989):162-77.

63 Marvin Soroos, 'A Theoretical Framework for Global Policy Studies,' *International Political Science Review* 11 (July 1990):309-22.

64 For a detailed examination of this decision, see Anthony Bergin, 'The Politics of Antarctic Minerals: The Greening of White Australia,' *Australian Journal of Political Science* 26 (July 1991):216-39.

65 Richard Woolcott, 'Challenges and Changes,' in R.A. Herr, H.R. Hall, and M. Haward, eds., *Antarctica's Future: Continuity or Change* (Hobart: Tasmanian Government Publishers for the Australian Institute of International Affairs, 1990), 26-7.

66 Lorraine M. Elliott, 'Continuity and Change in Co-operative International Regimes: The Politics of the Recent Environment Debate in Antarctica,' *Working Paper 1991/3* (Canberra: Department of International Relations, Australian National University), 21.

67 Hawke's 3 May 1989 speech to the Australian Mining Industry Council foreshadowed the decision later in the month: *DFAT Monthly Record* 60 (May 1989):192.

68 Bergin, 'Antarctic Minerals,' 235, for a discussion.

69 Chris Puplick, opposition critic on the environment, 'Government Dragging Its Flippers on Antarctica,' *News Release*, Canberra, 18 May 1989: cited in Bergin, 'Antarctic Minerals,' 228.

70 In the aftermath of the 1990 election, there was a sharp debate within the Australian Labor Party about whether second-preference ballots of Green movement supporters proved to be decisive in the unprecedented return of an ALP government for a fourth consecutive term. Clive Bean, Ian MacAllister, and John Warhurst, *The Greening of Australian Politics: The 1990 Federal Election* (Melbourne: Longman Cheshire 1991).

71 Gareth Evans, 'Protecting Antarctica: An Example of Courage,' *DFAT Monthly Record* 61 (March 1990):119-21.

72 Nick Cater, 'Australian Plan to Protect Antarctica Set to Win Approval,' *The Age* (20 November 1990), 5.

73 John Geddes, 'Canada Plays Major Role in UN's Conferences on the Environment,' *Financial Post* (28 August 1990).

74 Fen Osler Hampson, 'Climate Change: Building International Coalitions of the Like-Minded,' *International Journal* 45 (Winter 1989-90):64.

75 Fen Osler Hampson, 'Pollution Across Borders: Canada's International Environmental Agenda,' in Maureen Appel Molot and Fen Osler Hampson, eds., *Canada Among Nations – 1989: The Challenge of Change* (Ottawa: Carleton University Press 1990), 182.

76 Hampson, 'Pollution Across Borders,' 180-1.

77 David McRobert, 'On Global Warming, Canada Is Full of Hot Air,' *Globe and Mail* (18 February 1991).

78 Quoted in John Godfrey, 'Environment Leadership: Canada's Role,' *Financial Post* (26 March 1990).

79 For an examination of these differences and similarities in one issue area, see Andrew F. Cooper, 'Like-Minded Nations/Contrasting Diplomatic Styles: Australian and Canadian Approaches to Agricultural Trade,' *Canadian Journal of Political Science* 25 (June 1992):349-79.

80 Gareth Evans, 'Australian Foreign Policy: Priorities in a Changing World,' *Australian Outlook* 43 (August 1989):1-15, and 'Australia's Place in the World,' in Desmond Ball, ed., *Australia and the World: Prologue and Prospects* (Canberra:

Australian National University, Strategic and Defence Studies Centre 1990).

81 For two explorations of the impact of the constitutional discussions on Canada's foreign policy, see Gilles Paquet, 'The Canadian Malaise and Its External Impact,' in Fen Osler Hampson and Christopher J. Maule, eds., *Canada Among Nations – 1990-91: After the Cold War* (Ottawa: Carleton University Press 1991), 25-40; and Ivan Bernier, 'La dimension internationale dans le débat sur l'avenir,' in Hampson and Maule, eds., *Canada Among Nations, 1992-93*, 46-63.

82 This is well illustrated by the different approach Canada took to its polar region during this period: while Australia tended to focus on the broad symbolic aspects, the Canadian government sought to achieve a functional solution for its specific problems with transits of the Northwest Passage. For one discussion of the polar approaches of the two countries, see Donald Rothwell, 'Canadian Sovereignty in the Arctic During the 1990s,' *Australian-Canadian Studies* 10 (1992):81-109.

83 James Rusk, 'Mulroney Signs Ecopact,' *Globe and Mail* (12 June 1992).

84 Iain Wallace, 'Canada, the Environment and UNCED,' in Hampson and Maule, eds., *Canada Among Nations, 1992-93*, 141.

85 At Stockholm, the conference was split over the issue of compensation between proposals from the South for cash payments and the desires of the North for increased official development assistance. The Canadians proposed the substitution of trade benefits in the form of lowered tariffs, a proposal that was accepted by countries of both the North and the South.

86 Andrew Fenton Cooper and J.-Stefan Fritz, 'Bringing the NGOs In: UNCED and Canada's International Environment Policy,' *International Journal* 46 (Autumn 1992):796-817.

87 Notably David Dewitt and John J. Kirton: see their *Canada as a Principal Power: A Study of Foreign Policy and International Relations* (Toronto: John Wiley and Sons 1983).

Conclusion

1 Oran Young, 'The Politics of International Regime Formation: Managing Natural Resources and the Environment,' *International Organization* 43 (Summer 1989):335.

2 Ibid., 373.

3 Ibid.

4 Colleen Hamilton and John Whalley, 'Coalitions in the Uruguay Round,' *Weltwirtschaftliches Archiv* 125 (Winter 1989):547-62.

5 R.L. Rothstein, 'Regime Creation by a Coalition of the Weak: Lessons from the NIEO and the Integrated Program for Commodities,' *International Studies Quarterly* 28 (Summer 1984):307-28.

6 See, for example, Robert Jervis, Richard Ned Lebow, and Janice Gross Stein, *Psychology and Deterrence* (Baltimore: Johns Hopkins University Press 1985); and Robert Jervis, *The Meaning of Nuclear Revolution: Statecraft and the Prospect of Armageddon* (Ithaca: Cornell University Press 1989), esp. ch. 5.

References

Albinski, Henry S. *Australian External Policy Under Labor*. Vancouver: University of British Columbia Press 1977

Anderson, Kym and Ross Garnaut. *Australian Protectionism: Extent, Causes, and Effect*. Sydney: Allen and Unwin 1986

Andrew, Arthur. 'The Diplomat and the Manager.' *International Journal* 30 (Winter 1974-5):45-56

Ball, Desmond. 'Building Blocks for Regional Security: An Australian Perspective on Confidence and Security Building Measures in the Asia-Pacific Region.' Canberra Papers on Strategy and Defence No. 83. Canberra: Strategic and Defence Studies Centre, Australian National University 1991

Bergin, Anthony. 'The Politics of Antarctic Minerals: The Greening of White Australia.' *Australian Journal of Political Science* 26 (July 1991):216-39

Bernier, Ivan. 'La dimension internationale dans le débat sur l'avenir.' In *Canada Among Nations, 1992-93: A New World Order?* edited by Fen Osler Hampson and Christopher J. Maule, 46-63. Ottawa: Carleton University Press 1992

Boardman, Robert. 'The Foreign Service and the Organization of the Foreign Policy Community: Views from Canada and Abroad.' In *The Research Studies*, vol. 30: *Selected Problems in Formulating Foreign Economic Policy*, edited by Denis Stairs and Gilbert R. Winham, 59-103. Toronto: University of Toronto Press 1985

– *Global Regimes and Nation-States: Environmental Issues in Australian Politics*. Ottawa: Carleton University Press 1990

Boyce, P.J., and J.R. Angel, eds. *Diplomacy in the Marketplace: Australia in World Affairs, 1981-90*. Melbourne: Longman Cheshire 1992

Brown, Chris. 'Canada and Southern Africa: Autonomy, Image and Capacity in Foreign Policy.' In *Canada Among Nations, 1989: The Challenge of Change*, edited by Maureen Appel Molot and Fen Osler Hampson, 207-24. Ottawa: Carleton University Press 1990

Butler, Richard. 'Australia and Disarmament.' In *Australia and the World: Prologue and Prospect*, edited by Desmond Ball. Canberra: Australian National University, Strategic and Defence Studies Centre 1990

Cameron, Maxwell. 'Canada and Latin America.' In *Canada Among Nations, 1990-91: After the Cold War*, edited by Fen Osler Hampson and Christopher

J. Maule, 109-23. Ottawa: Carleton University Press 1991

Cameron, Maxwell A., Lorraine Eden, and Maureen Appel Molot. 'North American Free Trade: Co-operation and Conflict in Canada-Mexico Relations.' In *Canada Among Nations, 1992-93: A New World Order?* edited by Fen Osler Hampson and Christopher J. Maule, 174-90. Ottawa: Carleton University Press 1992

Capling, Ann, and Brian Galligan. *Beyond the Protective State: The Political Economy of Australia's Manufacturing Industry Policy.* Cambridge: Cambridge University Press 1992

Cheeseman, Graeme. 'Defence Policy and Organisation: The Search for Self-Reliance.' In *Diplomacy in the Marketplace: Australia in World Affairs, 1981-90,* edited by P.J. Boyce and J.R. Angel, 63-81. Melbourne: Longman Cheshire 1992

Clark, Joe. 'Canada's New Internationalism.' In *Canada and the New Internationalism,* edited by John Holmes and John Kirton, 3-11. Toronto: Canadian Institute of International Affairs 1988

Cohn, Theodore H. 'Canada and the On-Going Impasse over Agricultural Protectionism.' In *Canadian Foreign Policy and International Economic Regimes,* edited by A. Claire Cutler and Mark W. Zacher, 62-88. Vancouver: UBC Press 1992

Collins, Hugh. 'The "Coombs Report": Bureaucracy, Diplomacy and Australian Foreign Policy.' *Australian Outlook* 30 (December 1976):387-413

– 'Challenges and Options for the Department of Foreign Affairs in Its Fiftieth Year.' *Australian Foreign Affairs Record* 56 (November 1985):1077-89

Connors, Tom. *The Australian Wheat Industry: Its Economics and Politics.* Armidale, NSW: Gill 1972

Cooper, Andrew F. 'Australia: Domestic Political Management and International Trade Reform.' In *Agricultural Trade: Domestic Pressures and International Trade,* edited by Grace Skogstad and Andrew Fenton Cooper, 113-34. Halifax, NS: Institute for Research on Public Policy 1990

– 'Exporters Versus Importers: LDCs, Agricultural Trade and the Uruguay Round.' *Intereconomics* 25 (Winter 1990):13-17

– 'Like-Minded Nations/Contrasting Diplomatic Styles: Australian and Canadian Approaches to Agricultural Trade.' *Canadian Journal of Political Science* 25 (June 1992):349-79

Cooper, Andrew Fenton, Richard A. Higgott, and Kim Richard Nossal. 'Bound to Follow? Leadership and Followership in the Gulf Conflict.' *Political Science Quarterly* 106 (Fall 1991):391-410

Cooper, Andrew Fenton, and J.-Stefan Fritz. 'Bringing the NGOs In: UNCED and Canada's International Environment Policy.' *International Journal* 46 (Autumn 1992):796-817

Crone, David. 'The Politics of Emerging Pacific Co-operation.' *Pacific Affairs* 65 (1992):68-83

Cutler, A. Claire and Mark W. Zacher, eds. *Canadian Foreign Policy and International Economic Regimes.* Vancouver: UBC Press 1992

Dewitt, David and John Kirton, *Canada as a Principal Power.* Toronto: John Wiley 1983

Dobell, Peter C. 'The Management of a Foreign Policy for Canadians.' *International Journal* 26 (Winter 1970-1):202-20

Dobell, W.M. 'Interdepartmental Management in External Affairs.' *Canadian Public Administration* 21 (Spring 1978):83-102

Doxey, Margaret. 'Canada and the Evolution of the Modern Commonwealth.' *Behind the Headlines* 40 (November 1982):1-20

– 'Constructive Internationalism: A Continuing Theme in Canadian Foreign Policy.' *The Round Table* 311 (1989):288-304

Drysdale, Peter. *International Economic Pluralism: Economic Policy in East Asia and the Pacific.* Sydney: Allen and Unwin 1988

Drysdale, Peter and H. Patrick. *An Asia-Pacific Regional Economic Organization: An Exploratory Concept Paper.* Washington: United States Congress, Congressional Research Service 1979

Drysdale, Peter and Ross Garnaut, 'A Pacific Free Trade Area?' In *Free Trade Areas and U.S. Trade Policy*, edited by Jeffrey J. Schott, 219-31. Washington: Institute for International Economics 1989

Eayrs, James. 'The Origins of Canada's Department of External Affairs.' *Canadian Journal of Economics and Political Science* 25 (May 1959):109-28

– 'Canada: External Affairs.' In *The Times Survey of Foreign Ministries of the World*, edited by Zara Steiner, 95-115. London: Time Books 1982

Eden, Lorraine, and Maureen Appel Molot. 'The View from the Spokes: Canada and Mexico Face the U.S.' In *The Challenge of North American Integration*, edited by Stephen J. Randall, H. Konrad, and S. Silverman. Calgary: University of Calgary Press 1993

Elliott, Lorraine M. 'Continuity and Change in Co-operative International Regimes: The Politics of the Recent Environment Debate in Antarctica.' Department of International Relations Working Paper No. 1991/3. Canberra: Australian National University 1991

English, John and Norman Hillmer, eds. *Making a Difference? Canada's Foreign Policy in a Changing World Order.* Toronto: Lester 1992

Evans, Gareth. 'Australia Offshore – Diplomats and Traders.' *Australian Foreign Affairs Record* 59 (November 1988):457-9

– 'Australian Foreign Policy: Priorities in a Changing World.' *Australian Outlook: The Australian Journal of International Affairs* 43 (August 1989):1-15

– 'Australia's Place in the World: The Dynamics of Foreign Policy Decision-Making.' In *Australia and the World: Prologue and Prospects*, edited by Desmond Ball. Canberra: Strategic and Defence Studies Centre, Australian National University 1990

Evans, Gareth and Bruce Grant, *Australia's Foreign Relations in the World of the 1990s.* Melbourne: Melbourne University Press 1991

Evans, Paul. 'A North American Perspective on the Pacific in the 1990s: On the Pacific or of the Pacific?' *Australian-Canadian Studies* 10 (1992):61-80

Farrell, R. Barry. *The Making of Canadian Foreign Policy.* Scarborough: Prentice-Hall 1969

Findlay, Trevor. 'North Pacific Confidence-Building: The Helsinki/Stockholm Model. Peace Research Centre Working Paper.' Canberra: Australian National University 1988

- 'Asia-Pacific CSBMs: A Prospectus.' Peace Research Centre Working Paper. Canberra: Australian National University 1990
Finlayson, Jock A. with Stefano Bertasi, 'Evolution of Canadian Postwar International Trade Policy.' In *Canadian Foreign Policy and International Economic Regimes*, edited by A. Claire Cutler and Mark W. Zacher, 19-46. Vancouver: UBC Press 1992
Fox, Annette Baker. *The Politics of Attraction: Four Middle Powers and the United States*. New York: Columbia University Press 1977
- 'The Range of Choice for Middle Powers: Australia and Canada Compared.' *Australian Journal of Politics and History* 26 (1980):193-203
Gallagher, P. 'Setting the Agenda for Trade Negotiations: Australia and the Cairns Group.' *Australian Outlook* 44 (April 1988):3-8
Garnaut, Ross. *Australia and the Northeast Asian Ascendency*. Canberra: Australian Government Publishing Service 1989
Glazebrook, G.P. deT. *A History of Canadian External Relations*, vol 1: *The Formative Years to 1914*. Rev. edition. Toronto: McClelland and Stewart 1970
Gordon, J. King, ed. *Canada's Role as a Middle Power*. Toronto: Canadian Institute of International Affairs 1966
Granatstein, J.L. 'Canada's Royal Commission on Conditions of Foreign Service.' *International Journal* 37 (Summer 1982):408-12
- 'Peacekeeping: Did Canada Make a Difference? And What Difference Did Peacekeeping Make to Canada?' In *Making a Difference? Canada's Foreign Policy in a Changing World Order*, edited by John English and Norman Hillmer, 222-36. Toronto: Lester 1992
Granatstein, J.L. and Robert Bothwell. *Pirouette: Pierre Trudeau and Canadian Foreign Policy*. Toronto: University of Toronto Press 1990
Gray, Charlotte. 'War Games.' *Saturday Night*, March 1991, 10-13
Greenwood, Gordon, and Norman Harper, eds. *Australia in World Affairs*. Melbourne/Vancouver: Australian Institute of International Affairs 1974
Griffiths, Franklyn, ed. *Politics of the Northwest Passage*. Montreal and Kingston: McGill-Queen's University Press 1987
Gwyn, Richard and Sandra. 'The Politics of Peace.' *Saturday Night*, May 1984, 19-32
Hampson, Fen Osler. 'Climate Change: Building International Coalitions of the Like-Minded.' *International Journal* 45 (Winter 1989-90):36-74
- 'Pollution Across Borders: Canada's International Environmental Agenda.' In *Canada Among Nations, 1989: The Challenge of Change*, edited by Maureen Appel Molot and Fen Osler Hampson, 175-92. Ottawa: Carleton University Press 1990
Harris, Stuart. 'The Separation of Economics and Politics: A Luxury We Can No Longer Afford.' In *Academic Studies and International Politics*, edited by Coral Bell. Canberra Studies in World Affairs 6, Canberra 1982
- 'The Linking of Politics and Economics in Foreign Policy.' *Australian Outlook: The Australian Journal of International Affairs* 40 (April 1986):5-10
- 'The Amalgamation of the Department of Foreign Affairs and Trade.' *Australian Foreign Affairs Record* 59 (March 1988):71-4
- 'Regional Economic Co-operation: Trading Blocs and Australian Interests.'

Australian Outlook 43 (August 1989):16-25
– 'Economic Change in the International System: Implications for Australia's Prospects.' In *Agenda for the Nineties: Australian Choices in Foreign and Defence Policy*, edited by Coral Bell, 24-45. Melbourne: Longman Cheshire 1990
– 'Australia in the Global Economy in the 1980s.' In *Diplomacy in the Marketplace: Australia in World Affairs, 1981-90*, edited by P.J. Boyce and J.R. Angel, 30-50. Melbourne: Longman Cheshire 1992
Harris, Stuart and James Cotton, eds. *The End of the Cold War in Northeast Asia*. Melbourne: Longman Cheshire/Boulder: Lynne Reinner 1991
Hart, Michael. *A North American Free Trade Agreement: The Strategic Implications for Canada*. Ottawa: Centre for Trade Policy 1990
– 'Canada Discovers Its Vocation as a Nation of the Americas.' In *Canada Among Nations, 1990-91: After the Cold War*, edited by Fen Osler Hampson and Christopher J. Maule, 83-107. Ottawa: Carleton University Press 1991
Hasluck, Paul. *Diplomatic Witness: Australian Foreign Affairs 1941-1947*. Melbourne: Melbourne University Press 1980
Hawes, Michael K. *Principal Power, Middle Power, or Satellite?* North York, ON: York Research Programme in Strategic Studies 1984
Higgott, Richard A. 'Australia: Economic Crises and the Politics of Regional Economic Adjustment.' In *Southeast Asia in the 1980s: The Politics of Economic Crisis*, edited by Richard Robison, Kevin Hewison, and Richard Higgott, 177-217. Sydney: Allen and Unwin 1987
– 'Australia and the New International Division of Labor in the Asia Pacific Region.' In *A Changing International Division of Labor*, edited by James Caporaso, 147-85. Boulder: Lynne Reiner 1987
– *The Evolving World Economy: Some Alternative Security Questions for Australia*. Canberra: Strategic and Defence Studies Centre, Australian National University 1989
– 'The Ascendancy of the Economic Dimension in Australian-American Relations.' In *No Longer an American Lake: U.S. Policy in the Pacific in the 1980s*, edited by John Ravenhill, 132-68. Berkeley: University of California, Institute of International Studies 1989
– 'International Constraints on Labor's Economic Policy.' In *How Labor Governs: The Hawke Government and Business*, edited by Brian Galligan and Gwyn Singleton, 15-56. Melbourne: Longman Cheshire 1991
– 'The Politics of Australia's International Economic Relations: Adjustment and the Politics of Two-Level Games.' *Australian Journal of Political Science* 26 (March 1991):2-28
– 'Towards a Non-Hegemonic International Political Economy.' In *The New International Political Economy*, edited by Craig Murphy and Roger Tooze, 178-219. Boulder: Lynne Reiner 1991
Higgott, Richard A. and Jim George. 'Tradition and Change in Australia's International Relations.' *International Political Science Review* 11 (1990):423-38
Higgott, Richard A., Richard Leaver, and John Ravenhill, eds. *Pacific Economic Relations in the 1990s: Co-operation or Conflict?* Sydney: Allen and Unwin 1992
Hill, O. Mary. *Canada's Salesman to the World: The Department of Trade and*

Commerce, 1892-1939. Montreal and Kingston: McGill-Queen's University Press 1977

Hilliker, John. *Canada's Department of External Affairs*, vol. 1: *The Early Years, 1909-1946*. Montreal and Kingston: McGill-Queen's University Press 1990

Holbraad, Carsten. *Middle Powers in International Politics*. London: Macmillan 1984

Holmes, John W. 'Is There a Future for Middlepowermanship?' In *Canada's Role as a Middle Power*, edited by J. King Gordon, 13-28. Toronto: Canadian Institute of International Affairs 1966

– *Canada: A Middle-Aged Power*. Toronto: McClelland and Stewart 1976

– *The Shaping of Peace: Canada and the Search for World Order, 1943-1957*, 2 vols. Toronto: University of Toronto Press 1979, 1982

– 'Most Safely in the Middle.' *International Journal* 39 (Spring 1984):366-88

Ivanov, Vladimir I. 'Emerging Asian-Pacific Multilateralism: Its Impact on Regional Development and Stability Beyond the Cold War.' North Pacific Cooperative Security Dialogue Working Paper No. 6. North York: York University, February 1992

Jenkins, Glenn P. *Costs and Consequences of the New Protectionism: The Case of Canada's Clothing Sector*. Ottawa: The North-South Institute 1980

Jennett, Christine and Randal G. Stewart, eds. *Hawke and Australian Public Policy: Consensus and Restructuring*. Melbourne: Macmillan 1990

Job, Brian L. 'Canadian Interests and Perspectives Regarding the Emerging Pacific Security Order.' North Pacific Co-operative Security Dialogue Working Paper No. 2. North York: York University 1991

Keal, Paul, ed. *Ethics and Australian Foreign Policy*. Sydney: Allen and Unwin 1992

Keenes, Ernie. 'Rearranging the Deck Chairs: A Political Economy Approach to Foreign Policy Management in Canada.' *Canadian Public Administration* 35 (Autumn 1992):381-401

Kirton, John. 'Liberating Kuwait: Canada and the Persian Gulf War, 1990-91.' In *Canadian Foreign Policy: Selected Cases*, edited by Don Munton and John Kirton, 382-93. Scarborough: Prentice-Hall 1992

Kreuger, Anne. 'The Effects of Regional Trade Blocs on World Trade.' In *NAFTA, the Pacific, and Australia/New Zealand*, edited by John Higley, Robert Cushing, and Michael Sutton. Austin, TX: University of Texas Press 1993

Leaver, Richard. 'Restructuring in the Global Economy: From Pax Americana to Pax Nipponica?' *Alternatives* 14 (October 1989):429-62

– 'The Costs of Australia "Being Seen to Be There."' *Pacific Research* 3 (November 1990):5-7

– 'The Future of Northeast Asian Regional Growth: The Regionalist Alternative.' In *Northeast Asian Challenge: Debating the Garnaut Report*, edited by J.L. Richardson, 50-67. Melbourne: Longman Cheshire 1991

Lipsey, Richard. 'Canada at the U.S.-Mexico Trade Dance: Wallflower or Partner?' *C.D. Howe Institute Commentary* No. 20. Toronto: C.D. Howe Institute 1990

McCloskey, Jean. 'New Realities in the Pacific: The Political Perspective.' *Behind the Headlines* 46 (Winter 1988-9):1-13

McDougall, Barbara. 'Introduction.' In *Making a Difference? Canada's Foreign Policy in a Changing World Order*, edited by John English and Norman Hiller, ix-xvi. Toronto: Lester 1992

MacKay, R.A. 'The Canadian Doctrine of the Middle Powers.' In *Empire and Nations: Essays in Honour of Frederic H. Soward*, edited by H.L. Dyck and H.P. Krosby, 133-43. Toronto: University of Toronto Press 1969

Mack, Andrew. 'After the Cold War and the Gulf War: Prospects for Security in the Asia-Pacific.' Department of International Relations Working Paper. Canberra: Australian National University 1992

Mack, Andrew, and Paul Keal, eds. *Security and Arms Control in the North Pacific*. Sydney: Allen and Unwin 1988

Malik, J. Mohan. 'The Gulf War: Australia's Role and Asian-Pacific Responses.' Canberra Papers on Strategy and Defence 90. Canberra: Strategic and Defence Studies Centre, Australian National University 1992

Mathews, Trevor and John Ravenhill. 'The Economic Challenge: Is Unilateral Free Trade the Answer?' In *Northeast Asian Challenge: Debating the Garnaut Report*, edited by J.L. Richardson, 68-94. Canberra Studies in World Affairs No. 27. Canberra: Australian National University 1991

Matthews, Robert O. and Cranford Pratt, eds. *Human Rights in Canadian Foreign Policy*. Montreal and Kingston: McGill-Queen's University Press 1988

Maybee, Jack. 'Foreign Service Consolidation.' *International Perspectives* (July/August 1980):17-20

Millar, T.B. 'Managing the Australian Foreign Affairs Department.' *International Journal* 37 (Summer 1982):441-52

– *Australia in Peace and War*, 2nd edition. Canberra: Australian National University Press 1991

Molot, Maureen Appel. 'Where Do We, Should We, or Can We Sit? A Review of Canadian Foreign Policy Literature.' *International Journal of Canadian Studies* 1-2 (Spring/Fall 1990):77-96

Moore, Des. 'Economic Rationalism: Myth or Reality?' *IPA Review* 45 (1992):35-7

Nossal, Kim Richard. 'Personal Diplomacy and National Behaviour: Trudeau's North-South Initiatives.' *Dalhousie Review* 62 (Summer 1982):278-91

– *The Politics of Canadian Foreign Policy*, 2nd edition. Scarborough, ON: Prentice-Hall 1989

– 'Canadian Sanctions Against South Africa: Explaining the Mulroney Initiatives, 1985-86.' *Journal of Canadian Studies* 25 (Winter 1990-1):17-33

– 'Quantum Leaping: The Gulf Debate in Australia and Canada.' In *Allied Perspectives on the Gulf Conflict*, edited by Michael McKinley. Sydney: Allen and Unwin (forthcoming)

Osbaldeston, Gordon. 'Reorganizing Canada's Department of External Affairs.' *International Journal* 37 (Summer 1982):453-66

Ostry, Sylvia. 'The NAFTA: Its International Economic Background.' In *North America Without Borders? Integrating Canada, the United States and Mexico*, edited by Stephen J. Randall et al., 18-31. Calgary: University of Calgary Press 1992

– 'Changing Multilateral Institutions: A Role for Canada.' In *Canadian Foreign*

Policy and International Economic Regimes, edited by A. Claire Cutler and Mark W. Zacher, 337-44. Vancouver: UBC Press 1992

Ovenden, Keith and Tony Cole, *Apartheid and International Finance: A Programme for Change.* Ringwood, Victoria: Penguin 1989

Painchaud, Paul. 'Middlepowermanship as an Ideology.' In *Canada's Role as a Middle Power,* edited by J. King Gordon, 29-35. Toronto: Canadian Institute of International Affairs 1966

Paquet, Gilles. 'The Canadian Malaise and Its External Impact.' In *Canada Among Nations, 1990-91: After the Cold War,* edited by Fen Osler Hampson and Christopher J. Maule, 25-40. Ottawa: Carleton University Press 1991

Pratt, Cranford, ed. *Internationalism Under Strain: The North-South Policies of Canada, the Netherlands, Norway, and Sweden.* Toronto: University of Toronto Press 1989

– *Middle Power Internationalism: The North-South Dimension.* Montreal and Kingston: McGill-Queen's University Press 1990

Pusey, Michael. *Economic Rationalism in Canberra: A Nation-Building State Changes its Mind.* Melbourne: Melbourne University Press 1991

Randall, Stephen J. 'Canada, the United States and Mexico: The Development of Trilateralism.' *Frontera Norte* 3 (julio-diciembre 1991):121-36

Redekop, Clarence G. 'Trudeau at Singapore: The Commonwealth and Arms Sales to South Africa.' In *An Acceptance of Paradox: Essays on Canadian Diplomacy in Honour of John W. Holmes,* edited by Kim Richard Nossal, 174-95. Toronto: Canadian Institute of International Affairs 1982

– 'The Mulroney Government and South Africa: Constructive Disengagement.' *Behind the Headlines* 44 (December 1986):1-16

Reid, Escott. *On Duty: A Canadian at the Making of the United Nations, 1945-1946.* Kent, OH: Kent State University Press 1983

Renouf, Alan. *The Frightened Country.* Melbourne: Macmillan 1979

Richardson, J.L. ed. *Northeast Asian Challenge: Debating the Garnaut Report.* Canberra Studies in World Affairs 27. Canberra: Australian National University 1991

Riddell-Dixon, Elizabeth. *Canada and the International Seabed: Domestic Determinants and External Constraints.* Montreal and Kingston: McGill-Queen's University Press 1989

Rix, Alan. *Coming to Terms: The Politics of Australia's Trade with Japan, 1945-1957.* Sydney: Allen and Unwin 1986

Ross, Douglas A. 'Canadian Foreign Policy and the Pacific Rim: From National Security Anxiety to Creative Economic Co-operation.' In *Politics of the Pacific Rim: Perspectives on the 1980s,* edited by F. Quei Quo, 21-39. Burnaby, BC: Simon Fraser University Publications 1982

Rothwell, Donald. 'Canadian Sovereignty in the Arctic During the 1990s.' *Australian-Canadian Studies* 10 (1992):81-109

Roy, Patricia. 'Has Canada Made a Difference? North Pacific Connections: Canada, China, and Japan.' In *Making a Difference? Canada's Foreign Policy in a Changing World Order,* edited by John English and Norman Hiller, 125-62. Toronto: Lester 1992

Rudner, Martin. 'Canada, the Gulf Crisis and Collective Security.' In *Canada*

Among Nations 1990-91: After the Cold War, edited by Fen Osler Hampson and Christopher J. Maule, 241-80. Ottawa: Carleton University Press 1991

Sanger, Clyde. *Ordering the Oceans: The Making of the Law of the Sea*. Toronto: University of Toronto Press 1987

Schmitz, Gerald J. 'Human Rights, Democratization, and International Conflict.' In *Canada Among Nations, 1992-93: A New World Order?* edited by Fen Osler Hampson and Christopher J. Maule, 235-55. Ottawa: Carleton University Press 1992

Skilling, H. Gordon. *Canadian Representation Abroad: From Agency to Embassy*. Toronto: Ryerson 1945

Skogstad, Grace. *The Politics of Agricultural Policy-Making in Canada*. Toronto: University of Toronto Press 1987

Skogstad, Grace and Andrew Fenton Cooper, eds. *Agricultural Trade: Domestic Pressures and International Trade*. Halifax, NS: Institute for Research on Public Policy 1990

Snape, Richard, Jan Adams, and David Morgan. *Regional Trade Agreements: Implications and Options for Australia*, 2 vols. Melbourne: Monash University 1992

Stubbs, Richard. 'Reluctant Leader, Expectant Followers: Japan and Southeast Asia.' *International Journal* 46 (Autumn 1991):649-67

Thomas, Christopher. 'Reflections on the Canada-U.S. Free Trade Agreement in the Context of the Multilateral Trading System.' In *Canadian Foreign Policy and International Economic Regimes*, edited by A. Claire Cutler and Mark W. Zacher, 47-61. Vancouver: UBC Press 1992

Tucker, Michael. *Canadian Foreign Policy: Contemporary Issues and Themes*. Toronto: McGraw-Hill Ryerson 1980.

Viviani, Nancy. 'Foreign Economic Policy.' In *Hawke and Australian Public Policy: Consensus and Restructuring*, edited by Christine Jennett and Randal G. Stewart, 397-405. Melbourne: Macmillan 1990

Wallace, Iain. 'Canada, the Environment and UNCED.' In *Canada Among Nations, 1992-93: A New World Order?* edited by Fen Osler Hampson and Christopher J. Maule, 131-46. Ottawa: Carleton University Press 1992

Watt, Alan. 'Australia: The Department of Foreign Affairs.' In *The Times Survey of Foreign Ministries of the World*, edited by Zara Steiner, 34-45. London: Time Books 1982

Whitaker, Reg. 'Prisoners of the American Dream: Canada, the Gulf, and the New World Order.' *Studies in Political Economy* 35 (Summer 1991):13-27

Winham, Gilbert R. 'Canada, GATT, and the World Trading System.' In *Canada Among Nations, 1992-93: A New World Order?* edited by Fen Osler Hampson and Christopher J. Maule, 115-30. Ottawa: Carleton University Press 1992

Wirick, Gregory. 'Canada, Peacekeeping and the United Nations.' In *Canada Among Nations, 1992-93: A New World Order?* edited by Fen Osler Hampson and Christopher J. Maule, 94-114. Ottawa: Carleton University Press 1992

Wonnacott, Ronald J. 'U.S. Hub-and-Spoke Bilaterals and the Multilateral Trading System.' *C.D. Howe Institute Commentary* No. 23. Toronto: C.D. Howe Institute, October 1990

Wood, Bernard. *The Middle Powers and the General Interest*. No. 1 in the series *Middle Powers in the International System*. Ottawa: North-South Institute 1988

– 'Canada and Southern Africa: A Return to Middle Power Activism.' *The Round Table* 315 (1990):280-90

– 'Towards North-South Power Coalitions.' In *Middle-Power Internationalism: The North-South Dimension*, edited by Cranford Pratt, 69-107. Montreal and Kingston: McGill-Queen's University Press 1990

Woods, Lawrence T. 'The Business of Canada's Pacific Relations.' *Canadian Journal of Administrative Sciences* 4 (December 1987):410-25

Woolcott, Richard. 'Challenges and Changes.' In *Antarctica's Future: Continuity or Change*, edited by R.A. Herr, H.R. Hall, and M. Haward, 18-36. Hobart: Tasmanian Government Publishers for the Australian Institute of International Affairs 1990

Index

member, 59, 61
Pickering, Thomas, 120
Pine Gap, 135
Pitfield, Michael, 38, 190 n. 30; on
external affairs, 40-1
Poland, 18
Pollution Probe, 167
Portillo, Lopez, 108
Portugal, 129, 209 n. 3
Powell, Colin, 205 n. 48
Powell, Janet, 207 n. 73
Pratt, Cranford, 18
Privy Council Office, 38, 40-1
Promotion Australia, 190 n. 34
Protectionism, 22, 53-5; in Australia,
44, 45; in United States, 56
Punta del Este meeting, 52, 72
Putnam, Robert, 22, 99

Quebec, 22, 134, 168

Ray, Robert, 123, 124, 125-6, 134,
138
'Ready, aye, ready,' 207 n. 74
Reagan, Ronald, 58, 67, 88; and
Central America, 108; and North
American Accord, 107
'Red Book' on Cambodia, 150, 151
Regional Economic Expansion,
Department of (Canada), 36
Regional Industrial Expansion,
Department of (Canada), 37
Regionalism, 177-8
'Renewalists,' 12
Renouf, Alan, 191 n. 45
Resolution 661, 124, 204 n. 23
Resolution 678, 132, 140, 206 n. 49
Richardson, Grahame, 165
'Routine' diplomacy, 29, 168
Royal Canadian Engineers, 135
Royal Canadian Regiment, 135
Royal Commission on Conditions
of Foreign Service, 39, 40
Royal Commission on Government
Organization (Glassco Commis-
sion), 189 n. 19
Ruggie, John, 12
Russia. *See* Union of Soviet Socialist
Republics

Salinas de Gortari, Carlos, 108
Sanctions: Cuba, 108; Iraq, 120;
South Africa, 117
Saudi Arabia, 120, 132, 138, 205 n.
48
Secretaries Committee on Overseas
Representation, 47
Segal, Gerald, 85
Sembler, Mel, 125
Shultz, George, 102
Singapore, 85, 94
Single Integrated Market, 86
South Africa: Canadian policy on,
156-9; sanctions against, 117
South Asia Association for Regional
Cooperation, 154
South Pacific Regional Trade and
Economic Cooperation Agreement
(SPARTECA), 67
Southern Hemisphere Temperate
Zone Agricultural Producers, 66
Sovereignty-association, 22
Spain, 129, 209 n. 3
Springborg, 207 n. 73
Stevens, H.H., 189 n. 19
Strange, Susan, 14
Strong, Maurice, 167
Stubbs, Richard, 16
Suez crisis, 20, 207 n. 73
Sununu, John, 205 n. 46
Sûrété du Québec, 130
Sweden, 18, 34-5, 60, 146, 209 n. 3
Switzerland, 60, 209 n. 3

Taiwan, 85, 90, 93, 94
Tanzania, 158
Tariffication, 79-80
Test Ban Treaty, 145
Thailand, 94, 98, 102; as Cairns
Group member, 59, 61
Thatcher, Margaret, 119, 120, 128
Tiananmen massacre, 93
Timor, 18, 207 n. 67
Trade, Department of (Australia),
42-8 passim
Trade and Commerce, Department
of (Canada), 37, 38, 41-2, 189 n. 19
Trade Commissioner Service:
Australia, 46; Canada, 36, 39

Canada and International Relations

Set in Stone by Vancouver Desktop Publishing Centre

Printed and bound in Canada by D.W. Friesen & Sons Ltd.

Copy-editor: Joanne Richardson

Proofreader: Perry L. Millar